Under the editorship of

WAYNE C. MINNICK

THE FLORIDA STATE UNIVERSITY

"All life therefore comes
back to the question of our
speech, the medium through
which we communicate with
each other; for all life comes
back to the question of our relations
with one another."

Henry James

EFFECTIVE SPEAKER

EDWARD S. STROTHER

ALAN W. HUCKLEBERRY

BALL STATE UNIVERSITY

HOUGHTON MIFFLIN COMPANY • BOSTON

NEW YORK   ATLANTA   GENEVA, ILLINOIS   DALLAS   PALO ALTO

PREFACE

The Effective Speaker is written for the beginning student of public speaking. It attempts to give him (1) a body of rhetorical theory, (2) criteria for evaluating effective speaking, and (3) guidelines to help him make the most of his present abilities.

This book is also written for the teacher. We are aware that he has very little time for extended discussions of theory and that he must find a text to augment the principles he touches on. We are aware, too, that he prefers a text which is teachable, stimulating, based on instructional experiences, and well-grounded in principles established by tradition and confirmed by recent research. To say that we have captured all these qualities is overstepping the bounds of modesty; yet we have made the effort.

The table of contents will reveal rather conventional organization. We begin with definitions and statements of basic principles, describe in general terms the process of speech preparation, and then move to more extended discussions of the major variables in preparing and delivering a speech. Although we are conventional in this respect, we are unconventional in others: (1) we try repeatedly to analyze the reasons for speech failure; (2) we use more examples from classroom speeches than most of the introductory texts; (3) at the end of most chapters we present a classroom speech in full for study and criticism. We admit without shame or apology that the classroom examples are not great rhetoric; however, their frankness and authenticity are more engaging than many of the examples selected from *The Congressional Record* and other published sources.

A full measure of credit is due to many who have helped us. We must thank our students, both graduate and undergraduate, who have stimulated our thinking; Mrs. Lucille Royalty for her assistance in proofreading; Dr. Wayne C. Minnick for many helpful suggestions on both content and style; and, finally, the college speech staff at Houghton Mifflin for the careful editing always essential in bringing a book to life.

E.S.S.
A.W.H.

v

In writing *The Effective Speaker,* we have made several assumptions: that you are a freshman or sophomore in college; that you are around nineteen years of age; that you have been speaking for about seventeen years with moderate but not overwhelming success; that you are quick and energetic and want to speak better; and, finally, that you would rather practice the art of speech than read about it. We have planned our text to reflect these assumptions. May we offer some advice on how to use it?

First, read the text quickly in one sitting. If you find it interesting, you will not mind returning to it later. If you find it tedious, you will at least know what to expect as the instructor makes assignments. As you read, note (a) the general organization of the text and (b) the systematic treatment of the aspects of effective speaking.

Second, read the text to help yourself rather than to comply with assignments. Focus your study on the sections that deal with your own particular difficulties. If your instructor and classmates think your speech subjects are unsuitable, concentrate on the chapter devoted to that problem. If your critics report that you are weak in organization, language, or delivery, study those chapters carefully and work hard to remedy your deficiencies.

Third, if this text conflicts with classroom instruction, *follow the advice of your teacher.* We think we know you well, but your teacher knows you better. He is with you; he listens to you. And as a result of his direct contact with you, his training, and his responsibilities as a teacher, he will help you more than this or any other public speaking text.

Naturally, we wish you success — in this course and in the years to follow. After all, speech is our principal means of living with others. If we lose our tongues, we may in time lose our lives.

E.S.S.

A.W.H.

CONTENTS

ABOUT THE PHOTOGRAPHS

PART ONE

Getting Started

EFFECTIVE SPEAKING: AN OVERVIEW

THE FIRST CLASSROOM SPEECH

CHAPTER 1

EFFECTIVE SPEAKING:
AN OVERVIEW

When asked what to do to become an effective speaker, Winston Churchill replied jauntily, "Buy a cigar and a pair of spectacles." Even for an extraordinary man like Churchill, such a reply contained only a grain of truth. For learning to speak effectively is not just a matter of adding props; instead, it is a matter of careful planning and hard work. Good speech does not come to us at birth, nor is it some fortunate accident which happens in high school or college. On the contrary, it is a skill which results from a well-planned program of improvement.

Perhaps the point may be illustrated by analogy. Consider the young boy who has made up his mind to become a swimmer. Without knowing even how to stay afloat, he stands for a moment at the edge of the pool to speculate on the horrors of deep water. He closes his eyes, grits his teeth, holds his nose, says, "I *will* learn to swim!" — and plunges in. He avoids panic, remembers those rudimentary lessons from his Cub Scout manual, and stays afloat. With a little determination he succeeds in thrashing back to the safety of his jumping-off place. For the moment, at least, he declares himself a success because he did what he set out to do with that first leap into the pool. After a few weeks he can beat his way across the width of the pool, and by the end of summer he can swim its length. By September there is no question in his mind about his ability. He has become a swimmer.

But has he become a good swimmer? The answer, of course, hangs on our standard of goodness. To the non-swimmers, he is outstanding. To his fellow fifth-graders he is merely average. To the swimming instructor he is an "intermediate." He reaches his goal, but his goal is narrow and limited. His kick is labored, his arm stroke weak, his breathing unrhythmical, and his entire body lies low in the water. To become a good swimmer he will need to plan a deliberate program of self-improvement.

So it is with the speaker. At the risk of overextending our analogy, we may say that years ago we took a courageous plunge into a deep pool of words. By and large we have met with success. We get things done. Every day we engage in dozens of conversations at the expense of thousands of words. We attend conferences, discussions, lectures, symposiums, and debates. We meet to solve the problems of our society, to improve our schools, to increase the contribution of our churches, and to meet the challenges confronting our local government. Elsewhere men and women, working with the spoken word, plan the affairs of state and national government; and federal authorities meet with people of other nations to work out the affairs of the world. Our supply of words is inexhaustible, and our speech seems ever-enduring.

But is it *good* speech? To this we must answer "Yes," because, after all, we *do* manage to communicate. But at the same time, we must acknowledge our occasional failure — the times we have been misunderstood because we were groping for words or were caught in a tangle of disorganized thoughts — and plan deliberately for improvement. Deciding on a plan of improvement is not simple; it calls for many careful decisions about the people with whom we talk, our choice of speech materials, organization, language, and mode of delivery. But until we have made these decisions, we cannot take sensible steps toward effective speaking.

■ ## THE SPEAKER DEFINED

The speaker communicates thought and feeling by voice and body to secure a desired response from his listeners. Though this definition seems deceptively simple, it may have greater meaning if we divide it into its several parts and discuss each separately.

Communication. Obviously, there are many kinds of communication. The musician is a communicator. The sculptor, the painter, the actor, the dancer, the architect — all are communicators. In different media of expression all of them convey to others some attitude, emotion, or thought. Whatever the medium, these four elements are basic to all communication: (1) someone to *originate* the thought, (2) someone to *receive* it, (3) a *medium* for *expressing* the thought, and (4) the *thought* itself. If we remove any one of the four, communication in the fullest sense cannot take place.

Thought and feeling. Thought and feeling are the substance or raw material of communication. They are the things talked about. Without them there can be no communication. Or if the communicator and his audience do not refer to the thought *at the same time,* there is no communication *at that time.* If the musician plays to an ear that will not listen, if the sculptor presents his work to eyes that cannot see, if the poet writes for an intellect that cannot understand, there is no exchange of thought or feeling. And, similarly, if the speaker utters words that make no sense to his listeners or speaks to an audience deaf to sense, there is no thought and no communication.

Voice and body. These are the speaker's media of expression. The sculptor speaks with stone and wood; the painter with oil and canvas; the dancer with his body; the actor with voice *and* body. The speaker, then, may resemble the actor. Using his body, he shrugs to indicate indifference, frowns to indicate dislike, or throws out his arms to indicate resignation. But the speaker is not an actor or an oral reader. The actor and the reader are interpreters; they usually interpret or communicate the thought and feeling of others. The speaker, by contrast, is *not* an interpreter; he presents by voice and body the thought which is *his.*

A desired response. Again in this respect, all communicators have something in common. The architect who designs a church wants it to inspire a particular response. The poet or novelist writes for a clearly determined purpose. The speaker likewise speaks with a definite objective in mind. When there is no objective, when there is no purpose or reason for speech, communication becomes frivolous or inane.

Listeners. Though we can easily identify the listeners in a public speaking situation, we must not assume that listeners appear only in large audiences at our public auditoriums. They are present when an instructor gives an assignment, when the housewife tells her husband what to bring home for supper, or even when the brand new freshman asks for directions to the administration building. The speaker meets his listener on dozens of informal but important occasions during the day, and together they talk and listen — for a purpose.

The speaker, then, is one who

- communicates
- thought and feeling
- by voice and body
- to secure a desired response
- from his listeners.

Clearly, there are speakers who succeed and speakers who fail. It is important for the student of speech to recognize both if he is to meet with success.

■ THE INEFFECTIVE SPEAKER

Consider the speaker who fails. We are not thinking here of the student in a public speaking class but rather of the professional lecturer or the national celebrity who leaves us bored and unexcited. He arrives, puffed with enthusiasm for his own words. He tells a joke that hobbles, coins a phrase that bounces, and pauses, dark and somber, like a Hamlet lost in thought. He flails the air with awe-inspiring gestures. He either has many facts but little wit, or he has great wit but few facts. His organization resembles a twisted maze, and he seems to know nothing about using his voice effectively. Though weaknesses like these are easily identified, there are others which often escape our attention but nevertheless cause a breakdown in communication.

☐   **SPEAKERS FREQUENTLY FAIL BECAUSE THEY FORGET HOW DIFFICULT IT IS TO LISTEN**

Let us imagine that we are in an audience challenged by the many ideas of a good speaker, one who appeals to our reasoning. He wants us to receive and appreciate his information, to agree with him to such an extent that our attitudes are deepened or shifted from one extreme to another. He arouses us to such an extent that we want to participate, to ask a question immediately, to add to the information he has provided; but, unfortunately, we cannot speak. At best we may laugh or applaud at selected moments; beyond this we cannot actively participate at the moment the speaker stimulates us. We are forced by the nature of the occasion to remain still — with neither freedom to talk nor freedom to move.

The role we play in the presence of the public speaker is that of the passive participant. We cannot participate actively and enthusiastically in the *exchange* of thought; we can only receive. Because of this, we are easily distracted, and before the speech is ended our attention wanders to other interests. We remain courteous, of course. We keep our eyes open and our faces turned in the speaker's direction. We usually avoid excessive coughing and sneezing. We give all the outward appearances of listening, but in reality the speaker makes little impact on us.

Furthermore, we tend to listen with our prejudices and our doubts. When our minds are made up and our attitudes well-established, we usually accept whatever confirms our point of view and reject whatever contradicts it. Perhaps this is why more and more of us distrust anyone engaging in the act of persuasion. The bread man who knocks on our door assures us that his bread is superior to all others; but we have always been satisfied with the supermarket brands. The handsome young man at the Big-Buy Used Car Lot greets us with a "you-came-to-the-right-place" smile, but somehow we believe that all used car lots are about the same. The television admen pump endlessly their quasi-scientific demonstrations of stomach acids eating holes in napkins, aspirin dissolving in the human stomach, and nasal sprays quickly shrinking swollen sinus membranes. While our TV gangsters speak of the big double-cross, our Senate Investigating Committees join the social critics in renewed discovery of duplicity, graft, payola, deceptions, and ten percenters.

Whom can we believe? Where precisely can we find the man who will speak only the truth? We look for him on the speaker's stand, but maybe he sounds just a bit like the adman on a promotions drive. We think we hear the bold and extravagant claim instead of the simple truth. Then we remember the word our neighbor used: "Hood-winker!" We remember the advice of our ninth-grade teacher: "Don't get carried away; get the facts." Finally, in the rough and tumble of our own bewilderment, we listen with half our mental faculties and doubt with the other half!

Listening is hard work. The successful speaker will acknowledge that fact and make every effort to help his audience through the use of interest-getting materials, through materials related to the desires and needs of his audience, and through all those qualities of organization, language, and delivery that make listening easier.

☐   **SPEAKERS FREQUENTLY FAIL BECAUSE THEY ARE SELF-CENTERED**

A century or so ago, Americans were thrilled by the prospect of a celebrated speaker coming to town. Usually an active man, a drama-tist, a spellbinder, an entertainer in all essential respects, he was deter-mined that his oration would top even the finest entertainment. Though years have passed and times have changed, the tradition con-tinues. Many speakers still believe they are performers rather than communicators. Such speakers fall roughly into three groups: First, there is the speaker who has little to say but says it well. His voice is beautiful, his manner charming, but his speech is shallow, full of platitudes and empty rhetoric. Second, there is the person of note, with an enviable reputation in the literary world or the world of public affairs. When he approaches *us,* however, he seems to be coasting on reputation alone. He appears to have lost sight of *us* as he reads from a chapter of his book or repeats the speech which our newspapers and magazines have quoted with great frequency. Finally, there is the obvious showman. He speaks with the comedian's versatility of voice and body and wins the warm and welcome response of laughter. If his purpose is merely to entertain, we cannot call him a failure; but if his purpose is to inform or instruct on an occasion calling for seriousness, we must call him showman or even buffoon.

The effective speaker cannot run the risk of being indifferent or self-centered. He must be genuinely interested in his audience and show that interest in his words and in his voice.

□ ## SPEAKERS FREQUENTLY FAIL BECAUSE THEY USE DIFFICULT OR DATED LANGUAGE

All of us have heard the speaker who falls into this category. Usually a man with a scholar's grasp of his subject, he is careful to enrich his ideas with facts and to support his facts with sources. His vocabulary is extensive, and his sentences flow smoothly in rhythmical succession. He possesses many of the finest attributes of our most respected speakers, and yet he fails. Why? Perhaps the answer lies in his attempt to present a finely phrased essay or to recapture the style of the grand romantic past. He recalls the eloquence of Patrick Henry, Daniel Webster, and William Jennings Bryan, and so admires their rhetoric that he attempts to reproduce it.

Obviously, the effective speaker today cannot use the language or the style of the past. His listeners prefer language that approaches conversation *at its best,* with its warmth, simplicity, directness, and vitality. In the press of busy schedules, time and the consequent need for brevity become matters of major importance. No one has long to listen or, of course, to speak. Everyone must get back to work, and the campaigning candidate must make a thousand speeches between now and next November.

□ ## SPEAKERS FREQUENTLY FAIL BECAUSE THEY DO NOT PINPOINT THE DESIRED RESPONSE

Some speakers apparently feel that the purpose of a speech is merely to fill up a gap of time. They seem only to be putting in an appearance so that those in the audience who are curious about their looks or their point of view may satisfy their curiosity. They talk "about" something until their time is up; then, satisfied that they have complied with their part of the agreement, they say "Thank you" and depart.

Such speakers are aware that they must speak on a *particular* subject to a *particular* audience at a *particular* place for a *particular* period of time; but they fail to realize that they should speak with a *particularly desired response in mind.* They may speak capably "about" a matter of concern — "about" foreign policy, "about" medical care, "about" aid to education, or "about" the greatest threats to peace. But all these "abouts" mean very little unless they have a precise, pinpointed objective. Speaking "about" something may do no harm, and it may help to complete a ceremonial ritual and fill up a time gap. Apart from this triviality, such speaking accomplishes little.

The speaker needs to determine how he wants his listeners to respond. Does he want them to laugh? Does he want to deepen existing attitudes? Does he want to change audience opinion from "no" to "yes"? Does he speak primarily to make his audience uneasy or uncomfortable? Or does he speak so that all who hear will leap into action? He must answer such questions in advance if his speech is to succeed.

The effective speaker has a definite objective and pursues it forthrightly. He avoids all traces of aimlessness in his effort to win a favorable response.

□   **SPEAKERS FREQUENTLY FAIL BECAUSE THEY BELIEVE KNOWLEDGE OF A SUBJECT IS ALL THAT IS NECESSARY FOR SUCCESSFUL COMMUNICATION**

There have always been those who distrust the study of speech. Their distrust seems to grow out of their abiding faith in content as well as out of their failure to understand the purpose of speech training.

It is imperative, of course, that the speaker have something to say. His speech must be rich in content. He must observe. He must read widely and deeply on matters pertaining to his subject. He must think. But having done all these things, he still has no guarantee of success. He must also understand the people to whom he is speaking. He must find ways of making speech content interesting, clear, and vivid to his listeners. The speaker who learns this lesson and practices it will succeed. In contrast, the "get-tough" speaker who says, "It's my business to present the facts; it's yours to receive them" demonstrates his ignorance of the difficulties of communication and does his "facts" a disservice.

The content speaker labors under other mistaken impressions about the nature of speech. Misinformed, he is likely to believe that a *speech class is little more than a vocal finishing school,* where effective speech is achieved by mechanically learning and applying a few laws of platform behavior. He may even believe that speech is not so much interested in truth as in the *appearance* of truth — in falsehood, deceit, and insincerity. But training in speech is not the product of a finishing school, not a body of law, and not a lesson in deception. Good speech *is* concerned with making content meaningful through language and delivery that is natural and sincere.

Failure for whatever reason is regrettable, but there is little need to cry universal despair. Just as the student may observe failure, he may also observe success. And since success, not failure, is the chief concern of this book, the student should prepare not only to recognize weaknesses but also to identify the strengths of the effective speaker.

■   THE EFFECTIVE SPEAKER

Who is the effective speaker? What are the standards for judging good speech? Once the speech has been presented, what criteria can the listener use to determine the speaker's success? There are seven principles that will help to answer such questions.

☐   THE EFFECTIVE SPEAKER MUST HAVE
                                              A WORTHWHILE IDEA

Ideas may arise from many sources — from the speaker's observations, from his reading and listening, or from his discussions with friends and colleagues. But the worthwhile idea does not suddenly leap full-blown into the speaker's head; it is more likely to grow slowly as he matures and continues his research and his observations of life. In contrast, the trivial or frothy idea is commonplace and hardly worth exploring.

Between these two extremes of the "worthwhile" and the "trivial" is an endless list of ideas which *must* be expressed because they have a direct bearing on our immediate lives. The factory foreman must speak of the need for increased attention to safety because accidents continue to happen. The coach must deliver his emotional pep talk at half-time because his team is losing the game. And the after-dinner speaker must delight his audience with good humor because the occasion calls for laughter. None of these ideas is of the dimension of The Great Bomb or The Great Problem of Racial Integration; yet each has its place. Each is appropriate to the needs of the particular audience.

An effective speaker realizes that his listeners judge him on his choice of ideas — on the level of their significance as well as on their usefulness or appropriateness to the audience and the occasion.

☐   **THE EFFECTIVE SPEAKER MUST WISH TO
                    SHARE THE IDEA WITH OTHERS**

It is often good to be a thinker removed from everyone else. It is good for the student and good for the teacher. It was good for Galileo, Newton, and Einstein, for silence is the soil in which ideas grow. But sooner or later the silence must be broken. Our Galileos, Newtons, and Einsteins cannot afford to be mute. Their ideas must be made a matter of record. This can happen only when the man with the idea has a desire to stand up and be heard — to share his idea with others.

Closely associated with the desire to speak is the desire to fulfill the social responsibility of exchanging ideas on controversial matters. Without an exchange, without a thorough, comprehensive discussion of vital issues, there is little need for the guarantee of free speech. Where the exchange does take place, the private citizen is better prepared to vote and govern wisely. There are undoubtedly speakers who stifle their desire and shirk their responsibility to discuss certain issues because they are "too hot." Even on the college campus, students may avoid discussing faculty censorship of the student newspaper because the issue is "too delicate." In both instances the desire to speak may be present, but the desire and courage to fulfill a social responsibility are missing.

An effective speaker is eager to share his ideas with others. He realizes that on most issues there are at least two sides and that each side must be presented in its most reasonable light if the freedom to speak is to amount to anything.

☐   **THE EFFECTIVE SPEAKER COMMUNICATES**
                                            FOR A PARTICULAR PURPOSE

It is very difficult to speak without any purpose whatsoever. Even the individual who talks to himself has the goal of "talking it out" or "thinking it over" or "releasing the self." When two people exchange idle social chatter about the weather, there is the aim of breaking the ice and tearing down the social barrier that exists between them. Good speech is functional, and its practice indicates that the speaker is working toward a particularly desired response from his audience.

The *general purposes* of speech are to inform, to persuade, and to entertain. The teacher's chief aim is usually to inform, the political candidate's to persuade, and the humorist's to entertain. These general purposes become *specific purposes* when the speaker narrows his topic. The English teacher, for example, knows:

1. that he must inform (*the general purpose*)
2. that he must inform about literature
3. that he must inform about drama
4. that he must inform about recent drama
5. that he must inform about drama of the "absurd"
6. that he must inform about the absurdity of Harold Pinter's drama
7. that he must inform about Pinter's dialogue (*the specific purpose*)

In this sequence the speaker's purpose becomes increasingly specific as he moves away from the first and most general purpose.

The effective speaker decides in advance how he wants his audience to respond. He realizes that ideas unrelated to purpose will rattle like pebbles in a bass drum.

☐   **THE EFFECTIVE SPEAKER COMMUNICATES IDEAS PROPERLY DEVELOPED BY SUITABLE MATERIALS**

An idea is the beginning of speech content, but this beginning grows as the speaker selects additional materials to develop it. To develop is to *clarify,* to *reinforce* through evidence and analytical reasoning, or to *prove* the probability of an assertion. To reach these goals, the speaker will use materials appropriate or pertinent to the subject and the audience. They will be interesting and varied. They will be clear and concrete, free of ambiguity and double meaning. They will come from particular and authoritative sources rather than from the grapevine.

Suppose the speaker's controlling assertion is: "I believe that our private rights should have precedence over public rights." Such an assertion cries out for clarification. What does the speaker mean? Is he speaking of the right to vote Democratic or the right to wear a red necktie? Further development clarifies the point; he is speaking of the right to own property, to run the business which he chooses, to hire and fire whomever he likes, and to reject whatever union interferes with his policies. To reinforce such assertions, the speaker finds it necessary to rely on restatement, examples, statistics, and authoritative opinions. To *prove* the absolute truth of his assertions is quite another matter; at this point the speaker is faced with an impossibility. All that he can hope to establish is a probability of the truth, not the truth itself.

The effective speaker is a selective speaker. Once he has chosen his idea, he selects supporting material that is appropriate, clear, varied, and authoritative so that he may clarify, reinforce, and prove.

☐   **THE EFFECTIVE SPEAKER IS WELL ORGANIZED**

Since clear ideas, good intentions, and volumes of supporting material mean very little in the absence of good organization, the effective speaker — like the novelist, the dramatist, or the musical composer — must decide how to order his thoughts. Though the precise organization will vary according to the subject, the principles remain the same. The speaker selects his first words carefully to prepare his audience to receive his ideas. He creates an interest in his subject. Early in his presentation he reveals his controlling idea; and as he moves from one subdivision to another, he laces them together with transitions and shows how each is related to his central point. When all the major subdivisions have been explored, he pulls them together with a summary and concludes with an appeal for the desired response.

By the use of good organization, the effective speaker reveals much more than the clarity of his ideas. He reveals both the nature and the sources of his evidence. Further, he indirectly reveals a sense of honesty. He implies: "I make no attempt to send up a smoke screen to hide the issues. I want us to meet them head on."

☐   **THE EFFECTIVE SPEAKER USES
                               APPROPRIATE LANGUAGE**

Once the speaker has formulated his ideas, developed them by good supporting materials, and arranged them in the most reasonable order, he must express them in the most appropriate language. Appropriateness depends on three things — the nature of the audience, the occasion, and the kinds of ideas to be presented. The President of the United States, in delivering a Report to the Nation, will use a dignified, simple style. The evangelist or revivalist will use words that have emotional power. The college professor, speaking to colleagues in his field, will use language that is learned or sophisticated and often foreign to one trained in another specialty. All effective speakers, however, use words that are simple, precise, and concrete as well as words that provide color and excite action or belief.

But words do more than carry the thoughts and emotions of the speaker; they project an image of his personality and reveal his intelligence, his character, and his attitude toward society. Offensive words, words that are crude and vulgar, indicate an offensive personality and shock an audience accustomed to discretion. Words of taste and human understanding indicate a wholesome personality and usually invite a fair hearing.

☐ **THE EFFECTIVE SPEAKER COMMUNICATES BY GOOD DELIVERY**

Many students enter a speech class with the mistaken impression that delivery is their only concern. True, it is a major concern, but with most instructors it is the concern developed last. A speaker must first develop, organize, and phrase his ideas. Once that is done, he must rely on his voice and body to convey his thoughts. A platform speaker without skill in delivery is like a concert violinist without the violin. Neither can win a favorable response from his audience.

The speaker's delivery depends on two things: effective use of his body and effective use of his voice. Bodily communication includes the speaker's total appearance and behavior: his grooming; his posture; the way he sits, rises, and walks; the way he gestures with his hands and arms; and the way he expresses thought by the varying expressions on his face. Vocal communication includes such things as loudness or volume, pitch, timing, and quality. It also includes melody or variety and, of course, articulation and pronunciation.

The effective speaker knows that good delivery is no social or academic frill. He has respect for its importance. When speaking to an audience, he adapts his delivery to the nature of the occasion. Through movement and gesture, he suits his actions to his words and makes his words more meaningful. He uses a voice that is active, natural, and sincere to stimulate interest and win a favorable response from his audience.

SUMMARY

1. The speaker communicates thought and feeling by voice and body to secure a desired response from his listeners.
2. Speakers frequently fail because:
    a. They forget how difficult it is to listen.
    b. They are self-centered.
    c. They use difficult or dated language.

    d. They fail to pinpoint the desired response.
    e. They believe knowledge of a subject is all that is necessary for successful communication.
3. The effective speaker:
    a. Has a worthwhile idea.
    b. Has a genuine desire to share that idea with others.
    c. Communicates for a particular response.
    d. Uses suitable materials to develop the idea.
    e. Is well organized.
    f. Uses appropriate language.
    g. Communicates by good delivery.

EXERCISES

1. This chapter discusses five reasons for the failure of public speakers. To these, add five more which you believe are also important.

2. Listen to a chapel or convocation speaker. Evaluate his speech in terms of the seven criteria for good speech presented in this chapter. Be prepared to discuss how he fails as well as how he succeeds.

3. Without referring to any particular professor on your campus, join with your entire speech class in preparing an exhaustive list of the annoying characteristics of college lecturers. Which is mentioned most frequently? Least frequently?

4. Prepare a similar list of desirable characteristics of college lecturers. All things considered, how do college professors measure up to the standards of good public speakers?

5. Examine those everyday situations in which you are a speaker. In how many of them are you a *public* speaker? How do you measure up to the standards of good speech?

6. Prepare a two-minute speech of self-introduction. Present yourself in such a way that you will help your instructor and

your fellow students remember who you are. To be sure, your name is important, as are your major subjects, your home town, and your selected profession. But even more important are the attitudes you have toward people and things. What, for example, is your attitude toward college professors? Toward dormitory food? Toward those required P.E. courses? Or even assignments in speech?

You should have several objectives: (1) To speak in such a manner that everyone will remember your name. (2) To speak in order to assure everyone that it will be good to have your company. (3) To speak to break the ice, to remove the barrier of classroom stiffness. (4) To speak casually and informally, with notes if you like, but certainly without a manuscript. (5) To speak without concern for grades — especially if your instructor assures you that the speech will not be graded. (6) To speak so as to illustrate your likenesses to and certainly your differences from other persons.

7. The two brief speeches which follow were delivered by freshmen to comply with the preceding assignment. All the student speeches found at the end of each exercise are transcriptions of recorded speeches presented in a college public speaking classroom. Read them quickly; then answer to your satisfaction the questions which follow.

   A. My initials are S.A.S. — Sas. My friends call me Sassy — not, of course, because of my disposition or my manner of speech but simply because of those three letters. They stand for Shirley Ann Simpson. But perhaps I should tell you that I'm thinking of changing both the name and the initials to JINKS. Let me tell you why.

   I suppose all freshmen girls want to make a big hit their first few days on campus. I was no exception; so the minute my parents left the dorm I dashed back to join my roommate. As I opened the door to our room a pin fell out of the bottom hinge and the door went banging into the plaster wall. Well, Roomie and I tried to put the door together again, but since both of us are Home Ec. majors we failed and put in a call for the custodian. As fate would have it the custodian was busy — trying to get a tablespoon out of the garbage disposal; so Roomie and I went back to work. The pin went in, the door moved freely, and privacy was finally assured — but only after one badly skinned index finger. That's why I'm gesturing with a band-aid.

That evening, at our first candle-light dinner, I tried to make a big impression. I was careful with my conversation. I made certain to smile at pleasant remarks and laugh at the jokes. I took special pains to keep one hand in my lap — just the way Mom told me. But the meat presented a problem. How is a girl with a lame finger going to cut a tough steak? I tried, but the steak won. My finger slipped off the fork, the meat scooted out into the centerpiece, and my hand ended up in the candied yams.

It was a great day for Sas, or rather Jinks, or rather . . . what was it now? Oh, yes. Shirley Ann Simpson.

B. My name is Jim Barnett. I'm a first quarter freshman from Milford. I don't suppose many of you know much about Milford. As a matter of fact there isn't much to know; but if you ever drive through, take special note of the caution light. That's our one bright spot and it's busy twenty-four hours a day.

I'm planning to major in history. Why, I don't know. I guess it's because I've always liked it. Even in grade school I liked to read about history. I was always glad when Lincoln's birthday came along, because I knew all of us would get to learn more about the man who is probably our most famous American.

In high school I was a member of the honor society. I played second horn in the band. I was president of Future Farmers of America, active in the Methodist Youth Group, and when the choir director would let me, I sang in the choir.

I've never been very good at making speeches. My tongue gets twisted, my voice shakes, my lips begin to twitch, and . . . well, when you look at me like that, you can see what happens. Judging from the speeches I've heard today, I'm afraid I'm going to be at the bottom of the heap.

QUESTIONS

a. In your opinion is there any significant difference between the two speeches? What is the difference?

b. Judging from the printed speeches, can you predict that you would remember one speaker more easily than you would the other? Why?

c. What is the greatest strength and weakness of each of the two speeches?

d. In what respect will you make your speech of self-introduction superior to each of these?

8. *Alternate speaking assignment.* Instead of delivering a self-introduction, deliver a brief introduction of the classmate seated at your right. Keep the same objectives in mind.

CHAPTER 2

THE FIRST
CLASSROOM SPEECH

The speech class presents the student with a problem not encountered in other classes. In most of his classes the subject matter is approached gradually, bit by bit. In a conventional history class, for example, the instructor proceeds chapter by chapter or era by era; the geometry class progresses from simple to complex theorems; and it is much the same in classes of literature, science, business, or art. The student of speech, by contrast, begins with the total activity of speaking; there can be no piecemeal approach.

Because of this "wholeness" of approach, the beginning speech student is likely to demonstrate certain weaknesses which will discourage him but at the same time prove that he is normal. He may, for example, speak only to the instructor or to the windows, floor, or ceiling. He may deliver speeches which ramble and lack unity and coherence. Or he may be nervous or jittery. In short, he may not be able to win immediate response from an audience. Despite all these "normal" reactions, the student must make the effort to be superior even with his first speech. This chapter is designed to help him meet that challenge.

■   **PREPARING TO SPEAK**

Good preparation includes seven steps:

1. Analyzing the audience
2. Selecting an idea or subject
3. Determining the purpose
4. Gathering the material
5. Organizing the material
6. Finding the right words
7. Practicing the delivery

Each of these steps will be treated at length in subsequent chapters, but here they are briefly described to give the student an overview of the complete process of speech preparation and delivery.

☐   **ANALYZING THE AUDIENCE AND THE SETTING**

Some instructors will encourage the student to assume that the class audience is a group of apathetic or hostile listeners. Others will allow the student to assume that his audience is a Mothers' Club, a PTA group, or a National Convention of the Republican Party. Most instructors, however, have their students consider the classroom audience to be precisely what it is — a group of young people interested in becoming better speakers and listeners, and just as real and responsive to challenge or boredom as any other audience.

Before starting to prepare his speech, the student should learn as much as he can about his classroom audience. How many in the class are freshmen and how many are sophomores? What are they majoring in? Speech? English? Engineering? Business? What is the ratio of men to women? Do they come from nearby small towns or far-removed metropolitan areas? From the speeches of self-introduction, learn as much as possible about audience attitudes toward campus, community, and national issues. And what about the instructor? After all, he is part of the audience, too.

In addition to knowing about the listeners, the student speaker should know something about the room in which he will speak. He should bear in mind that a platform or stage, for example, will give him an air of formality no matter what the nature of his speech. If the room is wide and the audience scattered, he will find audience contact more difficult than in a narrow room. Windows open to the campus, doors open to the corridor, or other possible distractions for an inattentive listener should be noted. In short, the effective speaker will do all he can to make physical surroundings work for him and not against him.

☐   **SELECTING THE SUBJECT**

All too frequently the student says, "But I don't have anything to say. I just don't know what to talk about." Taking the easiest way out, he goes to the Periodical Room of the library and "borrows" an article from *Reader's Digest* — its idea, its development, its arrangement, and even its language. Such speech preparation is not only dishonest but thought-stifling as well. A class in speech is neither a class in reading nor a class in reporting on popular articles; it is a class in which a student starts with his own ideas or those which become his after wide reading or equally wide experience.

Many students solve the problem by choosing a subject pertaining to their college campus. Notice, for example, how the general area of campus problems could serve the student for the duration of the course:

1. Dormitory food
2. Roommates
3. Inadequate study facilities
4. Campus government
5. Girls (Boys)
6. Fraternity/Sorority costs
7. The governing board
8. Finding the right course
9. Finding the right professor
10. The price of used books
11. Abuse of the library
12. The autocratic professor

13. Changing a major
14. Learning logic
15. Waiting in line
16. Getting a government loan
17. Finding an adviser
18. Weekend social life
19. Segregation on campus
20. Haste and hustle
21. Pleasing the prof
22. Writing home
23. Religion on campus
24. Conformity
25. Finding part-time jobs

Every student can probably think of many more. At any rate, after looking over such a list, limited as it is, he can hardly maintain that he has nothing to talk about. Of course, the range of speech subjects should not be limited to the campus. National and international issues offer many worthwhile subjects for a speech as well.

Not just any subject selected at random will do. It must pass the tests of acceptability: (1) It should be interesting to the speaker. (2) It should be of interest to the audience. (3) It should be worthwhile or worth considering. (4) It should be adaptable to the time allotted.

☐   **DETERMINING THE PURPOSE**

Almost all our speaking is motivated by a purpose of some kind. We say "Hello," "Good morning," "Nice day," or "See you later" for particular reasons. In casual conversation we try to convince our friends that Illinois has a better football team than Ohio State; that Professor Casey is an outstanding teacher; or that a certain political candidate should not be seriously considered for office. At one moment we try to persuade, at another, to inform or entertain. But as we move from informal conversation to the modest formality of the public-speaking classroom, the *need* for a well-determined purpose becomes even more apparent.

The speaker's first responsibility is to determine his *general purpose*. Is it *to inform?* If so, he might instruct his audience about

a subject recently studied in an anthropology class. Is it *to persuade?*
If so, he might attempt to convince his listeners that more of them
should enroll in anthropology. Is it *to entertain?* If so, he might
relate an amusing experience he had during last summer's "dig."

The speaker's second responsibility is to determine the *specific
purpose* of his speech — the precise response he wants from his
audience. It should be phrased in a definite statement; it should be
closely related to the subject; and above all it should be kept clearly
in mind as the speech is prepared and delivered. Notice in the
following example how the subject is selected and narrowed; then
notice how the specific purpose grows logically out of the subject and
the general purpose.

Subject area:	Crime in the United States
Area limited:	Juvenile delinquency
Further limited:	Juvenile delinquency in New York's Chinatown
General purpose:	To inform
Specific purpose:	To help my audience understand why New York's Chinatown has little juvenile delinquency

The student's specific purpose is to describe the conditions in
Chinatown that inhibit juvenile delinquency, but he obviously implies
a secondary purpose: he wishes to persuade his listeners that areas
with serious delinquency problems ought to take a leaf out of Chinatown's book. The speech actually combines two general purposes,
informing and persuading, in order to make the specific purpose clear
and vivid. Because the student has refined the specific purpose so
precisely, a secondary general purpose is not confusing but helpful.
More often than not, a speech will combine general purposes for
the same reason. But the specific purpose will suffer unless one
general purpose is dominant, as it is in the speech above.

☐   **GATHERING THE MATERIAL**

In all probability the first speaking assignments will be simple
enough so that the student may rely on personal experience for

materials to develop his speech. The student who worked for the Continental Can Company during the summer may easily prepare a process speech on "Steps in Making the Pull-Tab Can." The student who worked for a railroad may talk on "How to Lose a Train." And the coed who is at college primarily to find herself a husband may prepare an amusing speech on "Husband Hunting." All of these topics are best and most easily developed by reference to personal experience. Notice, for example, how one student prepared a speech on college examinations:

> *Idea:* Final examinations for college classes should be abolished.

> *Idea:* They encourage the professor to teach so that he will be able to test.

> > Example

> *Idea:* They place too great an emphasis on learning in order to earn a grade.

> > Example

> *Idea:* They frequently cause nervous exhaustion or even a mental breakdown.

> > Example

This is an excellent example of how a speaker can use personal experience to good advantage. Here the student undoubtedly found himself at some time in the past angered by the necessity for final examinations. Out of the anger grew a conviction. The conviction, in turn, was based on three ideas, each of which the speaker could support with firsthand experience or irrefutable evidence.

As a speaker moves out of the area of personal experiences, he obviously must rely on other sources for material to support his point of view. For example, it is not likely that the freshman girl in America will have had much experience in guerilla warfare, but this is no reason for her to avoid the subject if her interest is keen enough. But where will she find material? There are several possible sources, among them (1) an instructor or a fellow student known to have had some personal experience fighting guerilas in Viet Nam; (2) a ROTC training manual or film; (3) articles and books in the library. Naturally, she takes notes to remind herself of what she has accomplished and what remains to be done.

☐   **ORGANIZING THE MATERIAL**

After a speaker has selected and narrowed his subject, determined his goals, and gathered all his supporting material, he must organize his speech. It does no good to shuffle through an assortment of notes and talk about the first idea that rises to the top. An effective speaker will construct a plan. For example, a speech based on an historical event will probably be arranged in chronological order. The speaker who sets out to solve a problem might first describe the *status quo,* proceed to analyze the probable causes of the problem, and end with a description and rationale of his proposed solution. Whatever the plan, the speaker should write out his specific purpose and keep it before him as a reminder of what he hopes to accomplish.

For at least three good reasons, a speech plan is usually prepared as an outline. In the first place, preparing an outline helps the student clarify the purpose of his speech. Second, it enables him to test the completeness, clarity, and logic of the speech in terms of that purpose. Third, the outline serves as an aid to effective delivery.

The three major parts of a speech are the introduction, the body, and the conclusion.

The body. Since the body is the heart of the speech and reveals the substance of each significant idea, it is best to begin here. Notice in the following preliminary plan how the speaker begins with a purpose statement and follows with a simple list of three points.

Specific purpose:	To help my audience understand why New York's Chinatown has little juvenile delinquency.
First point:	Children are trained to respect their parents.
Second point:	Children have good employment opportunities.
Third point:	Children appear to have a blood relationship with all other Chinese children.

He then will support his three points with examples or illustrations culled from the material he has gathered.

The introduction. The purpose of the introduction is to draw attention to the speaker and his topic and to prepare the audience for what is to follow. The simplest introduction is an honest, straightforward announcement of the subject or of what the speaker hopes to accomplish. "Mr. Chairman, today I would like to tell you why the residents of New York's Chinatown have virtually no problem with juvenile delinquency." Perhaps a better introduction is one that is less direct, more creative, and more likely to prick the curiosity of the audience. "Mr. Chairman, as I read this morning's *Star,* it struck me that nothing is as popular as crime."

The conclusion. A properly prepared conclusion pulls the several parts of the speech together so that they act as a single voice appealing for the desired response. A good conclusion provides a succinct summary of the major points, again reveals the purpose, or appeals for belief or action.

Now notice how the three parts are combined in a complete outline:

I. Introduction
   A. *Example:* Reference to *Morning Star*
   B. *Statistic:* Crime in U.S.
   C. *Statistic:* Crime by juveniles

II. Body (Purpose: To help you understand why New York's Chinatown has little juvenile delinquency.)

   A. Children are trained to respect their parents.

     1. *Quotation:* Chinese parent

     2. *Quotation:* Father John McLoughlin

   B. Children have good employment opportunities.

     1. *Statistic:* Number of boys employed

     2. *Explanation:* The nature of family businesses

   C. Children appear to have a blood relationship with all other children.

     1. *Example:* The teacher with a class of relatives

     2. *Example:* Boys from opposite sides of town

III. Conclusion

   A. Summary of three points

   B. Appeal for understanding and increased attention to our juvenile crime problem

The student has stuck to his purpose and has organized his materials well. If he follows his outline during delivery, he should be able to accomplish his purposes effectively.

☐   **FINDING THE RIGHT WORDS**

The language of any speech should be determined by the audience and the nature of the occasion. If the purpose of the occasion is to pay honor, deference, and respect, obviously the speaker will not use flippant and frivolous language. Similarly, if the purpose is to entertain, he will avoid language which is, to use Carlyle's words, full of "dead pedantries and somnolent impotencies." The student should remain a student and not try to imitate the elder statesman. He should speak informally and actively, with honesty and sincerity. Above all, he should use language that is both clear and precise.

"How do we begin? What are our first words?" If the class has a chairman to introduce each speaker, the first words are "Mr. Chairman." These may be followed by acknowledging "friends" or "ladies

and gentlemen." By all means, do not begin by announcing the title: "My title is *Tinkling Brass and Sounding Cymbals.*"

"Are we penalized if we make a mistake in grammar?" Yes. A teacher of speech, like all other teachers on campus, believes that good grammar is characteristic of the good student. Some teachers will weigh the matter lightly, some heavily; to insure a margin of safety, make sure your grammar is in good order.

"If we correct our mistakes are we still penalized?" Probably — though there is no satisfactory way to measure the extent. Most critics prefer their speakers to say things correctly the first time without fumbling around for the right word. An error that is caught and then corrected is probably better than an error that is uncorrected; but because it calls attention to the struggle for correctness, it interrupts the flow of communication.

"Are there words or expressions we should avoid?" Yes (see Chapter 6). At the outset of the course, avoid one- or two-word transitions, such as "next," "another thing," and "also." Avoid such catch-all terms as "everything like that." And when phrasing the conclusion, try to be more creative than to say "and in conclusion" and "now I appeal to you."

"What are our last words?" These will depend on the speech and its purpose. The speaker should *not* say, "That's all I have to say," or "I guess that about does it for today." Such remarks weaken the conclusion. Neither should the student end with "I thank you." He should end with strong words that round out the entire speech and clearly reveal its purpose.

☐   **PRACTICING THE DELIVERY**

Many speakers are reluctant to practice delivering a speech. Apparently they are afraid of being discovered talking to themselves, or they believe that an idea on paper is the same as an idea spoken. Neither of these notions, however, should be taken seriously; for practicing the delivery will help to fix the outline clearly in mind, help in finding words and phrases that are especially appropriate, and even acquaint the speaker with the sound of his own voice. But before practicing, he should know which of the four kinds of delivery to practice inasmuch as each requires a different skill.

1. *Impromptu* delivery is spontaneous, offhand, spur of the moment. It takes place without previous specific preparation. It does not rely on notes. Our conversational speech is impromptu. When a friend asks "How are you?" we do not rush to the library to prepare a four-minute speech; we answer spontaneously.

2. *Reading* or *manuscript* delivery is at the opposite extreme from impromptu delivery. It is appropriate when the speaker believes it necessary to phrase his ideas with great care in order to develop a tightly-reasoned thesis. A Senator might read a statement announcing his candidacy for office. The President might read an address reviewing an important administrative decision. The industrialist might read a report to the annual meeting of the shareholders.

3. *Memorization.* In delivering a speech from memory, the speaker repeats word for word the content of his manuscript. Many college speakers seem to find great comfort in memorizing a speech. They know exactly what they want to say; they don't have to worry about finding the right word; and they can usually make very good audience contact. There are, however, some serious drawbacks. Memorizing a speech requires much more time for preparation; it is more likely to cause the speech to sound mechanical or "canned"; and it may lead to great embarrassment when a minor disturbance in the audience causes the memory to fail. Most speech instructors will strongly advise against memorizing a speech.

4. *Extemporaneous* delivery is quite different from the other three. It is unlike impromptu because it follows very careful preparation; it is unlike reading because the speaker has only his notes to follow; and it is unlike the memorized speech because the speaker "finds" his words at the moment he needs them. To deliver a speech extemporaneously is to speak freely and easily from carefully prepared notes.

Of the four types of delivery, the one assigned most often is extemporaneous. The student should not write out a complete manuscript with the intention of trying to get by with a skillful and deceptive reading. He should not try to memorize and recite or, worse yet, speak impromptu without any preparation whatsoever. The only memory work involved in the extemporaneous speech is how to begin and end, what the sequence of ideas is, and perhaps a particularly apt phrase or two. The only thing the extemporaneous speaker reads is a direct quotation. The rest of the time he just "talks" in an informal or conversational tone. He tries to establish direct eye-to-eye, face-to-face, and person-to-person contact. He is active, animated, and enthusiastic, and he uses appropriate gestures and vocal variety. He is human and responsive to others. And certainly he is flexible, allowing himself freedom to refer to the event which preceded, to explain a point which seems to baffle his listeners, or even to adapt to signs of boredom or restlessness in his audience.

"How should we use our practice time?" There is no way to answer this question satisfactorily for everyone; work habits vary too much from person to person. The following suggestions are a composite of the advice of a number of effective classroom speakers:

1. *Prepare early.* If you have only one day in which to build a speech, decide within the hour what to discuss. If you have several days, decide the first day. Spend more time on developing an idea than on choosing one.

2. *Use as few speaking notes as possible.* Some students report that they prepare a full outline and then write out a complete manuscript. After reading the manuscript two or three times, they destroy it and practice from their outline. Other students prepare a full outline for the instructor and a simple list of key words for their speaking notes. Still others work out their speeches orally. They develop the flow of ideas first; then when it sounds good to them, they prepare the outline. Almost all the better speakers learn to reduce their notes to the fewest possible words.

3. *Practice aloud.* Some students mumble to themselves as they work at their desks. Some deliver the speech to a roommate and ask for comments. Others speak into a tape recorder or to a mirror, while others find a time when their classroom is vacant and practice with a classmate. The place is not important; getting accustomed to your own voice is.

4. *Practice more than once.* Oddly enough, only a few recommended practicing more than twice. Apparently the speech

grows dull and uninteresting if overworked in practice. Practice actively, creatively — not with your mind in neutral.

5. *Plan some movement.* Most effective speakers plan to move or gesture at least once during a short speech. They do not carefully rehearse all their gestures in advance; they allow them to arise spontaneously in the presence of the audience.

The good speaker will soon find that an oral practice session is no longer necessary. After the third or fourth speech he will have a pretty realistic appraisal of his ability. He may still mumble while trying out a phrase or testing his introduction or his conclusion; but he will have developed confidence in his ability to express his ideas clearly and effectively the first time through.

■   **LEARNING FROM CRITICISM**

The adage "We learn by doing" is, in most learning situations, only a half-truth. "We learn by doing — with objective evaluation" is much better even if it does not have the folksy ring of simplicity. In a speech course, most, if not all, speeches are evaluated. Sometimes the instructor will jot down hasty notes on the student's outline. At other times the entire class will discuss the strengths and weaknesses of the speaker. Regardless of the technique of evaluation, the student should learn to accept the judgments of others and be guided by them in preparing future speeches.

In addition to accepting criticism from others, the student must evaluate himself. He must learn to be objective about his strengths and his weaknesses. The "weakness" most frequently mentioned by beginning students is the malady called "stage fright."

■   **STAGE FRIGHT**

All of us have experienced stage fright of some kind. As performers, we have been keyed up on the opening night of a theatre production or music recital. As college students, we usually feel upset and fearful at the thought of going in to talk with a professor who seems distant, or a dean who appears Olympian, and even with a coed who acts cool or aloof. Stage fright is a very common experience; it is not the exclusive property of the student speaker.

Actually, the student should be grateful that he does experience a certain amount of stage fright. Many professional speakers and performers welcome it and become concerned when it is missing, because they have learned that fear is an energy-producing emotion. It pumps more sugar into the blood and more blood throughout the body. It tones up the muscles and makes us more sensitive to stimuli. It helps us be alert and active. With fear barking at our heels, we can run, jump, and fight harder than we can under normal conditions.

But what can the speaker do to combat or control paralyzing stage fright — the knocking knees, the tight throat, the feeling that he can't control his memory, voice, and body? Excessive stage fright is usually due to one of two things: (1) fear of public criticism, and/or (2) lack of confidence in one's material or skill in delivery. The first cause can only be explained away, but the second, of course, can be actively avoided.

1. *Persuade yourself that speaking in the classroom is a perfectly normal activity,* both for the speaker and the audience. Students have talked in college classes for at least twenty-five hundred years and nearly all have survived. Usually listeners *do* want to hear what a speaker is going to say, and, for the most part, they are willing to overlook minor shortcomings. They are not there to tear the speaker apart. Judicious criticisms will be offered with courtesy and understanding. Even the instructor, who may at times seem like an ogre, is really on the speaker's side. If he is hard to please, it is because of his desire to help. It is his responsibility to refuse to allow the student to get by with anything less than his best work.

2. *Be well prepared.* The student should develop good work habits so that he will be ready to speak confidently when the time comes. He should learn to allow himself time enough to prepare thoroughly, according to his own rate of working and the requirements of his subject. He should learn to devote proportionate amounts of

time to choosing and narrowing his subject, researching, thinking, organizing, and practicing according to the needs of his speech and his own special problems. He should learn to evaluate his topic and purpose so that he can go directly to the kind of specific support he will need — books, articles, experts, or friends — without wasting time on futile research. Having enough good supporting evidence will make it unnecessary to pad his speech with empty generalizations. When he is organizing, he should discipline himself to outline and write clearly and logically, objectively criticizing himself at every stage of his work. He should practice delivering his speech in a quiet place, where he can get used to the sound of his own voice and concentrate on troublesome problems in articulation and pronunciation. The fraternity common room will be too distracting and inhibiting, but an empty classroom should serve him well.

The student will have no reason to feel fearful if he has prepared his material and his delivery as well as he possibly can. No one enjoys making a fool of himself, and no one enjoys even the *fear* of being foolish. The best way to substitute security and confidence for both the fear and the foolishness is to be well prepared.

SUMMARY

1. The steps in good speech preparation are:
   a. Analyzing the audience
   b. Selecting an idea or subject
   c. Determining the purpose
   d. Gathering the material
   e. Organizing the material
   f. Finding the right words
   g. Practicing the delivery
2. The student should learn to accept criticism and use it constructively.
3. To control stage fright:
   a. Persuade yourself that speaking in the classroom is a normal activity.
   b. Be well prepared.

EXERCISES

1. Make a written inventory of your present interests and attitudes toward controversial issues. How many of these would be suitable for classroom speaking? Prepare a similar list of social issues to which you have given so little thought that your attitude is not clear. In your judgment, what is the best procedure for clarifying a fuzzy attitude?

2. Early in this chapter we were reminded that an idea or a statement should be developed or supported. Below are five pieces of supporting material. Write in a single sentence the idea each most likely develops:

   a. Forty-seven per cent of all automobile accidents are caused by drivers who were drunk or had been drinking.
   b. Over the nation one marriage in four ends in divorce. In Indiana the ratio is one to three. In California it is one to one.
   c. *The Statistical Abstract* reports that in 1940 there were 2100 recorded illegitimate births. In 1961 there were 5200.
   d. In September of 1959 the school board of Norfolk, Virginia, admitted seventeen negroes to previously all-white schools.
   e. In 1960 the U.S. graduated 38,000 engineers and 11,300 technicians. At the same time Russia graduated 117,000 engineers and 250,000 technicians.

3. Listed below are several statements which need support. Consider each statement; then indicate what kind of supporting material will be most useful to the public speaker.

   a. The nations of South America, Europe, and Africa no longer show respect for the United States.
   b. The splitting of the atom has contributed much to peacetime progress.
   c. Racial segregation in the public schools is on the way out.
   d. Getting satisfactory grades in a college course is substantially more difficult than in a high school course.

   e. The United States will continue to be troubled by unemployment for many years to come.

4. Select a speech recently printed in *Vital Speeches* or the *New York Times.* Prepare an outline of the speech and write a one-page evaluation of its effectiveness.

5. Go to hear a chapel or convocation speaker on campus. If this opportunity is not available, listen to a classroom lecturer. Did the speaker use a conversational tone in his delivery? If the answer is yes, describe the essential aspects of voice and manner. If the answer is no, describe what prevented it.

6. Below is a transcription of a first classroom speech. Read it and answer the questions which follow.

THE TEEN-AGE MARRIAGE

Last night I read another article on teen-age marriages. In it I read about the same material that all of us have read in *Ladies' Home Journal, Good Housekeeping, Parents' Magazine* or any of the monthlies except the sterling adventures of *Mighty Mouse* or possibly *Popular Mechanics.* And what do we read? Teen-agers are immature, irresponsible, and ill prepared. The girls aren't interested in keeping house and the boys don't know how to fix a leaky faucet. The girls spend more time putting their hair in spoolies than they spend in putting good food on the table; and the boys put in more time scrubbing the white sidewalls of the convertible than repairing the back steps. Reading these articles, we come to the conclusion that marriage is an arrangement between an old man and an old woman who have memorized Dr. Spock and been carefully brainwashed by the marriage counselor. Marriage — and all that normally goes with it — is not for teen-agers! So say the articles.

Well, I challenge the conclusion. Two years ago I was a teen-age husband and my wife was a teen-age mate. Both of us are twenty-one now and glad to be out of that dangerous age. Now when we read the latest articles on young marriage, we smile and say, "Isn't it great to be out of danger?" Sure, that first year had its dangers and so did the second. Let's mention just three of the less personal ones.

The first danger is the one I call "the danger of the sympathetic look." My wife and I saw it first on the faces of our parents; then we noticed it on the faces of their friends; then their friends' friends — and so on until it began to show on everyone's face. We saw it worn by people in the dime store, by the cashier at Kroger's, and even by the Salvation Army Santa Claus. It was a look that said, "You're married, aren't you? Oh, I'm sorry. Marriage isn't to be taken lightly, you know." The sympathetic look is frightening and if you aren't careful it can be persuasive.

The second danger is also presented by outsiders. It's the danger of "The Prophet of Doom." Any marriage is touch and go; it can succeed or fail regardless of age or maturity. But the Prophet says, "You're young and senseless and all the facts are against you." And we read that young marriages were annulled or that two out of five ended in the divorce courts. Our parents told us all their marital hardships. Our friends would drop by to say that Connie walked out on Ted or that Pete and Alice were going to get a divorce or that Sally was going to have a baby after only four months of marriage. We heard and read a lot that first year that made us think we didn't have a chance.

There is one more danger you might be interested in. It's well-known to everybody — especially to students in an eight o'clock public speaking class. It's the danger of laziness. Laziness is sometimes called fatigue or exhaustion or sleepiness or sore feet, but whatever it's called it has to be checked when two people are beginning to build a life together. How does it go? The wife is too tired to cook supper? The husband is too tired to help with the dishes or to help get ready for company? Or maybe both of them are just too lazy to be considerate of the other. It takes energy and consideration. It takes freedom from self-indulging laziness to live with someone else. And I think this is true whether you are fifteen or fifty.

Teen-age marriages can work. So the next time you read an article asking everybody to help stamp out teen-age marriages, stop a moment before you rush into action. Just remember that the dangers of marriage — any marriage — can be overcome. There's no need to wait until you are middle-aged and senile before you start the Great Adventure.

QUESTIONS

a. Is the subject appropriate to the interests of college students?
b. Is the speaker's idea clearly presented? Clearly developed? What is his chief means of development or support?

   c. Is the speech clearly organized? How would you evaluate the introduction? The conclusion?

   d. Is the language appropriate for a college audience? Does it read like a class theme or a class speech? What are the differences between a theme and a speech?

7. Deliver a three-unit speech similar in organization to the one above. Be sure to follow carefully each of the preparation steps discussed in this chapter. Prepare an outline to give to your instructor. Limit your speaking time to three or four minutes.

PART TWO

Preparing the Speech

CHAPTER 3

SPEECH
PURPOSES

Theoretically, whatever we do, we do for a particular purpose. We read books for a purpose. We prepare daily assignments; we write essays; we study; we play tennis; we even look for ways to avoid doing anything — but whatever it is, we do it for a purpose. We speak for a purpose, too. The small boy who asks, "What is that thing?" is calling for information. The little girl who squeals with delight on finding a dead beetle wants to share her discovery. And the boss who shouts, "Get out!" wants to rid the company of a loafing employee. Regardless of its length or intensity of feeling, each speech has some purpose behind it.

■   **REQUISITES OF SPEECH PURPOSE**

Though we usually reason that a speaker is free to determine his own speech purpose, this is not always true. If the audience has assembled to celebrate an occasion or investigate a particular problem, the speaker must shape his purpose to meet those demands. Of course, it may be argued that his loss of freedom is only partial, for he still has the liberty to select a personal point of emphasis, reveal a new synthesis of familiar ideas, or reinvestigate matters often ignored or forgotten. And there are, of course, times when an audience assembles to give the speaker an opportunity to say whatever is on his mind and, consequently, to select whatever goal he wishes. But regardless of whether he is a completely free agent, the effective speaker chooses a purpose which will meet certain requirements.

□   **THE PURPOSE SHOULD BE APPROPRIATE**

A speaker's purpose is appropriate when it meets the demands of the audience, the speaker, and the occasion.

A young man, let us say, has been invited to speak to the monthly meeting of the Senior Citizens Club, an organization of people past retirement age. He delivers, with all its technical jargon, a detailed speech on how to build a hot rod. A college professor of biology has been asked to speak to the county medical society. He urges his audience to support increased medical care for the aged and to express their feelings by writing their senator. A college class has been asked to deliver a speech to inform or instruct. The varsity fullback begins with, "Do you realize that learning to apply cosmetics demands real skill?" The inappropriateness in each of these examples is obvious. In the first, the speaker failed to adapt his material to the age of his audience. In the second, he failed to acknowledge deep-seated audience attitudes or convictions. And in the third, the speaker selected a purpose inappropriate to himself.

If each of these speakers had modified and adapted his purpose to his audience, success would not have been impossible. A young man can speak to the aged on the subject of hot rods, but it is doubtful that very many of them want to know how to build one. Perhaps the speaker should have centered his attention on "What makes a young man build a hot rod?" or "In defense of hot rodding," or "How the Rod Benders Club helps improve traffic safety." Even these topics would require further adaptation, but each of them has a better chance of meeting the demands of an audience of older people.

□   **THE PURPOSE SHOULD BE SIGNIFICANT**

As a rule, a speaker's purpose is significant if it is an attempt to increase the knowledge of his listeners, improve their understanding, or make some contribution to their personal welfare. This definition leaves room for debate because we cannot always agree on how to reach an understanding or improve personal welfare. What is significant to some may be trivial to others.

A young man asked to deliver an informative speech to his classroom audience selected the topic of rainy weather and spent his time developing three points: Rainy weather causes increased traffic accidents, makes it difficult to get from one campus building to another, and causes increased hardships for the custodians of buildings. The speaker was well prepared and knew exactly what he wanted to say; he did not, however, know *why* he wanted to say it. Though all his listeners agreed on the truth of his assertions, they still asked, "So what? What have you told us that we don't already know?" The problems of weather are very well known, and few of us can respond enthusiastically to ancient arguments. The speaker could probably have won a more favorable response if he had chosen a more interesting topic: "How weather affects classroom teaching," or "How rain affects student attention." Or perhaps the only way to win a favorable response would have been to avoid the threadbare topic of weather altogether.

A significant purpose necessarily begins with an awareness of the knowledge and attitude of the audience. When the audience is relatively uninformed, the significance of new knowledge is less difficult to present; but where the audience is learned, the speaker must tax himself to avoid the trivial. In either event, the effective speaker decides on a valuable goal to work toward.

□   **THE PURPOSE SHOULD BE PRECISE**

A precise purpose is limited to a single definite objective. If there is no apparent objective in the speech, or if the objective is multiple or complex, the speaker has not narrowed his purpose precisely.

A speech purpose often appears weak because the speaker attempts too much. His problem is not insignificance but oversignificance.

A minister, for example, may be inveighing against obscene literature on the newsstand, but he confuses his purpose if he brings an indictment against heroin and prostitution in the same sermon. A young sales executive may be asked to report on consumer reaction to a new product, and in the process he delivers a dissertation on effective advertising and the importance of package design. A student may be assigned a four-minute speech to inform, and he attempts "A complete history of air travel from DaVinci to the stratojet." In each of these examples the speaker's purpose is weakened because he is attempting too much.

If it is bad to attempt too much, it is worse to attempt nothing at all. A student describes the illnesses of his newly-acquired used car; another reports on his water-skiing accident; and another explains what he hopes to accomplish by graduation time. If these subjects are interesting at all, they are interesting primarily to the speakers. They have neither interest nor value for the audience until there is an apparent purpose behind the subject. The student could describe his used car so that others might buy more wisely; report a water-skiing accident so that others might understand the meaning of water safety; describe academic ambitions so that others might be impressed by the significance of a good education. An effective speaker selects a precise purpose and stays with it. He reveals his purpose early in his speech and repeats it in his final remarks. Neither he nor his audience can possibly doubt what he wants to accomplish.

The purpose of a speech is never determined in isolation; it is always associated with the occasion, the audience, and the subject. All of these, in turn, are associated with supporting material, arrangement, language, and delivery. In short, effective speech begins with a clear understanding of a speech goal which is held to throughout the speech and which is appropriate, significant, and precise.

■   CHOOSING THE GENERAL PURPOSE

Behind every speech there is one fundamental purpose — to win the desired response. Every speaker wants his audience to listen, understand, and respond in some manner. He wants to affect others as he himself has been affected; he wants to re-form or re-shape, to confirm or strengthen, the thoughts, feelings, and actions of his audience. In order to accomplish this, he must first determine which of three general purposes — to inform, persuade, or entertain — is required by the speaker, the audience, and the occasion.

☐ **SPEAKING TO INFORM**

The speaker who wants to inform will describe, define, report, explain, or supply a body of information which will lead to increased knowledge and understanding. The real estate agent may *describe* a house to a prospective customer. The politician may *explain* the several planks of his party platform. An attorney may *report* on the decisions of cases similar to the one being tried. Or the junior executive may try to *explain* why the Cleanmore Soap account was lost. They all seek *to inform*.

One of the first difficulties in informative speaking is describing terms, theories, and problems adequately. Consider for a moment a fragment which might appear in a speech to inform:

> Medical care for the aged is a form of prepaid medical care; and prepaid medical care is another name for socialized medicine. Socialized medicine, as we have learned from the example in England, is full of good intentions but, in reality, works against itself. It does not permit the patient to choose his doctor, nor the doctor to choose his patient. It fixes medical fees, determines where a doctor is to practice, and destroys his incentive.

This statement reads or sounds like descriptive material. The speaker uses the word "is" rather than "may" or "might" or "probably"; he uses short declarative sentences; he carefully avoids emotional language; he even suggests that he is supplying evidence by referring to the "example in England." On closer reading, however, we can see that the speaker is not giving us information; he is simply presenting a series of assertions, none of which is supported with factual or authoritative material. There is no reference to any specifically proposed piece of legislation dealing with medical care. When the speaker's purpose is to inform, he should stay with matters of fact and avoid matters of opinion. This speaker would have been more informative had he described the provisions of a particular bill, article by article.

A second difficulty arises in attempting to describe abstract topics. The speaker can describe a house easily enough by referring to the number of rooms, the color of the walls, or the condition of the roof. He can report on court decisions, lost business accounts, and party platforms; these things are observable and matters of written record. But how is he to inform his audience about a thing he cannot see? What will he say about the nature of loyalty? Freedom? Justice? There are several ways to do this. One is to rely on definitions commonly accepted by authority. Another is to refer to quotations which are appropriate to his purpose. Still another is to cite examples which bring the abstraction to life. His reasoning unites all these methods. He does not insist that his information on the unseen is the complete, absolute, and unchanging *truth;* rather, he implies that, after considering the best available evidence, it is *probably* true.

A third difficulty associated with the factual and informative speech is creating and maintaining audience interest. It is common on campus to hear, "Oh, he does nothing but pour out the facts for fifty minutes." We hear of "dull facts," "hard facts," "cold facts," and even "stupid facts." Though all of us realize that we could not live and prosper without them, we nonetheless continue to think of facts as inherently drab and uninteresting when presented by the public speaker. Knowing this, the effective speaker will select and use statistics and historical examples with considerable care.

This point may be illustrated by a student speech on the problem of urban renewal. After a rather poetic introduction depicting New York City silhouetted against a rising sun, he described a city that had grown ugly. He supplied his audience with figures on the population increase, figures on industrial increase, and figures on slums, education, and transportation. He presented such an encyclopedic array of "cold, hard facts" that he lulled his audience into utter boredom. He would have improved his speech substantially if he had taken a few essential precautions. (Though these principles will be discussed more completely in Chapter 5, they should be considered here if we are to understand materials in relation to speech purpose.)

a. *Select the most significant material.* It is pointless to try to say everything about anything. No one will ever have all the facts about urban renewal; even if he did, he would not have time enough to discuss them or his audience endurance enough to listen. In a short classroom speech, there is time only for those aspects of the problem which are most typical of urban growth; it is not necessary to include the number of minutes and seconds it takes to drive to Times Square from Grand Central Station at five o'clock in the afternoon.

b. *Select the most interesting material.* If the speaker must choose between two pieces of evidence which support a statement equally well, he should choose the more interesting. An example may serve better than a list of percentages, and an apt quotation better than an example.

c. *Relate facts to common experience.* Suppose the speaker's main point is the enormous cost of urban education. If he deals in thousands of children and millions of dollars, the problem immediately becomes remote. Most of us find it difficult to relate large sums of money and great masses of people to our own small financial dealings and limited social circles. The speaker would do better to talk of educating a single child. First, the cost — hundreds or thousands of dollars — is within everyone's understanding. Second, the speaker touches individually and personally every parent who has paid school taxes and educated a child. The speaker can arrive at the point of his speech — the astronomical cost of mass urban education — by setting the minds and imaginations of his audience to work out the conclusion for themselves in their own terms. He may, for example, suggest that his audience multiply the cost of educating one child by the number of children in the school system. He need never mention the actual cost. The mere suggestion of the multiplication task is staggering and expresses the speaker's intention more forcefully than "cold" statistics.

d. *Relate facts to human interest.* If the speaker's purpose is to contrast urban life with rural life, he has an excellent opportunity to use material with the "human touch." He might compare a discount house with the "general store," a presymphony dinner with a Grange supper, children in prams in Central Park with children running barefoot through the corn fields, *Hello, Dolly!* with the county regional high school's *H.M.S. Pinafore.* He might even recount the experiences and reactions of a family from Brooklyn who spent their vacation on a wheat farm in South Dakota, or a student from a Colorado ranch who spent his college years at Harvard.

    e. *Use some hypothetical examples.* Such advice may seem to contradict what we have said about the purpose of informative speaking, but properly used hypothetical examples can be a great aid. Naturally, the speaker should not create fictional testimony from fictional civic officials, or use "made-up" statistics. He should let his audience know when he is using a fictional example, and, further, he should see to it that his fiction illustrates the truth. The speaker talking about slum conditions, for example, might emphasize his point vividly by asking his audience to imagine the probable day-to-day existence of a hypothetical slum family of ten. If his factual evidence supports it, he could justifiably say that their only support is welfare, their "home" a single rat-infested room with poor ventilation, no plumbing, and one small coal stove.

☐   **SPEAKING TO PERSUADE**

    In a speech to inform, the speaker concentrates on the nature of the thing being considered. Ideally, he remains unprejudiced, unbiased, and thoroughly objective in his effort to present the facts. In persuasive speech, however, the speaker presents not only the facts but also *his personal judgment of the value* of those facts. His purpose is to get his listeners to accept his judgment and to believe or act as he wants them to.

    Persuasive speech comes into use when the speaker attempts to change the listeners' attitudes toward a controversial subject. Suppose, for example, that the speaker is much in favor of a state sales tax, and his listeners are much against. Realizing that he faces strong opposition, he attempts first to inform his audience, to show why his state needs additional funds and why the present tax structure is inadequate. In his second step he considers several of the tax reform bills presently in legislative committees. He reviews their strengths and weaknesses, and concludes, in his final step, that the most sensible solution is the sales tax. In effect he says, "Now that we have considered all the chief proposals, agree with me that my way is best and vote for the sales tax."

Often the speaker does not try to change an opinion so much as to deepen one which already exists. Perhaps the legislators are favorably disposed toward a sales tax but have a few serious reservations that will not allow them to vote for the bill. Perhaps, in their judgment, it might be unfair to the low-income workers, or fail to bring in sufficient revenue. The speaker sizes up the audience's attitude, speaks pointedly to undermine the areas of reservation, and attempts to lure his listeners away from neutrality and into positive action. Here the speaker works not for a change of attitude but rather an *intensifying* of attitude.

A third goal of the persuasive speaker is to maintain an existing attitude. At our political nominating conventions, let us say, the delegates from Illinois are committed to a particular candidate, but in the rough and tumble of vigorous politics the commitment begins to grow shaky. Or let us say that our football team, confident of victory a week before the game, begins to lose confidence as the kick-off approaches. Or, as a third example, let us say that our church membership, brimming with enthusiasm during the first weeks of the building fund campaign, begins to lose enthusiasm once the glamor and the excitement wear off. Each of these situations cries out for persuasive speaking. At the political convention the speaker addressing the wavering delegates says in effect, "Don't lose faith. Stay with us. Victory will be ours on the fourth ballot." At the pep rally, the speaker attempts to maintain the spirit of confidence; and at the church the minister reminds us of our religious responsibility for continued growth. When occasions like these arise, the purpose of speech is to re-energize or revitalize the attitude necessary for successful action.

The student of speech might ask, "But is it fair for a speaker to run around the country trying to influence people? Would it not be better to give them the facts and let them draw their own conclusions?" Such a question arises out of a misunderstanding of the nature of persuasion; it assumes that the persuader is more interested in the *extra*logical aspects of speech than in the logical, that he might use all the stratagems of the propagandists and ignore objective logical analysis. In reality, the persuader cannot ignore the facts. Indeed, if the speaker who informs and the speaker who persuades differ in knowledge, the difference should be in favor of the persuader. He should know the facts of the issue thoroughly, not only those which support his point of view but those which contradict it as well. Only through such knowledge can he defend himself against the factual onslaughts of his opponents.

But is the successful persuader a propagandist? Does he resort to highly emotional harangues? Does he deal in the half-truth, name-calling, or glittering generalities? No, he does not — or, rather, *should* not. Of course, persuaders differ greatly. The demagogue might use threat, the candidate a rosy promise, the politician a favor, the statesman a stylistic charm. None of these, however, measures up to the kind of persuasion advocated here. The most desirable aspects of persuasion may be reduced to these principles:

a. *The persuader begins with factual analysis.* He realizes that facts enable him to reason, and that his reasoning can be no better than his mastery of fact. The speaker who ignores facts or deliberately distorts them misses the most essential aspect of ethical persuasion.

b. *The persuader is fair.* He is not only "fair" with his facts; he is also fair with his opponents, fair with his audience, and fair with himself.

How should he treat his opponents? Should he refer to the President as one who has "deliberately betrayed" the American people? Should he indict American educators by saying that "They have a carefully worked-out plan to sell us out to the Communists"? Whenever we hear such nonsense, we should recognize the use of "name-calling" and the absence of reasonable argument. A sense of fair play encourages the persuader to respect his opponents, to acknowledge honest differences of opinion, and even to identify his opponent's strongest argument.

How should he treat his audience? Since this question is discussed at length in Chapter 12, it will suffice at this point to present the thesis statement of that chapter: The individual citizen is capable of governing himself when he has free access to essential information. The persuader who shows that he considers his listeners ignorant and incapable of acting sensibly and who consequently rejects the logical in favor of the emotional is likely to alienate his audience by insulting their intelligence. The speaker who shows confidence in the ability of his audience to understand facts presented clearly and rationally is in a better position to persuade.

And how is a speaker fair with himself? When he presents his own convictions, in spite of the convictions of his audience. Perhaps there are times when the speaker says, "Oh, I'd better not say that; they'd stone me! I'd better say the thing they are used to hearing." Whenever such a retreat is sounded, the speaker runs away from controversy; he deprives himself of the opportunity to grow in thought. The effective speaker welcomes the challenge of finding a way to relate his beliefs to the interests and opinions of his audience.

    c. *The persuader adapts to his audience.* All able speakers try to adapt their remarks to their audience, but because the persuader is attempting to win an audience to his point of view, he, especially, should develop the skills of audience analysis. He should find out as much as possible about the educational level and the political, religious, and social preferences of the members of his audience. He should try to determine how indifferent, hostile, or tolerant they are — to him and the issue at hand. With this background information, he can establish a common bond between himself and his audience. He could mention the common desire for security, status, progress, or freedom — whichever is relevant to his thesis and audience — as a goal of his proposition in order to get his audience to give him at least a fair hearing.

☐   **SPEAKING TO ENTERTAIN**

    The word *entertainment* usually suggests humor or laughter. Such a narrow use of the word would lead us to conclude that Bob Hope speaks to entertain, and that President Johnson does not. But to entertain is not necessarily to cause wild, uproarious laughter; it may be to provide a momentary escape from the tedium of everyday life, or to provide relief from seriousness of purpose. A speaker entertains if he causes laughter with tastefully chosen and appropriately used anecdotes. He entertains if he charms his audience with a reference to the unknown, the unfamiliar, or the quaint and novel.

    The inexperienced speaker often thinks he cannot entertain. He says, "But I can't be funny. I can't remember a joke for five minutes, and even when I do, I can't tell it right." Or he insists that he lacks the stylistic charm or the wit to turn a clever phrase or inject a touch of satire. It is true that not everyone who appreciates good humor can be humorous. Nevertheless, the student should accept the challenge and try to develop the skill.

Why? What value is there in humor? Quite aside from those occasions when entertainment is the order of the day — at banquets, club meetings, informal social gatherings — humor is often an integral part of speeches to inform and persuade. It helps us maintain our equilibrium by reminding us once again that we are human, fallible, subject to error — even laughable. It helps dispel the atmosphere of formality which often prevails as the speaker begins. It provides relief from the tensions of concentration. It creates renewed interest when attention wanders from the subject. All in all, humor is one of the most powerful weapons in the speaker's arsenal.

The subjects suitable for the humorous speech are innumerable. Robert Benchley could regale an audience with his famous "Financial Report." Mark Twain enjoyed great success with his speech on "New England Weather." And Will Rogers repeatedly chose the subject of Washington politics. Each of these, at first glance, seems pretty far removed from humor. Financial reports are dull; weather is commonplace; politics is serious business. But the humorist looks beneath the outer shell and finds the ridiculous within. The question, then, becomes not "What can I find that is humorous?" but rather "What can be made humorous in the subject at hand?"

One student answered this question satisfactorily in a speech on "Man and the Owl." Though he pretended his purpose was persuasion, it really was entertainment. He developed the thesis that the owl was superior to man because man wasted his night hours by sleeping while the owl remained productive and inquisitive. A second student spoke on the topic "Inside a Kid Brother's Head." She described her brother's mind as if it were a mad scientist's laboratory. As she developed her idea, she elaborated on "the memory mechanism," "the forgetting mechanism," and "the noise-making mechanism." A third classroom speech is quoted in full to illustrate what can be done with an ordinary subject and a little imagination.

> Thank you, Mr. Chairman, for that glowing introduction. Of course, you didn't include everything. You forgot to tell our audience that I flunked Beginning Badminton when I was a freshman. And you forgot to mention that I never did manage to make the required score of 110 in our class on Intermediate Bowling. I'm

sure you will agree that these two failures make me well qualified
for the subject I have chosen for this assignment. This morning I
want to describe for you the layout of our most recent addition to
our Practical Arts Building. As you are well aware this is the wing
devoted to the Underwater Basket Weaving curriculum.

But first a note or two of history. Underwater Basket Weaving
was first considered nothing more than a joke. If a student wanted
to describe a course as a crip, he'd say, "It's strictly underwater
basket weaving." But reality, you know, has a way of outstripping
our imagination and that is just what happened in the early sixties.
As far as I can determine, this study had its first real break in 1968.
A Miss Hazel Wrathmore, Professor of Disintegrated Studies, accidentally left a flower basket in her laboratory sink while she took
her nature study girls out to gather dried grasses for their winter
bouquets. Now as I understand it, the janitor later found the basket
in a sink full of water. Well, being a sensible man he pulled it out
and forced it dry under the sun tan lamp which he kept over the
chaise lounge in his office. When Professor Wrathmore returned,
she was so pleased with the tight weave and the rich hazel nut color
that she set her girls to the task of reproducing them. Naturally,
there were many failures, but the secret was finally discovered. The
first real Underwater Basket Weaving course was introduced in the
fall of 1971. Those first attempts at aqua weaving were primitive
— even crude as a matter of fact — but they were forerunners of
the beautiful baskets of today.

If you can follow me now as I explain this drawing, you will
understand the facilities that will be ready for use by the fall of '79.
Here, near the center of the room, is the conventional classroom
area where the students receive their orientation. Here they study
the merits of various materials — reed, wicker, rattan, and so forth.
They also study weaving patterns, basket design, and the basket as
a status symbol in the well decorated home. Directly to the front
of the classroom area you will note the two dressing rooms. Here,
of course, the weavers will put on their bathing suits to prepare for
the laboratory sessions. It used to be that a student had only to roll
up his sleeves and weave under ten inches of water, but this was
later proved improper when Dean Everglade reminded us that we
must educate the *whole* student. "Plunge the rascals in," he directed
the faculty. "Educate them all over." From that time on we have
needed bathing suits and snorkel tubes.

We plan to continue the program. If you look at the right wall here, you will see a series of cabinets. In each cabinet is a SCUBA outfit so we'll no longer have to weave while holding a clumsy snorkel between our teeth. But SCUBA has problems of its own. It will force the student to take prerequisites in Principles of SCUBA Diving, Air Tank Maintenance, and Pressure Regulator Repair.

Now here at this end of the room is the Weaving Tank. Students have already dubbed it "The Bucket" or "The Big Dipper." When the student, complete with his SCUBA equipment, plunges into the tank, he will pull a line of wicker from the spools hanging from above. When the baskets are complete they are handed to the instructor for inspection; then while still wet they are put into the sun lamp oven located over here in the corner.

The rest of this wall is made up of sliding glass doors opening on to a terrace of pink Italian marble. Here the students will rest and visit with each other while their baskets are drying. I suppose I should mention that this terrace was considered a frill by some members of the faculty, but their objections were overruled by President Moresize. He said, "Pleasant conversation between girls and boys in an academic community is a worthy use of leisure time. Leave the terrace in!"

I know your curriculum is crowded and I know that the work you have to do in Croquet Ball Refinishing is very demanding, but do your best to save a place for Underwater Basket Weaving. I'm sure you'll think it's fun.

A second troublesome problem for the beginning speaker is how to deliver an entertaining speech. When the speech is satiric or mock-serious, the delivery differs very little from that of any other speech. The humorist might play down gestures and wear a deadpan expression, or he might raise a brow and put his tongue in his cheek. When the humor is achieved by a series of short episodes, narratives, jokes, and wisecracks, however, the speaker uses the delivery of the story-teller, which is based on five principles.

1. *Know the material well.* The speaker cannot afford to forget essential details, mutter an apology, and then say, "Oh, I forgot to tell you . . . . " Possibly the greatest offense of all is to forget the punch line. A few essential notes for quick reference are preferable to the embarrassment of the forgetter's pause.

2. *Keep the story simple.* The long, "shaggy dog" story or the story heavy with excess detail hardly seems worth the effort when the point

is made or the laugh finally arrives. Taking care not to overlook necessary details, it is better to strip the story of all the nonessentials and concentrate on getting to the punch line quickly.

3. *Make the punch line decisive.* As the speaker delivers the punch line, he often increases his speed and his volume. Everyone should hear the line and hear it easily, without having to turn to a neighbor to ask, "What did he say?"

4. *Let one story lead to another.* As laughter begins to wane, the speaker tries to maintain the favorable atmosphere by telling another joke or story. To do this, of course, he must "gang up" his stories, one right after another, rather than spacing them widely.

5. *Let the story speak for itself.* When the response to a story is deafening silence, it is better not to attempt a recovery by explaining why it is supposed to be funny. It probably was cold, inappropriate, or poorly told; explanations will only make the matter worse.

■   **A SINGLE GENERAL PURPOSE**

The three speech purposes — informing, persuading, and entertaining — are often used in combination. Obviously, however, the speaker must decide on one general purpose before he marshals his evidence and chooses his methods. He then may use the other two speech purposes to support his general purpose. He may entertain to inform. He often cannot persuade until he has stated the facts. The successful professor, for example, seeks primarily to inform. But he uses persuasion and entertainment to motivate his students to accept the information he wishes to convey. He uses all three general purposes, but he carefully makes one predominant.

So it is with all speakers. There must be a single prevailing purpose. Only after this is determined can the speaker refine his objective and select the material to support his specific purpose.

■   **SELECTING THE SPECIFIC PURPOSE**

A specific purpose is the precise response desired from the audience during or after the speaker's final words. It is a statement of the *definite behavior* expected of the audience as it responds to the speech.

Too frequently speakers fail because they have no distinct notion of what they want in response. The effective speaker formulates a clear statement of what he wants a particular audience to believe, understand, feel, act, or enjoy.

Perhaps the need for precision will become clearer after studying each of the following examples:

1.	**Subject:**	Ice fishing
	General purpose:	To inform
	Purpose narrowed:	To describe a series of fishing experiences
	Specific purpose:	To help the audience understand and appreciate the rigors of ice fishing
2.	**Subject:**	Progress in wartime
	General purpose:	To inform
	Purpose narrowed:	To call attention to an often ignored idea
	Specific purpose:	To help the audience become aware of the scientific and technical progress made during wartime
3.	**Subject:**	The right of labor to strike
	General purpose:	To persuade
	Purpose narrowed:	To change the prevailing attitude
	Specific purpose:	To convince the audience, contrary to its opinion, that unions within vital industries have no right to conduct a nationwide strike
4.	**Subject:**	Access to news
	General purpose:	To persuade
	Purpose narrowed:	To deepen an existing attitude
	Specific purpose:	To remind the audience of the necessity of wide news coverage in a democratic society
5.	**Subject:**	The American image abroad
	General purpose:	To persuade
	Purpose narrowed:	To promote a definite action
	Specific purpose:	To motivate the audience to contribute to Radio Free Europe

6.	Subject:	The defeated man
	General purpose:	To entertain
	Purpose narrowed:	To stimulate laughter
	Specific purpose:	To amuse the audience with humorous anecdotes of men who have been done in by the trying circumstances of life

7.	Subject:	The Queen of Sheba
	General purpose:	To entertain
	Purpose narrowed:	To provide momentary escape
	Specific purpose:	To reconstruct the probable daily life of the Queen of Sheba

Once a specific purpose is determined and clearly stated in a simple sentence, it serves the speaker in two ways: (1) it guides him in his speech preparation, and (2) it is his statement of intent as he addresses his audience. The first of these has already been discussed. Let us turn now to the second. The speaker, of course, will not say, "Today I'm going to convince you, contrary to your present attitude, that unions have no right to strike." Nor will he say, "I'm going to motivate you to give money to Radio Free Europe." And, obviously, he will not say, "My purpose is to make you die laughing at all the funny stories I'm going to tell you." Such purposes may be in the speaker's mind, but to be useful they must be rephrased into *thesis statements*.

■ **PRESENTING A THESIS STATEMENT**

The thesis statement of a speech is an expression, direct or implied, of the basic *idea* to be developed by the speaker. Since it is designed for the audience and for their immediate understanding, it should be stated in a single sentence which is *short, easily understood,* and *precise*. Notice, for example, the difficulties presented in the following example:

It is my sole purpose to prove to you that the national forces of authority are gradually wresting from the American press its time-honored right and responsibility to examine all public events or all events directly associated with the welfare of the people and to relay these facts to our national citizenry so that it might govern with the wisdom of Solomon.

This thesis is too long-winded, complex, and full of vagaries. The words "prove to you" trigger our resentment and make us less willing to shift our point of view. "National forces of authority" is indefinite and vague. "Wresting" is an emotional word and full of unpleasant connotations about those "national forces." "Time-honored" is likewise emotional and full of pleasant connotations about the press. And so on until we come to the metaphor comparing our "national citizenry" to Solomon and all his wisdom. This statement is neither short, easily understood, nor precise.

Consider another version of the thesis as it might have been introduced by a second speaker:

A preliminary remark to prepare for the thesis	I would like to speak this evening about a problem in American society that is daily growing more acute. Whether we realize it or not, it affects all of us. It is the problem of keeping the American citizen informed. I am speaking of the Federal Government and its relationship to the press. My position on this question may be stated quite simply: *The current governmental control of the release of news seriously threatens the validity of American democracy.*
Thesis statement	
Limiting the thesis	I do not mean to suggest that our government resorts to deliberate lies or that it deliberately distorts events of history and mangles statistical accounts. I mean it guides public attitudes toward persons of note, toward scientific progress, toward international events. I mean, more than all else, that our government is providing increasingly less reliable information.
Restating the thesis	

Now the thesis is simple, understandable, and precise. We notice still other things from the speech context in which it is placed. (1) The speaker does not thrust this basic idea onto his audience without warning; he warms up to it by gradually becoming more precise. (2) The speaker realizes that the significance of the thesis may not be immediately clear; so (3) he is careful to limit his remarks by stating what he does *not* mean and (4) by expanding on what he *does* mean. When the thesis statement is presented directly rather than implicitly, it usually appears early in the speech. Sometimes it may be the very first sentence. Sometimes it will appear after an attention-getting step and a brief historical note. Sometimes the thesis statement will be delayed until very late in the speech or even until the conclusion. Perhaps the greatest determiner of its location is the audience. For example, if the above excerpt on government control of news were delivered by a journalist to a group of angry newspaper men, the statement might well come immediately. If the journalist were to address a group of citizens who had developed no strong feelings one way or another, he would present the statement early but after some warm-up. If the journalist were to attempt to persuade a hostile group or any group that believed news control is essential to public welfare, he would present it late — after all the evidence and reasoning had been examined. There is, of course, the possibility that the thesis would never be stated; it might simply be implied or suggested. In this case the speaker must make certain that the implication is clear enough to avoid confusion.

SUMMARY

1. Speech purposes must be:
   a. Appropriate
   b. Significant
   c. Precise
2. The general purposes of speech are to inform, to persuade, and to to entertain.
3. When speaking to inform:
   a. Describe rather than judge.
   b. Describe abstract topics by reference to authority or concrete examples.

    c. Combine factual materials with interest materials.
4. When speaking to persuade:
    a. Try to change, deepen, or perpetuate an attitude.
    b. Analyze the facts.
    c. Be fair.
    d. Adapt to the audience.
5. When speaking to entertain:
    a. Find humor in the subject at hand.
    b. Use the delivery of the good story-teller.
6. Though all three general purposes may be present in the same speech, *one* should predominate.
7. The speaker's specific purpose is the reaction he wishes to elicit from his audience.
8. The thesis statement reveals the specific purpose.
9. The thesis statement should be simple, understandable, and precise.

EXERCISES

1. During the classroom speeches which you have heard up to this point, what observations have you made with respect to *purpose?* Do the speakers definitely progress toward a specific goal? Do they speak as though they want a precise reaction from the audience? Or do most of them seem only to attempt to satisfy the instructor?

2. What general speech purposes would likely come into use in the following occasions?

    a. A high school commencement
    b. An outdoor Fourth of July celebration
    c. A victory banquet
    d. A large grievance committee meeting
    e. A national convention of doctors
    f. A debate between two political candidates
    g. A Ladies' Night at Kiwanis

    h. A university faculty meeting
    i. A sales meeting
    j. A group of students in a professor's home

3. In this chapter we have said that people respond to speech that informs, persuades, and entertains. Write a short paper in which you describe other social forces that influence human behavior. For example, a man can very easily be persuaded when there is a gun at his back. Are there similar nonverbal ways of persuasion? How many of these ways are appropriate to a democratic society?

4. In a speech to inform, a government official is heard to say, "I would like to explain in greater detail, but unfortunately this information is confidential." Later he says that details are "classified" and "top secret." In a class discussion arrive at some conclusions about the role of the government in presenting information.

5. Conduct a discussion on the uses of persuasion. At first glance the question may appear too simple to discuss, but consider such additional questions as: Does a speaker ever try to create uneasiness? Fear? Hate? Shame? Are any of these goals justifiable? If so, under what circumstances?

6. Conduct a discussion on the uses of humor. No doubt some humor exists solely for the laughter of the moment. At other times there appears to be instruction or persuasion behind the laughter. Discuss especially how humor is used in this second respect.

7. The following speech was delivered by a beginning speaker. Read it, then answer the questions that follow:

AN AFRICAN IN NORTH AMERICA

As one of the many hundreds of African students studying in the United States today, I'm going to take this opportunity to review just briefly what experiences the African student encounters in the

United States. It is indeed a very fortunate thing, perhaps a great honor to be able to go to study in some far and distant country. It is the dream of many young people to come to the United States to see for themselves the wonders and mysteries they so often hear being talked about. The opportunity of studying in American universities and colleges is an occasion which happens but once in a lifetime.

On arrival in the United States the African student is impressed by the beauty of the countryside, its magnificent skyscrapers, modern streets and highways, beautiful cars, buses and trains and many other things which make the American life more pleasant and easy. As his stay becomes longer and longer, the excitement about these things begins to fade away, and the student begins to realize what he come here for. He is here to pursue education and professional training. And as he goes about with his studies, he now assumes a very realistic attitude. He begins to observe a great deal of things, and maybe what he observes does not correspond with what he had been led to believe. He begins to examine little things which constitute big things and many questions begin to arise. He begins to wonder what Americans think of him as a stranger, a visitor, a guest of their government. He begins to wonder what Americans think of him as an African. He begins to wonder what Americans think of him as a member of a different race and creed. He wants to know to what extent the Americans follow the principles and ideals they have set for themselves — those of democracy, freedom, brotherhood of mankind, Christianity. Do they love their neighbors as themselves? A bigger question immediately crops up. Africa will arise one day to be a great nation in the world. What news and what messages shall I carry back to my people about America as I saw it? What lesson have I learned by coming to this country? This should pose a very complex situation to the American himself. What impression is the American public giving to the African students? What picture of himself is the American making in the eyes of Africa? Is it a good one? Or is it one that gives him pride and satisfaction?

Let us remember that our goal is to foster better international understanding and to create world peace and stability. It is the duty of all thinking men and women from all parts of the world to join hands in union and help build a world, a world of friends based upon partnership, democracy, and, above all, Christianity.

a. Is the speaker's purpose clearly established? What is his purpose?
b. What are the chief means by which he hopes to accomplish his purpose?
c. What things distract from his purpose?
d. What changes would you recommend?

8. *A speaking assignment.* Deliver a four-minute speech to inform, persuade, or entertain. After the speeches have been delivered, discuss the success of each speaker with particular reference to general and specific purpose.

CHAPTER 4

SUBJECTS
AND SOURCES

The greatest hurdle for many students is finding a subject to develop into a speech. For years students have been excusing themselves with, "I'm not an expert. I really have nothing to say. Who wants to listen to me?" And for years instructors have replied, "Nonsense. No one lives in a vacuum. You have thoughts, ideas, experiences, agonies, enthusiasms, and ambitions like everyone else, and all of them can be subjects for a speech." Moreover, a literate college student is continually expanding his concerns, developing new ideas and interests as he absorbs the cultural heritage to which his college or university exposes him. The real problem is not finding *a* subject for a speech but choosing one of the hundreds at his command.

■ SELECTING THE SUBJECT

In some circumstances speech subjects are highly restricted, if not predetermined. The speaker's subject in effect is chosen for him by the nature of the occasion. In the *tradition-dominated* occasion, for example, a minister, priest, or rabbi will deliver a sermon, the subject of which is naturally drawn from the Bible or parish problems; a guest speaker at an inauguration will obviously talk about the incoming official and his hopes and plans. The *subject-dominated* occasion usually revolves around a specific problem. The speakers at a town meeting called for raising school taxes will undoubtedly discuss the need for more money and the pros and cons of raising taxes. At a *speaker-dominated* occasion, the audience is there because of the speaker's personal eminence or reputation. He is free to talk on any topic he pleases.

Most classroom speeches, however, are not dominated by tradition, subject, or speaker. The student must choose a subject. He is not a minister in church, an educator before a town meeting, or the President of the United States. He generally has no specialized training or experience which make him an authority; he has not yet gained recognition as a spokesman for a particular cause. His audience will not be listening to him because of his knowledge or expertise on a matter of great importance, or because of his prestige. He will, in short, have to select a subject from the greatest repository of all — personal experience.

☐   **THE ROLE OF EXPERIENCE**

The student is correct in assuming that we are attracted to speakers whose reputations are well established, but he should recognize several fields of competence of his own. He may not be expert in problems of international relations, government, science, industry, and education, but *he is an expert on whatever has happened to him and on his own thoughts and feelings*. As a simple illustration of a speech based on experience, consider the following:

FOLLY IN A CHICKEN SHACK

Bertrand Russell once wrote the shortest history of man. Listen: "Since Adam and Eve ate the apple, man has never refrained from any folly of which he was capable. The end." The history of man is the history of folly.

A welfare agent has many opportunities to view man's folly. Consider the case which I investigated about three weeks ago. I stopped my car in front of the house — only it wasn't a house; it was a shed or rather a chicken shack. I hurried up a little path to knock on the planks that were supposed to be a door. Before I could knock, though, a thin little girl of seven opened the door and yelled, "We saw you drive up! Whacha bring us?" I said, "I didn't bring you anything. I came to talk with your mother and I mean to talk business." And I hurried past the girl into the dirtiest, most foul-smelling one-room shack I've ever known.

How can I describe either the room or my feelings? I can't, really. I was so mixed up with feelings of anger, pity, disgust, and nausea that what I tell you now is certain to be distorted. I do remember the stove — a small potbellied stove just inside the door. I remember the pile of coal which was heaped next to it on the floor. I remember that above the coal pile was their only window — and two panes had been knocked out and covered with cardboard. About four feet in front of the stove was a double bed — no sheets and a filthy bedspread lay half in the coal dust and half draped over the bed. A little tow-headed girl of four sat there wondering what all this was about. She was puzzled, maybe scared to death, and probably cold. She wore only a T-shirt and tennis shoes — not another thread. I walked over to the far end of the room to look behind a curtain that had been nailed across a corner, and there I found the cause of the odor — a lard can that was being used as a toilet.

That did it. I wheeled around to the mother and yelled, "You get that out of here and you do it right this minute."

She didn't say a word. She just stood there and stirred a pot of ham and spaghetti.

So I said, "You've got an outhouse. Why don't you use it?"

She said, "It's cold."

And I said, "Cold or not you use it. If you don't I'll have these children put in a home."

Well, she stopped stirring and walked over to me. She pointed the spoon at me and said, "*I wish you would* — and when you find the man they belong to, toss him in too."

I know — it's easy to laugh when it's told as a story. We always laugh at stories of the "no-count" man — until we're married to one; then it isn't funny. It wasn't funny to me either. There was nothing

I could do, so I hurried out to the car to make out my report and return to the office.

But I just sat there. I was shaking with anger and disgust and pity. And like Bertrand Russell I thought "What folly!" It was *my* folly because I have everything I want and more than I need; yet I give nothing to this woman. It was *her* folly because she has so much less than her own energy could provide. It was *our* folly because we are more concerned with 100-megaton bombs than we are with a decent life for simple people.

This speech was delivered in the classroom by a county welfare worker who returned to college after the last of her children had graduated from high school. Many times when she spoke in class she drew on her experience as a welfare worker. In this speech she used a welfare case. In other speeches she told about working with the police, truant officers, teachers, YMCA directors, and officials of the city and county. She was not an accomplished speaker in every sense of the word, but she did realize that her own experience was rich in speech subjects.

Every student has a similar richness of thoughts, feelings, and experiences that have determined his outlook and attitudes. One student has been involved in a serious automobile accident; another has become a national trapshooting champion. One has watched his closest friend become a shoplifter; another has submitted an original project to the science fair and won first prize. One has felt the effects of race prejudice; another has joined a peace march in Washington. Regardless of who the student is, something in his background has helped to shape his thought or fix his "stance of mind."

Consider, for example, a few of the subjects which might grow out of everyday experience. Any student could easily prepare a list like the one below in less than an hour.

Areas of Experience	*Related Subjects*
Teachers	1. She taught me to sing
	2. He lived by the Golden Rule
	3. She influenced me most
	4. He was most unreasonable
	5. Some teachers are neurotic

Areas of Experience	*Related Subjects*
Friends	1. A friend in need 2. "The friends thou hast . . ." 3. "The egghead and I" 4. My richest friend 5. Three lessons in friendship
Relatives	1. The uncle who fishes 2. A patriotic grandfather 3. Family reunions 4. Mother manages father 5. Father's theory of discipline
School	1. Cheating 2. Dormitory food 3. Required courses 4. Social restrictions 5. The campus newspaper
Society	1. My stand on integration 2. Is God dead? 3. Luxury living 4. Crime in our town 5. What I believe we need
Likes	1. Skin diving 2. Fort Lauderdale at Easter 3. Chocolate éclairs 4. Small motor repairs 5. Baking
Dislikes	1. Men who dance as though they were killing snakes 2. Women who play dumb 3. "Far-out" music 4. Abstract painting 5. My French professor

A warning is essential at this point. Simply "telling" a personal experience is likely to lead to shallowness. The student should examine the experience for significant detail and for the way it has helped establish an idea or attitude.

■   **NARROWING THE SUBJECT**

Narrowing a subject means choosing an aspect of a broad topic that may be treated thoroughly in the allotted time. General subjects like "The Railroad Industry," "The American Indian," or "Warfare" are much too comprehensive; they must be limited if the speaker is to do justice to the topic in the time available. Suppose, for example, that the sophomore music major decides to deliver a classroom speech on music. At first his thoughts are a jumble of ideas about music and dance in ancient Greece, medieval church music, the bawdy ballads of Elizabethan times, sedate seventeenth century court music, oriental music, American music. He finally decides on American music and breaks it down into folk music, New Orleans blues, swing, jazz, and rock-and-roll. When he chooses a category he can handle with reasonable thoroughness, he has started to narrow his subject. Should he choose "New Orleans Blues," he will probably still want to narrow it to a topic like "The Latest New Orleans Blues Hero."

The speaker narrows his subject not only for reasons of time, but also to focus his thinking and research. When the subject is limited, he can investigate it more deeply and present a fuller, better rounded speech. His ideas, supporting material, language, and delivery may all be more easily and quickly adjusted to his speech. The student speech below exemplifies a properly narrowed subject.

UNION MONOPOLY POWER

The people of the United States have been subjected in recent years to the ruthless monopolistic power which is wielded by labor unions. It is my purpose in this speech not to offer a solution which would curb union monopoly, but to give documented evidence to indicate that such a monopoly does exist, and that its effects on the economy are undesirable.

I shall now give four pieces of documented evidence of the misuse of union monopoly. John Davenport has written in a recent issue of *Fortune* magazine that Tom Coffey, a Nebraskan who owned a small trucking firm, was run out of business by the Teamsters' Union. Secondly, former Secretary of Labor James P. Mitchell has reported a charge in the *Congressional Digest* of August–September, 1966, that a group of men in Tennessee, including

Teamster officials, has been responsible for at least 173 violent acts in the short span of four years.

Mitchell continues by saying that several acts of union violence have been reported in Scranton, Pennsylvania. These acts include the dynamiting of a building, the bombing of a bakery, and the damaging of trucks. Professor Sylvester Petro, of New York University's School of Law, has written that in one case the Teamsters' Union "ran a trucking company out of business by refusing to let it have any drivers."

I have shown that union monopolistic power is not a theoretical concept, but a tragic reality. I have listed four documented cases in which unions have used their unique powers to their own advantage, cases in which these unions have harmed, or even ruined, their competitors. I have not even suggested a solution to the current problem of union monopoly, but I believe I have made it quite clear that such a problem does exist. Are you willing to let this problem continue and to grow even more destructive? In the name of the American economic system, I hope that your answer is in the negative.

This speech has its shortcomings. For its length, it is too rich in evidence and too thin in interpretation; its skeleton shows. Furthermore, in presenting only one viewpoint, it is not objective. It has, however, the advantage of a limited subject and purpose. The speaker obviously set out to say one thing and accomplish one purpose.

■   **TESTING THE SUBJECT**

During the process of choosing and narrowing his subject, the effective speaker tests it for appropriateness, interest, and value.

☐   **APPROPRIATENESS**

It is imperative that the subject be appropriate to the speaker, his audience, and the occasion. A Senator normally does not speak on fraternity pledging. The President does not speak against smoking unless he feels the national welfare is endangered. Both must give their attention to more significant matters of state. The young lady who has spent her life in a large city knows little if anything about life on the farm. If she should speak to her classroom audience on diseases particularly troublesome to swine, the class would probably react with: "But what could *you* know about hogs?" We react similarly when a politician poses as a scientist or a scientist as a politician, or when a theologian poses as a military tactician or a tactician as a theologian. The city girl would be more successful if she talked about the problem of rats and cockroaches in the slums. The politician should stick to his legislation and committees; the scientist to his quantum theory and experiments; the theologian to his Tillich and Teilhard de Chardin; the military tactician to his war games. In short, to be successful and convincing, each speaker should deal with subjects which are appropriate to him and his experience.

A subject must also be appropriate to the audience. The speaker should not assume that his audience is captive and that, being caught, it will be interested in any subject he chooses. Many audiences do not have the training or maturity to understand highly technical subjects. Women are usually not as much concerned with sports as are men, and men care very little about the dangers of back-combing the hair. Rural audiences are not immediately caught up in the problems of the slums and urban renewal, while city audiences are likely to sleep with their eyes open through a discourse on the corn borer. It follows, then, that choosing an appropriate subject will give the speaker a head start with his audience. This is not to say that the speaker whose field is urban renewal should *never* talk to farmers. The farmer should know of urban renewal as well as pigs and corn. It *is* to say that the urban renewal expert should adapt his subject to an audience of farmers — by keeping his language simple and nontechnical; by drawing some analogies between farming and urban renewal if possible; in short, by relating his subject to the interests of his audience.

Finally, a subject should be appropriate to the occasion. When the occasion is gay and festive, the speaker can ill afford to speak on the inevitability of war, death, and destruction. When the audience anticipates serious instruction, he cannot be frivolous and inconsequential. And, certainly, when the occasion calls for "a few words," the speaker should not throw himself into a speech that requires hours for completion. Common sense insists that the speaker adjust to the purpose or spirit of the occasion.

☐   **INTEREST**

The speaker should not only be genuinely interested in his subject; he should also see to it that his interest is apparent to the audience. As the student goes through his trial by fire deciding on a suitable subject, he may make a dozen or so false starts and succeed only in filling his waste basket with crumpled outlines. After a few such experiences, he learns that his best point of beginning is his own interest. If he is interested in his subject, he will build his speech with greater enthusiasm, and his interest and enthusiasm will inevitably show up in his delivery.

Is the subject interesting to the audience? This question has, in a sense, just been discussed in regard to appropriateness. While catering to audience interest is perfectly justifiable in certain instances — especially in speeches to entertain — in others it is not. The teacher, the minister, the lawyer — indeed, most speakers — are obliged to speak on certain subjects for certain purposes. The chemistry professor, for example, is not at liberty to say, "Well, today I'm going to teach volley-ball because it's more fun, or jazz because it's more interesting." He must teach chemistry, whether it is interesting to the members of his class or not. His duty as a speaker is to *make* his subject interesting. In other words, the speaker should be less concerned with selecting an interesting subject than with what he does with it once the selection is made.

☐   **VALUE**

Of all the criteria for choosing a subject, worthwhileness is the most important as well as the most difficult to describe. Worthwhile topics are relevant to the people who are listening. They are not necessarily lofty or super-serious, but they do have dimension or scope. They enlarge our experience and interests; they help us "see" more clearly or feel more deeply; they do not cater to our prejudices or waste our time on trivialities.

Consider the classroom speeches of the young man from Pennville, a town of about fifteen hundred people. His first speech was on "The Pennville Volunteer Brigade." For his second speech he discussed "The Home Fire Extinguisher." Later in the course he chose "Getting Off the Second Floor." These topics seem too insubstantial to justify an audience's time and patience, but the speaker managed to relate them to his audience. In his first speech, he compared a volunteer fire department to a fulltime big-city department, listing the obstacles a volunteer department must face and showing that it still can save property and lives efficiently. He dramatized it with "human interest" anecdotes drawn from his own experiences as a volunteer, and made it significant with statistics showing how great a portion of this country is protected by just such departments. In his second speech, he stressed the importance of keeping and knowing how to use a fire extinguisher and once again called on his own experiences to dramatize the importance of such safety measures. He handled his third speech in much the same way. In all speeches he capitalized on the implicit and actual humor of his topics. His listeners were enlightened, interested, and entertained.

Topics that are current and "of a certain magnitude" are worthwhile. This is not to say that every speaker should speak only of current events, but it is to say that current events should receive a generous amount of attention — especially in the college classroom. National and international events offer a never-ending supply of speech topics. At the moment, any of the following topics are "current" and "important": the latest scrap between the United States and Panama, Cuba, or the Dominican Republic; the latest crisis between the United States and Russia over wheat, Viet Nam, or West Germany; Franco's Spain; the English economy; DeGaulle's anti-NATO policies; the recurring friction between Israel and Jordan. At home, elections, the war on poverty, boosting the economy, raising the income tax, the draft, and race riots are worthwhile subjects for classroom speeches.

These topics are current now. In a year, by the time these words are before the readers' eyes, many will have become past history, and a new complex of current events will have become established. To say the least, the college student owes it to himself and his classmates to read, evaluate, and talk about the people and events which affect the world around him.

☐   **THE ROLE OF RESEARCH**

In the process of choosing and narrowing a suitable topic, the speaker realizes that in some respects he is generally well prepared. He may even find research unnecessary. On other occasions, however, he realizes that he has no factual background to support his opinions, no actual experience to rely on. When this is the case, he must attempt to deepen and extend his general knowledge by research. Consider, for example, the subject of Communism, still a favorite for classroom speeches. Most students know something about the subject. They have heard television and radio news commentators; they have read news items in the daily papers; they have listened to politicians, ministers, and educators; they may even have discussed the subject with friends and colleagues. Despite this experience, however, the student still feels uncertain when he tries to prepare a speech on the subject. The result is a series of clichés that all his listeners have heard repeatedly:

> As you know, the United States is shipping goods to Russia when everybody knows that Russia is our number-one enemy.
>
> We should not be helping Russia because we are only defeating ourselves.
>
> Why should we help them get any further ahead than we are in the space race?
>
> We are selling them the shovels that will dig our graves.

The truth of these ideas is not in question. Virtually all the speaker's listeners will automatically agree before the statement has been completed, but they remain passive, listless, and unexcited, because their experience is fully as rich as the speaker's. The response is probably, "Oh, we've heard all that before." The speaker obviously needs new, even exciting, information to jar his listeners out of passive agreement.

How is this done? How can we be sure that our experience is good enough to justify our speech subject? The only acceptable answer lies in further investigation, some formal, some informal:

THINK. The young speaker should develop the habit of assessing his own knowledge and experience. It is the only way to answer such questions as: "What do I — *I personally* — think about this question of censorship? Do I really have any sensible attitude toward trade with Russia? Can I honestly say that I know where I stand on mixed marriages, burning draft cards, or taking LSD? What do I know about these issues? What information do I have, or need, to support my stand?"

OBSERVE. In some respects the student speaker leads a sheltered life. He studies, goes to class, speaks, eats, and studies again. For weeks at a time he remains on campus, safe and isolated. He observes campus events, but seldom does he observe the events within the nearby community. Does the community have a Juvenile Court? What goes on there? What happens at a meeting of the City Council? Is the desk sergeant at the police station busy on Saturday nights? What is a murder trial like? And what goes on in the factory south of town? The list is endless, and each question may be answered, in large part, by going out to see.

DISCUSS. The speaker may profit greatly from a good, free-flowing discussion with others. Thinking and observing are not enough. He should experiment by testing his ideas in the fires of discussion. Once he has expressed an idea, he may realize that the opposition is brisk or that his own judgment is hasty. He may improve his own reasoning by listening to that of others. He should certainly arrive at a better understanding of the idea being discussed. Through discussion, the speaker gradually develops, defines, and refines his ideas and his powers of clear expression as well.

READ. An able speaker does not stop with what he thinks, observes, and hears. He reads extensively. He reads not only to strengthen his own point of view but also to become better acquainted with opposing points of view. He reads to broaden his thinking, to gain new understandings and insights. He reads to doubt — perhaps even to discard his point of view. Ideally, he reads systematically. That is, he begins with material that gives him a brief introduction to his subject, goes on to books dealing at greater length with selected aspects of the subject, and proceeds to read more extensively in closely related fields. As he reads, he is careful to take notes of the material that might later be of special use.

To see how research strengthens and improves a basic idea, examine the statements in the left column below, then contrast them with their researched equivalents in the right column.

	Idea	*Researched and Supported Idea*
1.	Because of inadequate attention to soil conservation we lose a lot of top soil every year.	The estimated annual loss of top soil is 500 million tons. If we were to ship this amount by train it would take nearly a quarter of a million trains of fifty cars each to do the job.
2.	Most people don't know what they are talking about when they say our present-day automobiles aren't as sturdy as the old timers. Actually, modern cars have a much longer life expectancy.	Our local scrap-baling company tells me that in 1927 cars were scrapped after an average of 6.8 years. In 1967, that average had changed to fourteen years. The modern car stays on the road twice as long as its ancestors.
3.	You need no expert to tell you that our modern colleges have turned into playgrounds for young men and women.	T. S. Russell describes the American college as a place where students do little more than "root, rush, and organize."
4.	You would be surprised at the number of children who lose their lives every year by fire.	Last year 1500 children under five years of age died in fires.
5.	But the situation in Panama is not simply a question of the Panamanian flag over a Canal Zone high school. We can be pretty sure that somewhere, somehow politics also enters the picture.	Analysts are pretty generally agreed that once the conflict of the flag broke into armed attacks, the Panamanian President saw an excellent opportunity to win reelection by taking a firm stand against the United States.

The student's experience, limited though it may be, puts him on the right track, but the *specific* experience that comes with research will support or negate an idea and enable the student to speak authoritatively on it.

■   **SELECTING SOURCES**

The inexperienced student in a speech class all too frequently runs to the library for an article in his favorite — or a handy — magazine. And just as frequently his speech meets with disaster. He may succeed in deceiving his classmates about his source, but he has less success in deceiving his instructor. After all, the instructor can read, too, and he is pretty well acquainted with popular magazines. Furthermore, the student should realize that an instructor of public speaking may hear as many as fifteen hundred student speeches a year; with only a moderately good memory he can quickly determine the student's originality. Even if the student were able to get by with a rehash of a single artcle, this would not make it right. To borrow an article, lift its content, and present it as though it is original is flagrant dishonesty. It is to the speaker what plagiarism is to the writer. It should be avoided at all costs.

Borrowing from sources is acceptable if the student follows three simple rules. (1) He should begin with his own personal attitude or point of view and then look for ways to support, expand, or even reject it. (2) He should develop the habit of reading in at least three different sources. (3) He should always cite the source of the material used in his speech. These, of course, are minimum requirements which will vary greatly depending on the speaker, the occasion, and the subject.

But with what book or magazine should reading begin? Obviously, the subject and nature of the speech will dictate the choices. In general, the most up-to-date material on most subjects will be found in periodicals. Students often want to know what periodical is considered the best, but there is no pat answer to the question; useful material may come from nearly any source. In the periodical section of the library are the current issues of newspapers and magazines dealing with contemporary issues. Here, too, are the scholarly journals containing "depth" articles on particular subjects. To locate a particular article, the student should consult *The Reader's Guide to Periodical Literature* and not turn at random through *The Atlantic, Harper's, The Nation, The New Republic,* or *Saturday Review.* He will certainly want to refer to *The New York Times Index* for pertinent newspaper articles. The three weekly news magazines — *Time, Newsweek, U. S. News and World Report* — are dependably good. At least one of them should be read consistently, week after week, but not to the exclusion of other magazines. Excellent information may also be found in *Good Housekeeping, McCall's, Ladies' Home Journal, Esquire,* and even *Playboy,* but the quality of the information or ideas included depends on the authority or prestige of the writer of the article.

Other useful sources of information are housed in the Reference Room of the library. Among the yearbooks, *The Statistical Abstract of the United States* (1878 to date), *The Statesman's Yearbook* (1864 to date), *The New International Year Book* (1907 to date), and *The Information Please Almanac* (1947 to date), are best for statistical information. To the uninitiated these titles may seem rather dry and uninspiring, but a few minutes with any one of them will be enough to change this impression. Such volumes record facts and figures pertaining to the year-by-year changes in industry, education, religion, and government.

The biographical encyclopedias are invaluable for dates and capsule lists of men's achievements. The *Dictionary of National Biography* (British) and the *Dictionary of American Biography,* both of which include people of all times in their country's history, are the oldest, most detailed, and also the most selective. Information about "lesser lights" can be found in the general annual *Who's Who* and in the national and specialized ones (*Who's Who in Brazil,* . . . *in Science,* etc.). The academic world does particularly well by biographical reference books; every scholarly society publishes a directory, and Bowker's *Directory of American Scholars,* in four volumes by fields, keeps up with changing appointments and addresses admirably.

Also in the library Reference Room are the encyclopedias. Every student is well acquainted with the general information found in the *Encyclopaedia Britannica* and the *Encyclopedia Americana,* but he is usually less familiar with the subject encyclopedias like the *Encyclopedia of the Social Sciences* or the *Encyclopedia of Religion and Ethics.* The encyclopedias and dictionaries of various types are especially useful when the student wants a brief but objective introduction to a subject.

A fifth source of information for the speaker is books — those which deal specifically with the subject at hand. Admittedly, the student who has only one evening to prepare a speaking assignment will not have time to explore his subject in depth; but when he has more time, he should delve more deeply into his subject. An excellent goal for every student is to keep *generally* well read, not only on those subjects especially appropriate to his academic major but also on the problems faced by the society in which he lives.

Selecting the proper sources is clearly an important part of speech preparation. But no source, however recent or prestigious, can of itself produce an effective speech. Sources are only the raw materials; the speaker is the craftsman. Until he puts the materials together logically and creatively, his research will lie inert and lifeless.

☐   **NOTE-TAKING**

A good method of taking notes is essential in the preparation of a speech. Too often we are careless about taking notes. We get in a hurry and fail to record the most telling detail. We write on the backs of envelopes, paper napkins, and blank checks — and then thoughtlessly throw them away. We sometimes fill a page with words written horizontally, vertically, diagonally, and tie them all together with an intricate maze of lines and arrows that defies analysis. And sometimes, of course, we avoid note-taking altogether.

Systematic note-taking can aid clear thinking and check a faulty memory. It can help in arranging materials in an orderly fashion *while* the material is being collected. It can help us determine the thoroughness of our investigation by reminding us of how much (or how little) information we have collected.

Study the following note card.

Football: Early Days

    Records show that as early as 1366 "football" was played in England. It was so rough, with one village against another, that it became outlawed. (Loaded dice were outlawed at the same time.)

    One monk wrote: "The game at which they had met for common recreation is called by some the foot-ball game . . . A game, I say, abominable enough, and, in my judgment at least, more common, undignified, and worthless than any other kind of game . . ."

Harry Coulton, Medieval Panorama, p. 85

The student followed the most frequently recommended system of recording his research:

1. He used a 3″ x 5″ (or larger) card.
2. He recorded the source of the information.
3. He recorded the quotation clearly and accurately.
4. He recorded only a single item on the card.
5. He put a subject index heading at the top of the card to help him keep order as he continued his research.

Any student serious about his investigations will, in time, develop his own method of note-taking. He may remain with the note-card system but prefer variations in the procedure indicated here. Whatever the system, it must be orderly, accurate, and thorough so that the speaker may use his research data with ease and confidence.

SUMMARY

1. In choosing a subject, the student speaker may consider himself a potential authority on any subject within his own experience.

2. The speaker narrows his subject so that he may treat it with reasonable thoroughness and confidence in the time allotted.
3. The effective speaker makes sure that his subject is appropriate to himself, the audience, and the occasion; is interesting to himself and his audience; is worthwhile.
4. He supports his general ideas with research: he observes, thinks, discusses, and reads.
5. He takes careful notes on his research.

EXERCISES

1. Prepare a list of subjects appropriate to you. The list might have three parts: significant events, hobbies or interests, attitudes toward social issues.

2. Prepare a content analysis of a speech delivered by a prominent speaker appearing on campus or in town. Does each sub-assertion develop his major assertion? Determine how each sub-assertion was developed — by simple statement of belief, by reference to personal experiences, or by research.

3. Examine one of the following reference books and deliver a short oral report on a single selected aspect of the book:

   a. *Adeline's Art Dictionary*
   b. *Ballet Annual*
   c. *Book of States*
   d. *Cambridge History of American Literature*
   e. *Chambers' Biographical Dictionary*
   f. *Current Biography*
   g. *Directory of American Scholars*
   h. *Dictionary of the Bible*
   i. *Encyclopedia of Jazz*
   j. *Encyclopedia of World History*
   k. *The Golden Bough*
   l. *Groves Dictionary of Music and Musicians*
   m. *Guinness Book of World Records*
   n. *Leaders in Education*
   o. *New Century Cyclopedia of Names*
   p. *Oxford Companion to the Theatre*
   q. *Social World Yearbook*
   r. *Study Abroad*
   s. *Theatre and Allied Arts*
   t. *Who's Who in Atoms*
   u. *World Almanac and Book of Facts*

4. Choose four publications below with which you are not yet acquainted. Spend fifteen or twenty minutes with each; then present a short oral report on their probable value to the college speaker.

a. *The American Mercury*	**k.** *Horizon*
b. *The Atlantic*	**l.** *The Nation*
c. *Atlas*	**m.** *National Review*
d. *Business Week*	**n.** *The New Republic*
e. *Commonweal*	**o.** *Newsweek*
f. *Congressional Digest*	**p.** *Punch*
g. *Congressional Record*	**q.** *The Reporter*
h. *Current*	**r.** *Saturday Review*
i. *Department of State*	**s.** *Time*
Bulletin	**t.** *U. S. News and World*
j. *Harper's Magazine*	*Report*

5. Read the classroom speech below; then answer the questions which follow.

DOMINATING PARENTS

We have all heard the expression, "Let go of the apron strings." We, as a group, are now at that stage of life where we must let go of these strings which bind us to our homes and parents if we are ever to lead normal lives. But just letting go is a two-way process; parents must let go, too. In fact, one of the biggest problems of young adults today is the problem of dominating parents. Dr. Hunt, professor of psychology, has this to say: "Breaking away from dominating parents is one of the most pressing problems of young adults." Let us take a closer look at this problem.

Parents often fail to accept the fact that their children sooner or later become adults. Parents continue to think of their children as infants. Consider an actual case study. There was a young man named Benny who had grown up with his widowed mother. Benny had been a spoiled child all his life. Every time he fell, Mama was there to help him. Even when he grew up, Mama was there. Benny married and when something went wrong in his new home, he continued to run to Mama; and Mama, of course, was glad to help him out. When he got in debt, Mama paid his bills, but one day Mama's money ran out, too. In short order Benny found himself without a wife, without a home, without a bank account, and hopelessly in debt — and probably all because Mama refused to let go of the strings.

But consider a second factor. Parents often see their children as extensions of themselves and not as separate individuals. This is why some of us are faced with the problem of parents who want to plan our careers. We want to be a lawyer, but father wants us to be a doctor. When it comes time for marriage we might select Johnny, but Mother thinks Johnny is a poor choice for daughter. Now, why do parents behave in such a way? I think there are two reasons for refusing to let go of the strings. First, we all know that people want to be needed. They need to feel that they are important, that their opinion amounts to something, or that others seek them out for advice and guidance. This is natural. Thus the parent often hates to see his child outgrow the need for parental advice. Think back on the case of Benny. Benny's mother was a widow. She had no one else to whom she could give attention; so she had to have a receiver. She had to keep Benny dependent upon her. In doing so she ruined Benny's life. There is a second reason for parental dominance. Parents often look to their children to fulfill their own frustrated ambitions. This explains why Dad wants his son to be a doctor. Dad didn't make it. Dad didn't quite become what he wanted to be. There were too many hurdles to leap. So, he reasoned, "Maybe my boy can make it — if I push hard enough."

Yes, parents often attempt to dominate the lives of their adult children. I appeal to you as a group of future parents, rear your child so that he will be prepared to live in an adult world. At the same time prepare yourself to face the fact that one day your son will or must become an adult. And above all, learn how to let go of the strings.

QUESTIONS

a. To what extent does the speaker seem to rely on personal experience?

b. Has the speaker made experience significant, or does it seem trivial?

c. To what extent does the speaker rely on research?

d. Has the speaker adequately narrowed his subject?

6. Prepare a four- to five-minute speech based on research from at least five of the publications listed in Exercises 3 and 4 above.

CHAPTER 5

IDEAS
AND DEVELOPMENT

Once the speaker has determined his subject and purpose, he then must decide how to say what he has to say as effectively as possible. If a single, flat, and undeveloped statement will communicate the idea and accomplish the purpose, there is little need for a deluge of words. Usually, however, ideas cannot be handled so simply; they need expansion. The speaker needs to treat an idea so that it unfolds and reveals his precise meaning. He has to anticipate the reaction of his audience, to determine ahead of time where they are likely to misunderstand, refuse to believe, or lose interest.

To avoid the pitfalls of confusion the speaker should learn to (1) state his controlling ideas simply, (2) develop those ideas, and (3) support them with evidence and reasoning.

■   **STATING IDEAS**

Consider for a moment a thought as it might be expressed in a classroom speech:

Now another factor that we have to consider when we speak of slum conditions is the question of crime. Crime runs rampant and here you can find everything from forced rape to armed robbery to outright murder. Still another factor is the health of its residents.

The first weakness we notice is the lack of development. The "factor" of crime is introduced with one sentence and dismissed with a second. The speaker does not substantiate his statement about crime. We all know that crime includes rape, robbery, and murder, but the speaker tells us nothing about the incidence, increase, or decrease of such crimes. Before we could be impressed or persuaded to do anything about improving slum conditions, we would have to hear much more detail.

The second weakness is the lack of precision in stating the two ideas. If we were to hear these sentences at the moment of delivery, we might not take the trouble to object to them. We hear similar imprecision with such frequency that we have grown used to it and almost automatically assume we know the speaker's meaning. When we examine the sentences in print, however, we remember that the word "factor" means nothing more than "thing," which probably means "*any*thing." Even if we could agree on the meaning of this word, we would have difficulty agreeing on the meaning of the sentence: "Another factor is the question of crime." How can a "factor" be a question? How can crime be questionable? What does the speaker mean? The next sentence, "Crime runs rampant," is not enough help. Does the speaker mean there is a higher crime rate in the slums than in other parts of the city? Or does he mean that crime rates are on the increase? Does he want to reason that crime is bred by slum conditions? All we can really assume is that crime is there. This hardly impresses us, because evidence seems to indicate that crime is everywhere. The same careless use of "factor" occurs in the last sentence. The important point is this: The speaker should learn to phrase his controlling ideas clearly and precisely.

A controlling idea is best expressed in a *declarative sentence* — one which makes a statement or an assertion, one with which we can agree or disagree. It says: "The crime rate is increasing," or "We need to eradicate our slums," or "We should appropriate money for urban renewal." To each of these we may say "I agree" or "I disagree." The *interrogative* sentence, of course, asks a question —

"How can you describe slum conditions?" or "What should be done about them?" To these we cannot reply, "I disagree." The same is true for the *imperative* sentence, like "Rid the nation of its slums!" or "Tear down those ancient buildings!" Interrogative and imperative sentences are useful to the speaker at other times and for other purposes. Neither, however, is suited to the statement of a controlling idea.

A controlling idea is best expressed in a *simple sentence*. To add gravity and importance to an idea, a speaker frequently chokes its meaning with excess words and passionate overtones, thus:

> But I would say that while the slums of our larger cities are a menacing shadow over all our large metropolitan areas — and perhaps our rural areas as well, in view of the cancerous disposition of slum conditions — it is my belief, based on twenty-three years of experience with the budget, that we cannot well afford the billions of dollars it would cost to make every city first class.

In this example an idea ceases to be an idea; it becomes an entire oration, and not a very neat one at that. The idea becomes recognizable if we remove the argument, the restricters, and the qualifiers, and simply say: "This plan for urban renewal is too expensive."

Finally, a controlling idea should have *a single purpose*. This should be no problem if the idea is expressed in a simple, declarative sentence and if the speaker sticks to the point. In trying to stick to the point the beginner sometimes loses control of his supporting materials and confuses his purpose. At one moment he may be describing the actual circumstances of slums; then, before he is aware of it, he slips over into matters of judgment and begins to draw hard and fast conclusions — even though he is still under the impression that he is describing actuality itself. At the risk of making statements that may seem too hard and fast, let us say that the purposes of all controlling ideas may fall into one of three categories.

1. *To present statements of fact.* Statements of fact are concerned with actuality, with the existence of things, or with agreed-upon laws, theories, and concepts. They will declare:

1. Slums do exist in American cities.
2. Slums are increasing in American cities.

3. The rate of juvenile delinquency is very high in slum areas.
4. Health, safety, and sanitation facilities are inadequate in slum areas.

Each of these sentences is simple and declarative with a single purpose — to establish fact. None of them is concerned with an evaluation of proposed legislation, and none is rooted in opinion, speculation, guesswork, or blind prejudice.

2. *To present statements of value.* Statements of value, as the words suggest, are concerned with the worthwhileness of a program or a proposal. The speaker states the desirability, strengths, and weaknesses of an idea, person, place, or thing. For example:

1. The President's plan for urban renewal is sufficient for slum removal; or
2. The President's plan for urban renewal has many weaknesses.
3. Several state plans for urban renewal are adequately meeting the needs of their cities; or
4. State revenues do not allow sufficient funds for adequate aid to large cities.

Unlike statements of fact, statements of value judge, appraise, or give an opinion about the value of the subject in question. It is not to be assumed that matters of value are unrelated to matters of fact; on the contrary, a good value judgment must be based on facts.

3. *To present statements of policy.* A policy statement by the public speaker proposes the acceptance or rejection of a course of action. The chief clues to a policy statement are reference to a particular proposal and use of the word *should*. For example:

1. We should adopt the President's plan for urban renewal.
2. We should vote for Senator Smith's bill for urban renewal.
3. We should adopt the proposal for school aid to urban slums.
4. We should endorse the principle of state aid or municipal self-help.

We see that the purpose of presenting a policy is not divorced from the other two purposes. First, the speaker presents the facts about an issue; then he advances to a discussion of relative values; and, finally, he proposes acceptance of a policy or course of action. All three purposes are not always present. There often is not time to be this objective or comprehensive, but even when time and purpose are limited, *the speaker should at least speak as though he is aware of the facts and the values that bear on the policy.*

We may summarize this discussion by saying once again that the speaker should state his controlling ideas in simple, declarative sentences, each of which has a definite purpose. When we look back over the examples, however, another point becomes apparent: controlling statements are simple indeed, quite uninteresting, and often devoid of human feelings. They are little more than capsules of intellect or pellets of thought. If an audience is to survive, it must be fed more than a diet of pills; it must have the substance and bulk that come with well-developed thought. Consider the following diagram:

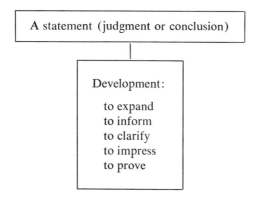

Here we have a speech unit, a statement and its development. The short classroom speech might consist of a single unit. The longer speech of ten or fifteen minutes might easily consist of three or more. And the complex speech will consist of several units and sub-units. Regardless of its length and complexity, however, the principle remains the same: There must be an appropriate development of each idea.

■   **DEVELOPING IDEAS**

There are many different ways of developing ideas, and each may be used individually or in combination. The methods most commonly used are: specific detail, explanation, comparison, narration, example, statistics, quotations, restatement, and visual aids.

☐   **SPECIFIC DETAIL**

To develop an idea by specific detail is to list or describe its smaller parts. Details may be sensory, appealing especially to the sense of sight, or they may be logical, referring to reasons, causes, effects, or goals. President Lyndon B. Johnson in his first address to Congress stated that, despite the recent assassination of John F. Kennedy, the country was still "capable of decisive action." He continued by listing the specific details, expressed here as goals:

> From this chamber of representative government, let all know and none misunderstand that I rededicate this government to the unswerving support of the United Nations, to the honorable and determined execution of our commitments to our allies, to the maintenance of military strength second to none, to the defense of the strength and the stability of the dollar, to the expansion of our foreign trade, to the reinforcement of our programs of neutral assistance and cooperation in Asia and Africa, and to our Alliance for Progress in this hemisphere.[1]

A student developed a classroom speech on conformity by presenting specific details from Orwell's *Nineteen Eighty-Four*.

> A nation of people who give up all claim to individual identity ceases to become a nation. It becomes a machine — oiled, operated, wound-up and shut off by a tyrannical "Big Brother." Its citizens are no longer able to think for themselves nor act for themselves. Rational thought and speech are unwholesome luxuries so they are replaced by "doublethink" and "newspeak." And wherever the citizen goes — at work, on the street, in his home — he knows that "Big Brother is watching."

[1] *Department of State Bulletin,* December 16, 1963, p. 910.

The chief value of such detail is not to prove but to clarify, and to get and hold the attention of the audience.

☐   **EXPLANATION**

To explain a thing or concept is to discuss its meaning. The speaker may describe a thing in terms of the broad category to which it belongs. He may show how it differs from similar things within that category. He may explain its function or operation. Or he may list its ingredients or components.

Secretary of State Dean Rusk, in evaluating the United Nations, uses this last technique in describing the nature of the world community:

> World community is a fact
> — because international communication is a fact;
> — because international transport is a fact;
> — because matters ranging from the control of communicable disease to weather reporting and forecasting demand international organization;
> — because the transfer of technology essential to the spread of industrialization and the modernization of agriculture can be assisted by international organization;
> — because modern economics engage nations in a web of commercial, financial, and technical arrangements at the international level.[2]

Senator Bartlett describes France largely in economic terms. He gives each term further significance by comparing or contrasting it with other nations:

> In terms of the United States, of Red China, or of Russia, France is not a powerful nation. Her national income is one-tenth our own. She now spends a higher percentage of this income on arms and defense than does any country of NATO with the exception of our own. She contributes in economic assistance to underdeveloped countries four times the contribution of the United Kingdom and close to one-half our own.[3]

[2] *Department of State Bulletin,* January 27, 1964, p. 113.
[3] *Congressional Record,* February 19, 1964, p. 3009.

□   **COMPARISON AND CONTRAST**

As we can see from the previous example, a comparison is a very useful means of developing an idea. When we compare one idea with another, we put them side by side and show their similarities and/or differences. We indicate the similarities existing between unlike things when we want to clarify or amplify. A bellows, for example, is not identical to human lungs, yet many teachers compare them: "Our lungs are like bellows. They pull the air in; then with muscular energy they force the air out." When we want to make a point of uniqueness, we contrast the differences:

> But a bellows is wood and leather, while our lungs are of delicate, membranous tissue. A bellows has a single cavity, while our lungs contain thousands. A bellows is used only to produce a stream of air, while our lungs exist primarily to feed the needed oxygen into the blood stream.

When the speaker uses a comparison as proof rather than clarification, he relies on a *literal analogy*. This is a comparison of similar things, one familiar to the listener, the other unknown or less familiar. For example, Senator Javits, defending our American aid to South Vietnam, compared the Vietnamese to South Koreans,

> We should reiterate our determination to try to find a viable, freely elected government for South Vietnam, pursuing very much the same policy that we pursued . . . in South Korea, and for the very same reasons.

But Senator Gruening was quick to object to the comparison:

> Has the Senator noted the marked difference in the attitude of the South Koreans from that of the South Vietnamese? The South Koreans were opposed to the Communists. They fought bravely and incurred many losses. The United States went in there to help those who wanted to help themselves. There seems to be a lack of will on the part of the South Vietnamese to wage a fight against the Communists. It contrasts with the will to fight of the Koreans. That is the basis of our difficulty in Vietnam.[4]

[4] *Ibid.,* p. 3156.

Testing the analogy. This example helps to illustrate the test of an analogy. *The two things being compared must be alike in all essential respects.* Mr. Javits reasoned that the South Koreans and the South Vietnamese were alike — both had the desire for freedom, and both were victims of Communist attacks. Mr. Gruening, however, considered the analogy weak because of the dissimilarity in their willingness to fight. Though Mr. Javits later denied the truth of this charge, his case was nevertheless weakened.

□   **NARRATION**

One of the most effective methods of development is narration. A simple story, fable, joke, or anecdote will not only drive home an idea, it will create interest as well. Here, for example, is a story used in a speech by the Rev. Robert J. McCracken, pastor of Riverside Church in New York City:

> A father and mother, humble farmer folk, sent their son to college and sacrificed to keep him there. He worked hard, won prizes and at length was about to graduate. They went to the ceremony and took their places, self-consciously, among the commencement throng. Their son was salutatorian, and they beamed with pride over the applause that broke out as he sat down. But when the applause continued on and on until the boy had to bow a second time in acknowledgment, the father could keep still no longer. Nudging his wife he said, "Mary, by all odds, that's the best crop we ever raised."[5]

In much the same way, Edward Olson of the National Conference of Christians and Jews used a story in his speech to school teachers and administrators in Fort Wayne, Indiana.

> . . . something like the Indiana farmer I heard about. A neighbor said to him one day, "Well, Jake, what are you going to plant this season?" Jake said, "I don't know." Persisting, the neighbor asked, "Corn?" "No," said Jake. "I'm scared of the corn borers." "How about wheat?" "No, that's not safe — too much wheat rust around."

[5] Lester Thonssen, ed., *Representative American Speeches: 1959–1960.* New York: The H. W. Wilson Company, 1960, p. 33.

"Then, how about planting potatoes?" "Oh, no — the potato bugs'll get them." "What are you going to plant?" "Nothing, I'm going to play it safe." Well, there are educators in many parts of the country, including some right here in Fort Wayne, who are not going to take that negative defeatist attitude . . ."[6]

Senator Keating used the *historical* narrative in his speech commemorating the uprising of Jewish people in the Warsaw ghetto. After relating the early abuses suffered during World War II, he closed with a description of the final dramatic events of the story:

> On April 19, the Germans came once again to the Ghetto to ship more of the Jews to their death but this time they were rebuffed. After meeting several more efforts of resistance, the Nazis resorted to burning down the buildings block by block, so as to turn the Jews out. Thousands did burn to death, thousands more died of starvation, disease, and injuries. A few managed to hide in the underground bunkers they had dug, until finally the last of these bunkers was seized, three weeks after the uprising. The remaining buildings were dynamited, reducing the Warsaw Ghetto to ashes and rubble.[7]

While narration is one of the most important methods of development, it seems to give the student speaker a great deal of trouble. He frequently chooses a joke, for example, not because it illustrates his point but simply because it is a joke. Sometimes he relies on a story that is much too long for his speech. Properly handled narrative materials are, above all else, appropriate; they are simple, without complexities of plot or subtleties of dialogue; they are definite in meaning, colorful, and rich in action.

☐   **EXAMPLE**

An example is a recounting of a specific event or occurrence. It may be an historical happening that has been observed and recorded, or it may be a hypothetical example created by the speaker. A well-known example is usually handled quickly without attention to small

---

[6] *Vital Speeches,* November 15, 1960, p. 79.
[7] *Congressional Record,* February 19, 1964, p. 2992.

details; an example which is unknown or might be misunderstood must usually be developed in greater detail.

The use of the undeveloped example is illustrated in a speech by Dr. Donald E. Anthony of Kent State University:

> The government of the United States has ever since it was founded engaged in activity which is inconsistent with laissez-faire philosophy. Throughout our history we have been more or less committed to protective tariffs. Very early the banking system came under the control of the federal and state governments. Today we have a maze of state and federal laws regulating nearly all forms of business activity.
>
> Even before the era of the New Deal, we had blue-sky laws, workmen's compensation, federal food and drug acts, the Federal Trade Commission, the National Banking Act, the Norris-LaGuardia Act, state utility commissions, the Interstate Commerce Commission, state and federal child labor laws, the Sherman and Clayton Anti-Trust Acts, and many other regulations upon our economy.[8]

Anthony quickly lists the several acts in a mass and the results are effective — indeed almost overwhelming in the apparent rush to prove the statement. But because the audience was familiar with the examples, Anthony felt no need to develop them.

An example expressed in narrative form was used by Secretary of State Dean Rusk as he was being interviewed by Professor Eric Goldman of Princeton University. Mr. Goldman asked how President Johnson compared with the late President Kennedy in decision making. Mr. Rusk replied that both were "men of action," both were "very conscious of the unfinished business," and both were "interested in what is required of us in a particular situation." Then he went on to provide an example of the speed with which President Johnson could act:

> Before he could be completely clear about exactly what the question was, he, for example, dispatched Mr. Mann and Secretary Vance to Panama, to have two of his top representatives right there on the scene to deal with the situation on the spot. He made immediate arrangements for this to be considered by the Organization of American States and a decision as to how to deal with it in the

[8] *Torch,* January, 1961, p. 42.

United Nations Security Council. He gave other instructions about the security of American life and property in the Zone itself. He telephoned President Chiari to get agreement that this is a matter that ought to be settled by discussion and not by violence.[9]

A third illustration of the use of example comes from a classroom speech:

> The accounts I have read of the misery of slum children are things that can't be forgotten. I read of the fourth grader who explained to her teacher that she missed school because the rats had killed her baby sister. I also read of the little girl who painted a picture of her apartment building with great streaks of red because this was the color she saw coming from the mouths of the old men who slept in the corridors. Then there was the boy whose legs had been broken by a baseball bat — he refused to say who did it because he hated the police more than he hated his attackers.

The use of example as a method of development is, of course, very popular. All of us have been in conversations in which someone has said, "Like what, for instance?" or "Give us an example." At times we use an example to explain or clarify; often we use it to prove and persuade.

Testing the example. If the example is used to establish probable truth rather than simply to explain or clarify, it must pass the test of acceptability: *Is the example typical or pertinent to the statement being supported?* An example is typical if most of the other examples support the same statement; it is atypical if the majority of examples contradict it. Mr. Rusk gave us a single example of President Johnson's quick and decisive action. He suggested that it was typical, and another example tends to confirm it. Johnson was quick to handle matters of state at the time of Mr. Kennedy's assassination: he was quick to convene Congress, to declare a day of mourning, and to let the world know that we were going to follow the same national policies.

Supporting by example seems to be a matter of numbers — the greater the number the greater the proof. But this is not always the case. Many times we have only one or two examples to work with.

[9] *Department of State Bulletin,* February 3, 1964, p. 167.

What happens when an atomic bomb is dropped on a large city? Only two examples are available, but that is more than enough. What happens when a popular Catholic aspires to become President? Again, only two examples are available, and the results contradict each other. What happens when a man consumes a fifth of bourbon in a short evening? There are thousands of examples, but one is enough. An example should first be typical and pertinent; then additional examples, if available and necessary, should be presented as well.

□   **STATISTICS**

The public speaker uses the word statistics for all figures — ratios, percentages, and grand totals. Figures are especially useful because they usually dramatize the extent or frequency of events. A single event, let us say, is a single example. When this example is viewed repeatedly at different times and places, it becomes a statistic. A student speaker, by way of illustration, began her speech with a dramatic example of a high school girl who was going to have a baby; then she made her point much stronger with statistics:

> This is no longer an unusual story. It happens so often that we have lost our sense of shock. The story is old and the plot is thin and the characters are always the same — young, immature, not yet out of high school. I wish you could take the time to read the last issue of *Parent's Magazine* because there you could read the statement of the Chicago Board of Education. They reported that 576 girls under sixteen and some as young as eleven dropped out of school because of pregnancy. Last year in the United States there were 50,000 girls of high school age who gave birth to children — out of wedlock.

To make the most of her statistics, the speaker moved from a single example to the number of examples in one city and finally to the total number in the nation.

But if the speaker is to use statistics wisely, he must take certain precautions.

1. *Large figures should be presented in round numbers.* A figure like 9,654,983,081 is clumsy, to say the least. Any audience would forget the first digit by the time the last arrived. In a speech the figure

would become "over nine and a half billion." Notice how this principle was followed by the late John Foster Dulles:

> Of the Chinese Communist prisoners taken in Korea, two thirds rejected repatriation . . .
> In Korea about 2 million have gone from the Communist north to the south.
> In Vietnam nearly 1 million went from the Communist north to the south.
> During the Hungarian rebellion, 200,000 escaped to freedom.
> In Germany over 3 million have gone from east to west.
> Indeed, the evidence suggests a "law" of popular gravitation to democratic freedom.[10]

2. *Statistics should be interpreted.* They should be presented in terms that are meaningful to the listeners, terms that are common to the experience of everyone. Few of us have ever seen a billion dollars, or a million, or even a few hundred thousand, but all of us have seen the things that money will buy. Notice that President Kennedy was aware of this:

> This Congress has already reduced this year's aid budget $600 million below the amount recommended by the Clay committee. Is this nation stating it cannot afford to spend an additional $600 million to help the developing nations of the world become strong and free and independent — an amount less than this country's annual outlay for lipstick, face cream, and chewing gum?[11]

Kennedy interprets a large sum of money in terms of three very familiar items. He makes the point psychologically significant by contrasting our desire to help others through foreign aid with our desire to indulge ourselves by a remarkably high expenditure for luxury items. It asks, in effect, "What is better? Face cream and chewing gum for ourselves, or food and freedom for underdeveloped nations?"

Mr. Henry C. Alexander shows the same skill in interpreting figures:

> . . . the total store of gold held for monetary purposes in all the free world amounts to some 36,000 metric tons. At the U.S. Treasury's

---

[10] A. Craig Baird, ed., *Representative American Speeches: 1958–1959.* New York: The H. W. Wilson Company, 1959, p. 40.
[11] *Department of State Bulletin,* November 25, 1963, p. 809.

official price of $35 an ounce, it is worth about $40 billion. That's less than half of what our Federal government spends in a year. You could stack all of it solidly in a room about 40 feet long, 40 feet wide and 40 feet high — a space no larger than a small ballroom.[12]

The figures are interpreted for us in four different ways — in terms of weight, monetary values, government expenditure, and space.

3. *Statistics should be used sparingly.* Statistical support is the most telling and the most revealing of all available kinds of material; even so, the speaker cannot run the risk of boring his audience with an endless list of figures. But how is one to know when he has too many or too few statistics? Unfortunately, there is no textbook rule. The answer varies according to the occasion and to the necessity for numerical data. A county treasurer presenting a monthly report to a group of city officials will necessarily use more statistical information than the average English teacher trying to impress his students with the need for careful reading. But whether a treasurer or a teacher, the good speaker learns from experience how many statistics he can comfortably handle with a given audience and subject.

□   **QUOTATIONS**

When a speaker quotes, he borrows, with proper acknowledgment, the words of someone else: the novelist, the poet, the historian, the newswriter, the scientist, the Senator — anyone whose words are particularly suited to the idea under discussion. Supporting material of this kind may be more easily understood if we divide it into the *informal* and the *formal.*

INFORMAL QUOTATIONS

An informal quotation helps to clarify or amplify the speaker's idea and adds a note of literary style. It does not provide logical support. It may win belief psychologically, but it does not prove the truth of a statement. This idea is well illustrated in a Kennedy speech to the National Press Club during a very busy campaign for the Presidency:

[12] *Vital Speeches,* January 1, 1961, p. 169.

Much has been said — but I am reminded of the old Chinese proverb: "There is a great deal of noise on the stairs but nobody comes into the room."

The President's State of the Union message reminded me of the exhortation from King Lear that goes: "I will do such things . . . what they are I know not . . . but they shall be the wonders of the earth."

*   *   *   *   *

"The President is at liberty, both in law and conscience, to be as big a man as he can." So wrote Professor Woodrow Wilson.

*   *   *   *   *

It is not enough merely to represent prevailing sentiment — to follow McKinley's practice, as described by Joe Cannon, of "keeping his ear so close to the ground that he got it full of grasshoppers."

*   *   *   *   *

. . . he [Lincoln] said to those present: "If my name goes down in history, it will be for this act. My whole soul is in it. If my hand trembles when I sign this Proclamation, all who examine the document hereafter will say: 'He hesitated.' "

But Lincoln's hand did not tremble. He did not hesitate. He did not equivocate. For he was the President of the United States.[13]

For his quotations, the speaker used a proverb, a literary quotation, a homey folk saying, and the recorded words of two past presidents. Though none of the quotations really proves the speaker's assertions, all of them were selected for a specific purpose. The first two introduce a touch of humor at the expense of his political opponent. The third helps to inform the audience about the power of the President. The fourth again is humorous. And the last creates a tone that is atmospheric, serious, almost reverent. Taken together, they do much to entertain, to clarify and stimulate, but they also project an image of the speaker himself. They reveal him as a man who made literature and history a part of his life.

[13] Thonssen, *op. cit.*, p. 33.

FORMAL QUOTATIONS

A formal quotation reveals facts or an interpretation of facts. A
Secretary of State is in an excellent position to know the facts about
Communist acts of sabotage in Argentina, but the student is not. It
stands to reason, then, that the student speaking on this subject will
quote information released by the State Department. The formal quotation, whether of fact or opinion, tends to prove the truth of a
statement.

Here is an example of how a student supported her statement on the
subject of college cheating with a formal quotation:

> Locating the cheater is no longer a problem; he can be found in
> any classroom of any college in America. Mr. Philip E. Jacob in
> his book *Changing Values in College* refers to cheating as the most
> obvious "chink in the moral armor of American students." He
> states that cheating is admitted by 40% of the students at a large
> number of colleges . . . This figure is astounding enough but it
> goes up in the opinion of the authors of *The First Two Decades of
> Life.* They claim that the figure may run anywhere "from two
> thirds to an astounding 85 percent." Apparently cheating is now a
> way of life. As the *Christian Century* put it, "It's not all right; it's a
> necessity."

The speaker begins with a statement: Cheaters exist in large numbers. She supports the statement with two quotations of fact and two
of opinion. The question remains: Does she prove her point? The
answer rests on the acceptability of the authorities or sources quoted,
which in turn rests on affirmative replies to the following questions:

1. Is the authority a recognized expert in the subject on which he
   is quoted?
2. Is the authority in a position to know? Was he there at the time?
   Or does he have channels of information that keep him informed?
3. Is his evidence in agreement with other evidence? Does he
   agree, for example, with other experts? Or do the statistics
   support him?
4. Does the expert stand to profit from expressing his fact or
   opinion? Is he free from prejudice?

Most students listening to the testimony on cheating would be unable to answer questions 1, 2, and 4, but question 3 is another matter. Because the testimony supports what most students have long suspected and what many students have been able to observe, the evidence does appear to be believable. Hence, the authorities are acceptable.

Beginning speakers are frequently at a loss when trying to deliver testimonial material. Perhaps the greatest problem is making an oral reference to the testimony without getting both tongue and brain twisted. A student might say: "According to two eminent psychologists, Merry and Merry, in their book, *The First Two Decades of Life,* published by Harper & Brothers in 1958 on page 517 . . . ." To get all this into a single sentence and maintain interest and clarity is impossible. Sources are important, but a speaker should not sound as though he is reading a formal footnote from a research paper. He should use only what is essential to the idea, purpose, and occasion and delete all items an audience can neither remember nor use.

A second problem is the "quote — end quote" convention. In court or in a formal committee hearing, the word "quote" at the beginning and "end quote" at the end of a quotation is useful. In a public speech, however, the device is mechanical and distracting. The speaker is more interesting if he shows that he is quoting by momentarily looking down at his notes or suddenly shifting his voice into a different tone or inflection. Testimony should be demonstrated rather than indicated with "quote — end quote."

A third problem is length. Some students, unless carefully advised against it, will read two or three paragraphs or even pages to illustrate their point. With testimonial material, however, more than a paragraph is usually too much of a good thing. The public speaker is not a public reader. He should choose only testimony which is brief, succinct, and right at the heart of the matter. Three or four sentences will usually suffice; often one will do.

☐   **RESTATEMENT**

Restatement is a form of rephrasing an assertion or question. We are acquainted with the friendly announcer who asks: "Are you troubled by morning backache? Do you feel grouchy when the alarm rings? Do you snarl and snap when the little woman says good morning? Then take . . . ." Obviously, this is restatement by the use of questions. The best restatement clarifies and improves on the previous expression. Notice how Dr. Rufus Clement uses this technique in the closing moments of his speech "How Would You Have Us?" delivered at the annual convocation of the United Negro College Fund:

> Finally when the decisive goal had been scored by an American — I found my elation mounting so high that I suddenly discovered that I was standing, and to my utter amazement there were tears streaming down my face. As this happened, I stopped and my other self said to me, Are you a fool? Why do you weep? Why, why, why are *you* so glad? There isn't a single Negro on the Winter Olympics team. These are not your people, this is the United States of America and has nothing to do with you. And just as suddenly I put down all this riotous, turgid voice within me and said, This is *my* team, this is *America, I am represented there, this is my country also.*[14]

Here, the first example of restatement occurs in the middle of the quotation and dramatizes an idea. The second series of restatements negates the first, expresses national pride, and asserts that America is for all Americans regardless of race. The speaker intentionally puts his strongest and most impressive restatement last.

☐   **VISUAL AIDS**

The modern college student needs no introduction to the visual aid. Since the introduction of educational television, the mass class, the language laboratory, and the teaching machine, every student is aware of the many devices that supplement the lectures of his professors. These same devices are used by the speaker outside the classroom — especially when his purpose is to inform or describe. Following is a brief annotated list of the visual aids available.

[14] *Ibid.,* p. 188.

1. *Blackboards* are especially helpful when there is little advance notice to prepare more elaborate visual aids. Since the speaker can easily make changes as he talks, a blackboard is also useful in illustrating a process or describing how change takes place.

2. *Demonstrations* are especially useful in discussing processes. Instead of merely talking about soil erosion, for example, a speaker could easily demonstrate his meaning with a flat box of dirt and a glass of water.

3. *Diagrams* are useful in demonstrating business or governmental organization. They easily show the span of administration, the level of authority, and the flow of communication.

4. *Graphs* are excellent for indicating degree, extent, or totals. The *line graph* is especially good for illustrating annual change (automobile sales, for instance); *bar* and *figure graphs* are excellent for comparing gross figures (the production of steel in a given year in various countries). The *circle graph,* sometimes called the "piece of pie," is useful in showing the parts of a whole (how a tax dollar is spent).

5. *Maps* graphically pinpoint geographical location, population distribution, topography — indeed, regional differences of any kind.

6. *Models* are attention-getting because they are three dimensional. A speaker cannot bring a battleship onto his platform, but a model is a reasonable substitute.

7. *Objects* may include anything small enough to bring into the room that is appropriate and necessary to the speech. They are particularly useful in demonstrations.

8. *Pictures,* of course, are also excellent substitutes for things too large for the speaker's platform. Pictures have the added advantage of presenting many different things in series — people, homes, places, etc. — in a brief time.

9. *Slides and film strips* have all the advantages of pictures plus the added advantage of greater size of the image.

Regardless of the kind of visual aid being used, the speaker must remember that he himself is the greatest aid. He must do the interpreting, and he must give direction and purpose to the material. To do this he must be sure that the projector is in good working order; that models and charts are large enough to be seen; that all materials are properly coordinated with his remarks; and that he treats the audience, not the aid, as the most important thing in the room.

☐   **METHODS COMBINED**

Though we have investigated several ways in which the speaker may develop a statement, they are not the only ones. As a matter of fact, the more we listen critically to the way we talk with one another and the more we analyze the manuscripts of prominent speakers, the more we realize that the speaker may use *any* method. Several methods are often combined. The speaker rarely uses *only* the example method, for instance; he usually combines it with one or more of the others. Anyone who attempts to describe the combination as a *single* method will soon realize that he is playing an impossible game. Consider, for example, this excerpt from a speech which appears in full at the end of Chapter 6:

> A few years ago, a Gallup Poll was taken and mothers across the country were asked two questions. First: Would you like for your son to become President? And almost ninety percent said, "Yes," they'd like for Johnny to become President. They then asked the second question: "Would you like for him to become a politician?" Almost the same percentage said, "No," they didn't want their son to become a politician. Somehow or other, they apparently figured their son could become President without any of the stigma of being a politician.

This excerpt is an *example;* it reports *statistics;* it *quotes* majority and minority opinion; it has specific *detail;* the entire passage is *narrated.* In short, it combines the characteristics of several methods of development.

The choice of developmental methods is not arbitrary. The speaker cannot say: "I have a statement and I think I'll develop it with narration, because I enjoy telling stories." The statement may not be suited to narrative development. Scientific subjects, for example, lend themselves to development by examples and statistics, not narration. Historical subjects, on the other hand, naturally lend themselves to narration and quotation. Current events are best developed by example, statistics, and quotations. The method to be used grows out of an investigation of a subject; it grows out of experience with the subject; it is indigenous to the subject.

■   **REASONING WITH SPEECH MATERIALS**

Throughout the preceding discussion we have examined methods of developing or expanding a statement. A particular method of development which needs special consideration is *reasoning,* the process of drawing conclusions from evidence. In this section we shall investigate *evidence* and the two fundamental types of reasoning, *induction* and *deduction.*

☐   **EVIDENCE**

Student speakers are often confused about the nature of evidence. Consider this example:

Statement: The crime rate in America is alarming

because

?Evidence?:   juvenile delinquency is increasing.

The remark about juvenile delinquency is not evidence. The student may say, "Why not? After all, it is a development of the broad subject of crime, and it is a matter of common knowledge that juveniles are committing more robberies and more criminal assaults than ever before." Evidence is not "development," "common knowledge," hearsay, or general belief. Evidence has three essential characteristics: (1) It is fact or expert opinion which (2) has been recorded and which (3) is used as the basis for inferring conclusions. A speaker's supporting material must have all three before it can be considered evidential.

1. *Evidence is fact or expert opinion.* "Juvenile delinquency" is

not a fact. It is a label our society applies to the criminal behavior of young people under a certain age (the specific age varies legally from state to state). A fact is not a label; neither is it general behavior. It is a specific thing or event that has actual existence. It is a fact that Robert W. received three years for breaking into a grocery store. It is a fact that Ted X. admitted hitting a gasoline station attendant. It is a fact that Steve Y. was found carrying a concealed weapon. These specific facts, taken together, constitute the broad category "juvenile delinquency."

Legally, an expert's testimony is fact, as well. If Dr. A. finds Willy Z. mentally incompetent and unable to stand trial, the court must take it as fact. If the crime laboratory reports that Charlie Q. failed the drunkometer test when he was arrested, the judge accepts it as fact that Charlie Q. was drunk at that time. We all accept as fact the opinions of experts with firsthand experience in other fields as well as law. We go to scientists for opinions on nuclear energy and accept them as facts. However, no matter how expert the scientist is in his own field, we tend not to accept as facts his secondhand opinions on educational methods or abstract art. For facts in those fields we would ask for the opinions of an educator or art historian.

2. *Evidence is recorded fact.* When we want a factual basis for our reasoning we do not rely on hunches and guesses; we turn to the spoken or written record. The speaker interested in juvenile delinquency may glean facts from a taped interview with the local Juvenile Prosecutor, from the daily ledger and annual report of the police station, and from the number of convictions recorded by local courts. He is not at liberty to accept verbal statements as fact unless they are recorded.

3. *Evidence is fact and expert opinion used as a basis for reasoning.* It is a relatively simple matter to repeat facts. Theodore Roosevelt holds the world's public handshaking record; according to the *Guinness Book of Records* he shook 8,513 hands in a single day. The same source reveals that a group of students from a college in Wisconsin holds the piano-smashing record; they smashed a piano with hammers and axes and put it through a nine-inch hole in four minutes, fifty-one seconds. Such facts are merely "interesting" until they are called upon to support a statement. Crimes are committed; they are

observed; the facts are recorded; but the record is virtually useless until prosecutor, counsel, judge, and jury reason from it to reach a verdict.

☐   **INDUCTIVE REASONING**

Inductive reasoning is reasoning from particular instances — evidence — to a valid general conclusion. Whenever we use *any* factual material to support the probable truth of a statement, we are reasoning inductively. We are aware, of course, of many kinds of reasoning: circumstantial, causal, reasoning by example, by analogy, by definition, by correlation, and what have you. They all work from facts to generalizations, so they are all forms of inductive reasoning.

Examine how inductive reasoning works with a testimonial narrative:

Narrative Fact 1

> Well, the defendant, Robert W., asked if I would help him kick in this grocery store and I said, "No"; so he asked me if I'd drive my car for half the take. I said "Yes," I would; so I drove him to Third and Spring — up the alley — with the lights out. I waited outside while Bob pried open the door with a tire tool. He was inside maybe two minutes; then he came running back and said, "Let's go, let's go. It looks good, real good."

Conclusion:

> Robert W. broke into the grocery at Third and Spring.

Of course, if the witness who reported this incident were prejudiced or if he perjured himself, his evidence would be discarded. To add

weight to the witness's testimony, however, the prosecutor introduces more evidence:

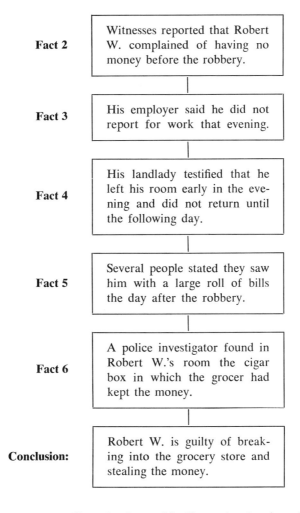

Fact 2	Witnesses reported that Robert W. complained of having no money before the robbery.
Fact 3	His employer said he did not report for work that evening.
Fact 4	His landlady testified that he left his room early in the evening and did not return until the following day.
Fact 5	Several people stated they saw him with a large roll of bills the day after the robbery.
Fact 6	A police investigator found in Robert W.'s room the cigar box in which the grocer had kept the money.
Conclusion:	Robert W. is guilty of breaking into the grocery store and stealing the money.

It is important to realize, simple as this illustration is, that *the conclusion is not a fact;* it is a judgment, an inference drawn from facts,
which is true beyond a reasonable doubt.

Similarly, the student speaking on juvenile delinquency must supply factual evidence which will lead to the conclusion that delinquency is increasing:

Statement:	Juvenile delinquency is increasing.

	There were more local juvenile convictions in 1968 than in 1967.
Evidence:	The national figures were higher in 1968 than in 1967.
	The Judge of the Juvenile Court said that court records showed more juvenile cases in 1968 than in 1967.

Conclusion:	Juvenile delinquency is indeed increasing.

In this example, the student is trying to prove the probable truth of a statement by evidence. He reasons from the specific to the general: he reasons inductively.

☐   **DEDUCTIVE REASONING**

Deductive reasoning is arriving at conclusions from conclusions previously drawn. This is a formal or structured kind of reasoning which proceeds from a generalized truth to a specific truth. Let us assume that we have conducted a study of all major American cities. We have examined the evidence on juvenile crime in each city, and we arrive inductively at a generalization: "All major American cities record an increase in juvenile crime." Now, the question is, "Does Chicago record an increase?" If we put our conclusions into the deductive pattern it reads like this:

All major American cities record an increase in juvenile crime.
Chicago is a major American city.
Chicago records an increase in juvenile crime.

The first statement is a conclusion previously drawn by induction or established by evidence. The second statement is true by definition or by agreement. The third statement is valid because it logically follows from the two preceding statements. If the first two statements are true, the third must be.

The name for the three-line structure of deductive reasoning is the *syllogism*. The example we have just studied is a *categorical syllogism* because it reasons from all the examples within the category of "major American cities." We could arrive at the same conclusion with the *hypothetical syllogism:*

If Chicago is a major American city, it records an increase in juvenile crime.
Chicago is a major American city.
Chicago records an increase in juvenile crime.

Again, the conclusion is the logical result of the first two statements. As with the first example, we cannot logically conclude, "Therefore Chicago shows a decrease," or "Chicago hasn't reported in yet." There is only one possible logical conclusion if the first two statements are true.

The third kind of syllogism is the *disjunctive* or "either . . . or" syllogism; the reasoner must make a choice between two possibilities:

Either Robert W. or Charlie Q. robbed the grocery.
Charlie Q. did not.
Robert W. did.

Though this is not the usual way of establishing guilt, it does help us to understand the disjunctive syllogism. If we can be certain that we have exhausted the list of suspects and if we can be sure that the two did not accompany each other, we have an acceptable first statement; then if the second statement is true, the conclusion will follow logically.

How is the public speaker to use syllogistic deduction? It is doubtful, of course, that anyone would prepare and deliver a speech composed only of syllogisms; the speech would be too mechanical and cold to interest an audience. The syllogism can help the speaker examine his thinking during the planning stages of his speech. He may cast his major assertions into appropriate syllogisms, and if he finds errors, he may redirect his thinking and prepare a more logical speech. The syllogism is equally useful for the listener. At the moment he hears the reasoning of the speaker, he may quickly reconstruct the arguments into syllogisms to test their soundness.

SUMMARY

1. Controlling ideas are best expressed in simple, declarative statements which reveal a single purpose.
2. Controlling ideas present statements of fact, value, or policy.
3. Ideas can be developed with specific detail, explanation, comparison and contrast, narration, example, statistics, quotations, restatement, and visual aids.
4. When developing an idea through comparison or analogy, we must make certain that the things being compared are alike in all essential respects.
5. When developing an idea by example we must be certain that the example is typical of or pertinent to the idea being discussed.
6. When developing an idea by statistics we should (1) round out large numbers, (2) interpret them in meaningful terms, (3) use them sparingly.
7. When developing by formal quotation, we choose an authority who is (1) a recognized expert, (2) in a position to know, (3) in agreement with other known authorities, and (4) free from prejudice.
8. Evidence is recorded fact or expert opinion which is used as the basis for reasoning.
9. Inductive reasoning is reasoning with evidence from particular details or "facts" to general conclusions.

10. Deductive reasoning is reasoning from conclusions previously drawn. It proceeds from the general to the specific in one of three kinds of syllogisms — categorical, hypothetical, or disjunctive.

EXERCISES

1. Prepare a list of fifteen short, simple, declarative statements which reveal your attitudes and on which you can prepare classroom speeches. Five should be statements of fact, five statements of value, and five statements of policy.

2. Many times student speakers present statements without expanding them. Such statements might include the following:

   a. Capital punishment is just plain murder.
   b. Capital punishment is sadistic.
   c. Capital punishment does nothing to prevent crime.
   d. Capital punishment is primitive.
   e. Mercy killing is a form of murder.
   f. Mercy killing is the usurping of God's rights by man.
   g. Mercy killing is based on the infallibility of a doctor's judgment.
   h. Birth control is interference with God's ways.
   i. Legalized abortion is murder.
   j. Crime comics are a major cause of juvenile crime.

   Evaluate each of these statements; then choose one, take a stand on it, and defend your point of view by using the best supporting material you can find.

3. Choose a speech from a recent issue of *Vital Speeches* and prepare a two-page analysis of its methods of developing ideas.

4. Discuss briefly some of the implications of the following quotation:

   > If you go buzzing about between right and
   > wrong, vibrating and fluctuating, you come
   > out nowhere; but if you are absolutely

and thoroughly and persistently wrong, you
must some of these days have the extreme
good fortune of knocking your head against
a fact, and that will set you all right again.

— THOMAS HUXLEY

5. Locate the error in each of the following syllogisms:

   a. All major American cities show an increase in juvenile
      crime.
      The city of Juarez is in Mexico.
      Juarez has very little crime.

   b. If Odin, Illinois, is a major American city it has had an
      increase in crime.
      Odin is not a major American city.
      Odin has had no increase.

   c. Either Chicago has had an increase in crime or its govern-
      ment has taken vigorous action to avoid it.
      Chicago has shown an increase.
      Its government has taken no vigorous action.

6. Prepare a four-minute persuasive speech in which you use at
   least four pieces of evidence. Make certain that your evidence
   supports the point you want it to support and that you cite all
   sources.

7. Prepare a four-minute speech to instruct or inform. Use at
   least three visual aids.

8. The following speech, as it appeared in the *Congressional Record,* was delivered by Senator Kenneth Keating on the floor of
   the Senate in March, 1964. What is Keating's main purpose?
   His subject? His controlling idea? Study the speech carefully
   to understand the use of developmental materials and to see
   how the speaker arrives at his conclusion through inductive
   reasoning.

   Mr. President, I wish briefly to report today on some mail which
I have received on the proposed civil rights legislation. I have
heard from thousands of New Yorkers on this subject. I very
frankly state that my mail has been running about equally divided

in favor of and in opposition to the bill. At one point, 2 or 3 weeks ago, the mail ran 10 to 7 against the bill.

This may come as a surprise to many supporters of civil rights, as it did to me. New York has been the leader in enacting civil rights legislation. We have on our statute books very progressive laws in this area. In fact, we have been so far ahead of most of the rest of the country that the enactment of Federal legislation in this area would have little practical effect in the State of New York.

We already have public accommodations laws. We already have a Fair Employment Practice Act. We do not discriminate against persons who seek to register to vote, because of their race, creed, or color. I have never heard of that happening in the State of New York. We do not build or operate segregated facilities with Federal money. We have no "separate but equal" laws on our statute books.

Why, then, is there so much opposition to the bill from the State of New York?

I believe the answer can be stated in two words: misinformation and hysteria. Both have been engendered by racist propaganda, which has been widely distributed in Northern States. There is an organization which calls itself the Coordinating Committee for Fundamental American Freedom, Inc. — a very high-sounding name. It has apparently begun a campaign to discredit the bill. It has mailed propaganda to northern homeowners, and has inserted paid political advertisements in northern newspapers. The principal financial contributor to the Coordinating Committee is the Mississippi State Sovereignty Commission. According to lobbying reports filed with Congress in the third quarter of 1963, of the $23,000 budget of this coordinating committee, $20,000 came from the Mississippi group.

In the fourth quarter of 1963, the receipts were $110,000. More than 90 percent of this amount came from the sovereignty commission, headed by the Governor of Mississippi and financed by funds regularly appropriated by the Mississippi Legislature. I hope these facts will be borne in mind if any of this literature is received by homeowners and other citizens, or if any such propaganda is read in hometown newspapers. Incredible as it may seem, these groups have been singularly successful in convincing many people that the passage of the bill would be a national disaster.

A man from Long Island called my office last week and was so choked with rage when speaking to a member of my staff that he was barely audible. The man threatened to spend every penny of his savings to defeat me at the polls if I continued to support the bill. He voiced the following objections to the bill:

First. The bill would require him to fire white employees with seniority, in order to hire Negroes.

Second. The bill would abolish the system of union seniority.

Third. The Federal Government would assume control of curriculum content of the schools and would discharge any employee whose views differed from those of Robert Kennedy.

Fourth. The Federal Government would move buses into New York for the purpose of transporting white children to schools in Harlem.

Fifth. He would be forced, against his wishes, to sell his home to Negroes.

Sixth. The financial foundation of the Nation would be jeopardized by Federal reprisals against recalcitrant banks and lending organizations.

Seventh. The pensions to disabled veterans and aged social security recipients would be summarily cut off because of any discriminatory action by a State official.

A careful note was made of these statements because they are indicative of what appears in my mail. The assertion is made again and again in these letters that the bill would destroy union seniority; that the bill would do away with the seniority system in unions; and that it would do all the other parade of horribles I have mentioned. The statements are repeated over and over, which makes it clearly evident that they are the result of a propaganda effort.

Every single one of these allegations is patently false, as would be obvious to anyone who had taken the time and trouble to read the bill. Some of the mail I have received is so far off base that if it were not discouraging, it would be amusing.

One man wrote a long letter suggesting that all Negro Americans be shipped off to Africa. When I replied that I disagreed vehemently with everything he said on the question, I received a second letter which repeated the same arguments but had this postscript:

> I have marked my second letter to your personal attention, since I am sure that my first letter was answered by a Negro on your staff.

Probably one of the most distorted letters, if not the most distorted, that I have received to date came from a nationally known and highly respected patriotic organization, of which I have the honor to be a member. I am proud of my membership in it. The writer of the letter stated that in 1928 the Communists launched their civil rights program to create social disorder in the United States by agitating the racial situation. He further stated that in 1928 the Daily Worker published, as a part of the Communist Party platform, the following demands:

First. The abolition of racial discrimination; second, the abolition of Jim Crow laws; third, voting rights for Negroes; fourth, integration in the Nation's schools; fifth, abolition of discrimination in Government employment; and sixth, the admittance of Negroes to railway stations, restaurants, and hotels. Then he wrote:

As Senator, you took a solemn and binding oath to uphold the Constitution of the United States of America. Which will your vote be, Senator? For the Constitution and against the civil rights bill, or for the Communist Party and its civil rights bill? The choice is yours.

Then he sanctimoniously signed the letter:

Yours for God and country.

This man is the "Americanism chairman" of this unit of a fine, patriotic organization.

Such nonsense, such clearly dangerous claptrap, practically defies reply. I suppose the thing to do is to reply to the gentleman, as I shall do, sending him a copy of the Constitution of the United States, with the 14th amendment underlined in red. Perhaps that will give some color to his allegations. Perhaps I shall send him a copy of the Republican and Democratic Party platforms adopted in 1960. I shall be inclined to say that I shall vote for the Constitution and for the bill now before the Senate. Quite frankly, I suppose this particular gentleman is rather beyond hope.

Here are a few other examples of the confusion which exists. A man in Bronxville asks:

Does this mean that once this bill is enacted, the Friendly Sons of Saint Patrick will no longer be able to reserve the grand ballroom of the Astor Hotel for the night of March 17, to the exclusion of those not of Irish origin? Similarly, a stadium or sports arena is defined as a place of public accommodation. Does this mean that the Jehovah's Witnesses will no longer be permitted to occupy the Yankee Stadium for their convention? And it no doubt would bar Constitution Hall in Washington to the DAR. Perhaps it is intended to.

I received a postcard from Claverack, N. Y., containing a stamp which many of us are accustomed to seeing:

> Get the United States out of the U. N., and the U. N. out of the United States.

The statement on this postcard charges that:

> The bill would liquidate constitutional government and establish a dictatorial tyranny.

A man from Albany says that my statement in the RECORD on February 26 in support of the bill:

> Sounds more like that of an agent of the President of Ghana.

A resident of Brooklyn fears that the bill would bar his:

> Rights to engage in private social activities in which he traditionally participates.

I do not exactly know what the gentleman has in mind, but unless his private social activities involve violating the political and human rights of other Americans, I know of nothing in the bill that would interfere with his social activities. I assure him that the bill would do him no harm.

I have a communication from a man in New York City which expresses considerable disturbance over my support of the bill and ends by saying:

> My family and I will vote for Khrushchev this November if he runs against you.

I do not anticipate that Mr. Khrushchev will run against me. But it is difficult for me to believe, bad as my record may have been in the minds of some, that constituents of mine are ready to support Mr. Khrushchev.

The writer of the next communication particularly opposes the

bill because he says "minority groups have become too cocky."
Then he adds: "like the new heavyweight champion, Lucius Clay."
All this is presented as a warning to Americans of good will in
all parts of the Nation. We may differ, and we do differ, with
others in regard to the merits of particular provisions of the bill;
but I hope those who do not favor the bill are not lending themselves to such hatemongering and smearing, which apparently are
so prevalent in the State which I have the honor to represent.

Mr. President, I would issue a warning that we are being deluged
with propaganda and are being subjected to an unbelievable barrage
of misinformation. I respect the right of anyone who differs with
me to express his views; but I do not intend to remain silent. I
shall continue to make public such documents as these; and I do
not intend to fail to reply when fear is instilled, lies are uttered, and
misinformation is spread. I think it is the duty of all Senators and
citizens to speak out with the truth.

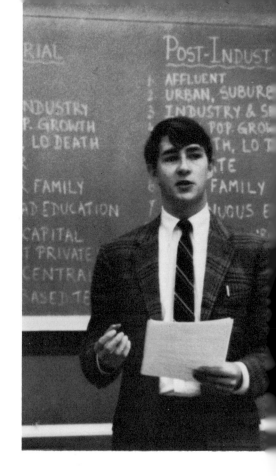

CHAPTER 6

ORGANIZING
THE SPEECH

In the third act of Shakespeare's *A Midsummer Night's Dream,* Peter Quince has trouble with his group of players as they rehearse an interlude for "the duke and the duchess on his wedding day at night." As distraction and distemper mount, Quince says to Francis Flute: "Why, you must not speak that yet; that you answer to Pyramus: *You speak all your part at once, cues and all.*" So it is with many of us. We try to spill out all our thoughts at one moment, with the result that our listeners are thoroughly confused.

This chapter deals with order — with organization, sequence, and balance. A sense of order enables the speaker to put all parts of his speech in their proper relationship. It enables him to use each idea in its most logical and advantageous place. It enables him to detect the weak spots in the development of his speech and to shore them up with additional materials. And at the moment of speaking, this concern with order helps the speaker stick with his ideas so that he will not be tempted to "speak all [his] part at once, cues and all."

■   **THE BASIC ORDER**

The most basic order is the *speech unit*. As we learned in Chapter 5, a speech unit is a statement together with its development. It may range in length from a brief remark to a short talk of three to five minutes. We find it in informal conversations, in the classroom, in business and industrial conferences, in governmental committee meetings — in any situation where discussion prevails.

Notice the single speech units in the conversational examples below:

Student:	*I think I'd better stay in tonight.* I have eighty pages of Trevelyan to read and two criticals to write. I have to review Emerson and Thoreau for American Lit. And to top it off I have to study for a quiz in Chem-Phys.	**Statement** **Development**
Buyer:	*We could be comfortable in this house.* It has four bedrooms, each with walk-in closets. It has two full baths, a large living room, a family room, a kitchen with all appliances furnished, a fenced-in play-yard, and a two-car garage. *It's just right for our family.*	**Statement** **Development** **Statement**
Teacher:	Let us review: Your purpose must be definite, your subject properly selected, narrowed, and developed. Your ideas must be effectively arranged and well delivered. *When you have mastered these techniques, you will be an effective speaker.*	**Development** **Statement**

These examples are not penetrating, but they do help us understand the most basic order available to the speaker. Notice that the statement may precede its development, it may follow, or it may do both. Notice also that the speakers rely on their experiences rather than documented evidence to tell them when to study, how to select a house, or how to instruct a student.

The level of difficulty increases slightly, but the same principle prevails in informal discussion. Notice how ideas are expressed at a meeting of a City Council:

Mr. Green:	Well, what would you say about our parks?	
Mr. Banks:	There are a good many things.	
Mr. Green:	For example —	
Mr. Banks:	For one thing, *we need to increase the recreational facilities of the parks we already have.* Of the seven parks, for example, only three have tennis courts. Five of them have ball fields, but after the slightest rain two of these are out of commission. Of the seven parks there is not one with a picnic shelter, not one with a swimming pool, and not one with any kind of recreational supervision. It is true that all seven parks have swings, but they are in such a miserable state that they are of little use. *We ought to do something and soon.*	**Statement** **Development** **Statement**
Mr. Green:	Yes, we do have our weaknesses.	
Mr. Banks:	We certainly do!	
Mr. Green:	But when you stop to consider the limited funds available, *we have made progress.* Our budget, you will remember, is less than $40,000. Out of this we must pay the Park Commissioner and the three maintenance men. We must keep the machinery — a truck, a tractor, and mowers — in good condition. That leaves us around $15,000 to maintain the grounds and equipment. Despite all this, if you will bother to check, we had not one single tennis court three	**Statement** **Development**

| | years ago and now we have nine. Our *progress* is nothing to write home about, but it *is there.* | **Statement** |
| *Mr. Banks:* | Well, it's still not enough. | |

Again, in each of the two longer segments of this discussion, we find a single speech unit — an assertion and its development. Both speakers could have developed their points of view in other ways. In addition to their local examples and statistics they could have read research reports or compared their park system with the systems of similar communities. They could have used expert testimony to define the ideal park or to justify the little progress already made. With more time at their disposal, they perhaps could have used any of the several developmental methods discussed in the preceding chapter.

Now, examine a single-unit speech — a speech with but one idea — as delivered on the floor of the Senate. Senator Williams of Delaware, aware of the Surgeon General's study and report on lung cancer and cigarette smoking, had just introduced an amendment that would repeal the price support for tobacco. The Senators from the twenty-three tobacco states were understandably alarmed. As one of the spokesmen on the side of tobacco, Senator Ervin of North Carolina defended the economy of his state:

Statement: *. . . Many things must be evaluated by research before a reliable conclusion can be reached.*

Development: At one time doctors noted that in areas of the country in which the people ate a great quantity of corn or corn products pellagra was widespread. Instead of conducting research — as ought to be done in the case of tobacco — the doctors said, "Pellagra is caused by eating corn." This was a public statement of position made at that time. That is what the departments of health stated. Some doctors refused to accept this apparently obvious conclusion and insisted that there should be more research into the question of the diet of people suffering with pellagra. As a result of the research that followed it was found that pellagra was not caused by eating corn but, on the contrary, it was caused by not eating green vegetables containing niacin. Yet those who had assumed the original position based their assertion that pellagra was caused by eating corn on statistics as reliable as the data on which the report of the Surgeon General's Committee was based.

Development: For a long time doctors noticed that people who suffered from malaria lived in the neighborhood of swamps. So they came to the conclusion that the decomposition of vegetable matter in swamps caused bad air or miasma. So to the disease was given the name "malaria," which was derived from two Latin words which mean "bad air." Publicly, in committee meetings, and in medical conventions, the doctors declared with absolute assurance that malaria was caused by breathing bad air generated in swamps by the decomposition of vegetable matter. Later research demonstrated that there is no relationship whatever between malaria and breathing bad air generated in the swamps. It revealed that malaria is caused by the bite of a female anopheles mosquito which has previously bitten an infected person.

Statement: As the Senator from Kentucky has pointed out, the report does not purport to be conclusive; *it suggests that further research is needed.*[1]

Senator Ervin's speech was only five minutes long, but before he yielded the floor, he supported his assertion by quoting from the *Wall Street Journal* and from an opinion of Dr. Joseph Berkson, a medical statistician from the Mayo Clinic. Senator Ervin's speech is presented here not to emphasize sectional economics, show bias, or favor smoking, but to illustrate the single speech unit — the simplest and most basic element of public speech.

[1] *Congressional Record,* March 4, 1964, p. 4185.

Now let us assume that we are preparing a speech considerably more complex than Senator Ervin's. Instead of one speech unit we have several. We may even have too many ideas for one short speech. We have some information to support some ideas and no evidence to support the others. So we think more deeply; we observe life around us; we talk things over with our friends; we read. Soon we realize that some of our most important ideas fall into related groups. When these relationships become apparent, we are ready to discard the other ideas and prepare an outline.

■   **CONVENTIONS OF OUTLINING**

First of all, we should understand that there are three distinct divisions in every complete speech: (1) the *introduction,* (2) the *body* or discussion, and (3) the *conclusion.* The introduction establishes a favorable atmosphere for the discussion to follow. The body contains the thesis or controlling idea, along with all sub-ideas and their development. The conclusion reviews or emphasizes the controlling idea and calls for a particular belief, understanding, or action. In this section we shall discuss outlining only the body. The introduction and conclusion are organized a little differently and will be handled in the next chapter.

The relationship of ideas within an outline is indicated in two ways — by symbols (numbers or letters) and by the width of the margins. The major divisions in an outline are usually shown with Roman numerals (I, II, III, etc.) and are placed flush with the left margin of the page. Succeeding subdivisions are indicated with capital letters (A, B, C, etc.), then arabic numerals (1, 2, 3, etc.), and then lowercase letters (a, b, c, etc.). Each succeeding subdivision is uniformly indented a few spaces further from the left margin. For further subdivisions one has a choice of symbols. The numbers and letters may be repeated, altered by placing them in brackets ([I], [A], [1], [a]) or parentheses. Since most classroom speech outlines seldom go beyond six divisions, arabic numerals within parentheses (1) are generally the last designative symbols shown.

Study the skeleton outline which follows:

I. _____

   A. _____

      1. _____

      2. _____

         a. _____

            (1) _____

            (2) _____

         b. _____

            (1) _____

                (a) _____

                (b) _____

            (2) _____

   B. _____

      1. _____

      2. _____

II. _____

   A. _____

   B. _____

Here are two major ideas, I and II, each with two first-order sub-ideas, A and B. Idea A under idea I apparently has much more detail than idea B — so much that it is subdivided down to the fifth-order sub-ideas (a) and (b). Roman numerals and narrow margins indicate the highest, most general, most comprehensive level of content. Wide margins and small letters in parentheses indicate the most specific breakdown of an idea. Similar letters or numbers are used for all ideas of equal value. Idea A under idea I, for instance, may carry more weight than idea B, it may be more sophisticated or more human, but the reader knows at a glance that the two have equal value in relationship to the parent idea, I.

When the student has an outline before him, he can check his understanding of the relationship of the parts to the whole by seeing if entries with equal margins and comparable symbols are, in reality, coordinate. Examine the following outline to see if the items are divisions of the same larger unit or idea, reasonably equal in importance, and comparable in language structure.

I. The problem of our parks
   A. Poor location
      1. Four in industrial areas
      2. One in a flood area
      3. Two in good locations
   B. Good swimming pools
   C. Poor park equipment

Are points A, B, and C parallel in structure? Are points 1, 2, and 3 parallel? Is this a complete outline? If not, why?

There are two kinds of outlines, the *topic* and the *sentence*. The topic outline is one in which every division and subdivision is a word or group of words which immediately reveal the point of discussion. An example of the topic outline follows.

EDUCATIONAL FALLOUT

Purpose: To inform my audience of the reasons for dropping out of high school.

Introduction

  I. Number of graduates in 1963
 II. Number of drop-outs

Body

  I. Lack of interest in curriculum
    A. Attitude toward college preparation
    B. Attitude toward business courses
    C. Attitude toward trade school
 II. Inability to adjust
    A. To administrative rules
    B. To assignments
    C. To social life

    III. Desire to earn money
        A. To help parents
        B. To become independent
            1. By owning a car
            2. By buying own clothes
            3. By earning own spending money

Conclusion

    I. Number of drop-outs unemployed
    II. Need for solving the drop-out problem

With controversial subjects or problems like this, it is best to represent every topic by a phrase or a clause rather than a single word. In the example above, words like "adjustment," "rules," "assignments," and "social" would not reveal the point of view of the speaker. Single-word entries, on the other hand, are especially well suited to non-controversial, largely descriptive subjects, like football or chess:

THE OFFENSIVE TEAM	CHESS
I. Backfield	**I.** The pieces
A. Quarterback	**A.** Pawns
B. Fullback	**B.** Bishops
C. Left Half	**C.** Rooks
D. Right Half	**D.** Knights
II. Line	**E.** Queen
A. Center	**F.** King
B. Guards	**II.** The moves
C. Tackles	**A.** Diagonal
D. Ends	**B.** Straight
	C. Two-and-one

The topic outline is the favorite among students because it is simple and easy to set down on paper. It is popular too because it provides ready-made speaking notes.

    The sentence outline is well suited for argumentative or persuasive speeches. It presents every division or subdivision in a complete, simple, declarative sentence; it expresses an idea as well as the speaker's viewpoint in regard to the idea. Look at the following sentence outline for a speech on soil erosion:

WE'RE BEING WASHED AWAY

Purpose: To persuade my audience that soil erosion must be controlled.

Introduction

I. We are gradually being washed into the sea.
  A. The annual loss of top soil is estimated at 500 million tons. (K. B. Pomeroy, *American Forest*)
  B. In the Minnesota Valleyland rain in six hours' time ripped out a gulley 15 feet deep and 150 feet wide. (L. C. French, *American Forest*)
  C. Over a half billion tons of rock material are annually removed from the Mississippi drainage basin. (H. D. Thompson, *Fundamentals of Earth Science*)

II. In human terms, the consequences of soil erosion are staggering.
  A. As topsoil is washed away, agricultural lands become arid and infertile, causing a decline in quantity and quality of crops.
  B. Forests dwindle, depriving us of wood products and their derivatives.
  C. Natural mineral deposits are wasted.
  D. Floods mean instantaneous loss of life, property, and crops.

Body

I. There are three causes for soil erosion.
  A. Land owners have stripped the land of its timber.
  B. Farmers have used improper plowing on slopes and ridges.
  C. Government officials have been slow in taking flood control measures.
    1. They have failed to control at the river mouth.
    2. They have failed to control on lowland banks.
    3. They have failed to control the river tributaries.

II. A three-part solution is essential.
  A. We should offer the land owner more incentive to reforest his land.

B. We should improve educational and research programs in farming methods.

C. We should immediately secure federal, state, and local funds for flood control.

III. The benefits from these measures are, by now, obvious.

    A. Agricultural, forest, and mineral productivity will perhaps be able to keep pace with the expanding population.

    B. Natural resources, property, and lives will be conserved.

Conclusion

I. Soil erosion is such a far-reaching problem that we must take the steps I have proposed.

II. I ask for your help.

    A. Support educational research programs in agriculture and forestry.

    B. Take an active part in conservation organizations.

    C. Work for appropriate federal, state, and county legislation.

The items in this outline are expressed in complete sentences, and each sentence is a clear and precise reminder of the idea to be developed. Obviously, the speaker will need examples, statistics, and quotations to back up every idea except the first one, but the outline as it stands is complete and logical enough to guide him directly and quickly to the kinds of support he will need. The sentence outline undoubtedly demands more careful preparation than the topic outline, but the increased benefits often make the effort worthwhile.

■   **PURPOSES OF AN OUTLINE**

An outline is not a straitjacket imposed on our thoughts. It is a flexible support for them, growing out of our changing ideas and guiding but bending with them. A good outline serves at least three purposes: (1) it helps the speaker arrange his ideas and supporting material in an orderly, logical sequence and thus achieve his specific purpose; (2) it makes clear to the audience the relationships, progress, and direction of the ideas in the speech; (3) it provides the notes the speaker will use during delivery.

☐   **ESTABLISHING ORDER**

Most of us have opened our center desk drawers and found a jumble of papers, broken pencils, pictures, paper clips, appointment books, glue, stamps, gummed labels, a paper punch, a stapler, rubber bands, and two sea shells. When we can stand it no longer, we clean the drawer. We put the paper clips, labels, stamps, and other small articles into their own boxes and arrange them neatly in the drawer. We sort, discard, and file the papers. We make a list of the things we need. In short, we restore order to the drawer — at least temporarily.

This is exactly what the speaker does with his ideas when he makes an outline. He sorts his jumble of ideas and notes, discarding irrelevant ones, putting similar ones together, taking stock to find out if he needs more of any kind.

The speaker knows, let us say, that he wants to talk on the subject of automation in modern industry. He has read and taken notes. As his ideas begin to take shape, he jots them down:

1. Automation means controlling an operation or process mechanically, impersonally.
2. It will replace human labor.
3. It will increase the rate of unemployment.
4. It will provide more leisure time.
5. It will increase the need for on-the-job training.
6. It will create a shorter work week.
7. It will cause the worker to feel less human.
8. It will cause more turnover of labor.
9. Salary increases will be harder to get.
10. Management will have to spend more on educational programs.
11. It will eventually lower the cost of manufactured goods.
12. There will be fewer disputes between labor and management.
13. It will enable more workers to have two jobs to increase their income and have a higher standard of living.
14. It will assure more quality control.
15. It will further destroy pride of workmanship.
16. Management will have to invest more in equipment and supplies.
17. It will increase the need for further formal education.
18. More women will be employed.

19. Job seniority will become increasingly less important as greater emphasis is placed on job skill.
20. More men will move into positions now held by women.

As the speaker studies the list, he sees first of all that he has too many ideas to develop in a speech of moderate length. Also, no dominant purpose is evident in the jumble. But he does notice relationships between some of the ideas, so he groups similar ideas under main headings:

I. How automation will affect management (5, 8, 10, 11, 12, 14, 16)
II. How it will affect labor (2, 3, 4, 6, 7, 9, 12, 13, 15, 17, 19)
  A. Women (18, 20)
  B. Men (20)
III. How it will affect labor-management relations (8, 9, 12, 19)
IV. How it will affect the consumer (11, 14, 15)

He looks over his list and realizes that he could develop any one of these four topics into a speech. Having read widely on each of them, he finds them all important; but since he has worked during the past two summers in a factory back home, knows the laborer's problems with automation firsthand, and is vitally interested in them, he decides to cut his list down and arrange his ideas thus:

Purpose: To convince my audience that automation will have a dehumanizing effect on the laborer.

I. The manager will become more and more concerned with the machine.
  A. He will invest heavily in automation.
  B. His research money will go into further refinements of automation.
  C. His educational programs will be motivated by a desire to protect the machine.
II. The laborer will become attached to his machine.
  A. He will work with a machine rather than with other men.
  B. He will feel that his machine helps him earn his higher wage.

C. He will decide that his own skills are no longer as important as those of a machine.

By trial and error and gradual elimination, the speaker has arrived at a feasible rough outline for his speech. He has synthesized, arranged, and related his ideas in a logical order to support his purpose.

But a working outline like this is not the last of the speaker's preparations before going to work on delivery. Speech preparation simply is not that neat and orderly. All the steps — choosing a subject, defining a purpose, researching, and organizing — take place at the same time and not in strict order. Before starting to outline, of course, the speaker has chosen a tentative subject and general purpose and has done some research. While outlining, he has further narrowed his subject and defined his specific purpose. His rough outline serves as a check on the soundness of his subject and purpose. It shows up irrelevant or repetitious ideas, illogical relationships between ideas, inadequate, superficial, or contradictory supporting material.

Examine the following outline:

THE ADVANTAGES OF FRATERNITIES

Purpose: To inform my audience of the advantages of fraternity life.

  I. The founding of the first fraternity
 II. The arguments against fraternity life
    A. Expense
    B. Snobbism
    C. Too much social life
III. The new Theta Sigma house
    A. Lounge
    B. Kitchen
    C. Dining room
    D. Study hall
IV. The advantages of living in the new Theta Sigma house
    A. Good food
    B. Pleasant surroundings
    C. Chance to study

In this outline, the speaker either has the wrong purpose statement or the wrong ideas to develop it: parts I, II, and III are completely irrelevant to his purpose. The founding of fraternities, the disadvantages of fraternity life, and the new Theta Sigma house might make excellent topics for other speeches, but they are distractions in the speech as announced. Second, the last division — the one which comes nearest to the point — distorts the purpose. Instead of speaking on the advantages of fraternity life in general, the speaker proposes to speak on the particular advantages of living in the new Theta Sigma house. The two ideas are distantly related, but they are not the same. So much is wrong with this outline that the speaker discards it and starts again:

THE ADVANTAGES OF FRATERNITIES

Purpose: To inform my audience of the advantages of fraternity life.

  I. You develop deep friendships that last for a lifetime.
 II. You make business acquaintances who may help you with future jobs.
    A. Those now in school
    B. Alums of own chapter
    C. Alums of other chapters
III. You are helped socially.
    A. To get dates
    B. To learn social graces
 IV. You are helped with school work.
    A. Upperclassmen help freshmen.
    B. A file of past examinations is kept for reference.

The speaker's original outline showed him clearly where his thinking was illogical and superficial, and it guided him to proper organization of his ideas. Thinking more deeply changed his attitudes; new attitudes caused him to approach his subject from a different angle. Then he rearranged and reoriented his outline in the light of his changed attitudes. If his subject had been more complicated, he might have had to go back and do more research for additional or different supporting materials. The point is that only when all changes and improvements have been made can the speaker consider his outline finished. By then his subject will be fully narrowed, his purpose clearly defined.

☐   **INSURING AUDIENCE UNDERSTANDING**

The speaker must stick to his outline during delivery if he expects his audience to understand what he has to say. If he follows his outline, they will receive his thoughts in order, with the ideas in logical sequence and relationship.

Obviously, if the speaker departs from his outline — forgets an example and doubles back to pick it up after he has gone into another point, or introduces a new idea not even in his outline — he will probably confuse himself and will undoubtedly confuse his audience. They will wind up with the speaker's original jumble of purposeless ideas. It is not enough that the speaker's meaning be clear in his own mind; he must make it clear to his audience or fail to achieve his purpose.

By following a well-planned outline, the speaker continually indicates the direction and progress of his thought. Every succeeding idea is related to the previous one, builds on it, and inevitably leads to the next. As he speaks, his audience is able to follow the development of his ideas, relate them properly, and see clearly where the speech is leading.

☐   **PREPARING SPEAKING NOTES**

The best way a speaker can assure himself of sticking to his outline is by using notes during delivery. The kind he uses is purely a personal matter. Some experienced speakers, especially those with photographic memories, do well without notes. They may even contend that notes restrict their spontaneity and interfere with audience contact. But most speakers prefer to have some kind of notes in hand. A topic outline can be used as notes; a sentence outline would probably have to be cut down to brief topics. But whether the speaker uses a separate card for each note or puts them all onto one piece of paper, he should arrange them in exactly the same order and sequence as the outline.

Some speakers use a full set of notes with all ideas, sub-ideas, and developmental materials included. Others are satisfied with a simple list of words. As an example, see how the following note card could serve as a reminder for all points in the speech on the advantages of fraternity life (p. 141):

```
Introduction:    Per cent organized
                 Number of frats

        Body:    Purpose — advantages
                 I. Friendship
                II. Business
                     A. Now in school
                     B. Alums — own
                     C. Alums — other
               III. Social
                     A. Dates
                     B. Social graces
                IV. School work
                     A. Upperclassmen
                     B. Exam files

Conclusion:      Summary
                 Appeal — keep open mind to advantages
```

This note card could even be abbreviated to the four main headings of the outline. But the point is, it follows the outline exactly.

Despite the great variation in practice, here are a few principles which all effective speakers observe in regard to the use of notes while speaking.

1. *Use notes when necessary.* For a very short speech of a single unit there may be little reason for notes. The student should accustom himself to getting along without notes during short speeches so that he can concentrate on maintaining direct contact with his audience. Notes may be superfluous even when the speech is longer if the subject is quite familiar to the speaker. Notes are useful, however, when the speaker is dealing with a complicated subject. For example, he

needs verbatim notes of the quotations he wishes to use or detailed statistical information. The speaker should always use notes if he thinks he might present his ideas out of logical order. Notes *must* be used if the speaker knows he is prone to lapses of memory.

2. *Use as few notes as possible.* Notes are to jog the memory, not substitute for it. If the situation calls for reading a speech manuscript, the speaker should read without fear of penalty; but if the situation calls for extemporaneous speech, he should use few notes and as few words as possible in his notes. If the idea is expressed on the card in only a word or two, the speaker needs to spend only a fraction of a second in picking up the cue and can easily maintain eye contact with his audience. Reading five-word sentences takes the speaker's attention away from his audience too long. A few speakers try to convert their notes into complete sentences, as in the following example:

I. I dislike dormitory cooking because
   A. It specializes in leftovers.
      1. Last Monday we had broccoli spears.
      2. Tuesday we had chopped broccoli.
      3. Wednesday we had broccoli *au gratin.*
      4. And tonight I bet we have cream of broccoli soup.
      5. We will continue to have broccoli until it is gone.
      6. And then we'll start in on a four- or five-day cycle of asparagus.

These are not notes. This is a complete manuscript containing every word the student wants to say. Items 1-6 under A could have been no more than one word, "broccoli," or possibly two, "broccoli example."

3. *Use notes that are clear.* All of us have heard the speaker who says: "This is embarrassing! I have a note here but I can't make it out! Ha! Ha! Can't read my own writing. Ha! Ha!" We laugh at him, of course, but out of discomfort and embarrassment rather than humor. If a speaker is sincerely interested in presenting his ideas or points of view, he will write or print plainly. He will make the letters large enough so he can keep the notes away from his face and not allow them to interfere with communication with his audience.

■   **PATTERNS OF ORGANIZATION**

If you were confronted by a pile of stones and directed to sort them, what would you do? You might, of course, divide them into big ones, little ones, and middle-sized ones. If you were a geologist, you might divide them according to genetic classifications. If you were a skilled mason, you might divide them into porous and nonporous, hard and soft, or round and flat. In short, you would probably sort the stones according to your knowledge and purpose. The same is true when the speaker arranges a number of speech units. He puts the ideas into their most natural or logical order according to his own background and the purpose of his speech. If the speaker has a thorough understanding of his controlling purpose and of the ideas and material he wishes to use, order will follow naturally.

Public speakers use six common patterns in organizing speeches: (1) simple list, (2) time, (3) space, (4) related divisions, (5) causal, and (6) problem-solution.

☐   **SIMPLE-LIST ORDER**

As its name implies, the simple list is the least complicated method of organizing ideas. The speaker may include as few as two or three miscellaneous and seemingly unrelated items. The shop foreman, for example, might say to a group of new workers:

I. You must wear your safety goggles.
II. You must not shut down your machinery until you are relieved.
III. You must wear sleeve guards if you are a press operator.

This is a simple list of ideas related to one another only in that the foreman thinks they are important rules to tell a group of men working for the first time in industrial production. The football coach might use the same organization in diagnosing the team's last defeat, and the theatre critic might do the same in analyzing the failure of last night's opening. A dean of students might give entering freshmen a simple-list talk on how to succeed in college.

The simple list may also contain closely related items like characteristics, weaknesses, strengths, or types. The student, for example, might organize a speech on teachers like this:

    I. The "thinker"
   II. The "dervish"
  III. The "pontiff"
  IV. The "motormouth"
   V. The "joe"

The speaker relates all these classifications within the category of teachers. In a sense they are related divisions (see page 148), but they are not necessarily interdependent; neither can the general category "teachers" be considered a "whole" entity with limits and only a certain number of parts. This list of teacher-types could go on and on.

Certain precautions are necessary when the simple list is used. First, the list should be short. If a speaker were to announce that he wanted to discuss eighteen topics, the listener would quickly despair. Even five items is pushing the upper limits; three or four are nearly ideal. Second, if the list must be long, the items should be regrouped under larger headings in related-divisions order. A long list of teachers, for example, might be regrouped under the categories of "popular" and "unpopular"; "secure" and "insecure"; "traditional" and "progressive." Third, give serious consideration to the sequence of ideas in a list. Usually it is best to put the most important item last and the second most important first. Listeners tend to remember the last point of a speech first and the first point second. Placing your most important point last will also help you end your speech on an upbeat. At other times, for instance in a speech to inform, it will be wise to begin with those items that are familiar and simple, and gradually work toward the unfamiliar and complex. For example, if the speaker is talking about harmony in music, he could first explain the harmony of a simple and familiar song and then go on to discuss more difficult pieces and advanced harmonics.

The simple-list-order speech is often used to describe the newest car, the oldest professor, the latest fad, the latest word from home, the most recent presidential election. Many list items will be personal opinions. If you must add a subjective judgment, let your audience know it is yours. Such expressions as "in my opinion" or "to my way

of thinking" will usually be enough. At times you may even have
to admit: "I don't presume to know all the facts that bear on this
question. My knowledge is limited." A confession of inadequacy
may lose a vote or a decision, but it will gain you a measure of respect.
Stand firm on your opinion if it is soundly supported by evidence.
Tread lightly if your opinion is supported by nothing more than your
emotions or intuition.

☐ **TIME ORDER**

Time — often called chronological — order is most frequently used
in organizing (a) narratives ("My Summer in Southern Europe"),
(b) historical events ("Kennedy's Fatal Trip to Dallas"), and (c)
descriptions of process ("Growing Your Own Geraniums"). The
following outline describes in chronological sequence the process of
propagating plants by stem cuttings.

    I. Prepare the cuttings.
       A. Cut shoots below soil line in early spring.
       B. Insert shoots into moist sand.
   II. Transplant to pots in six weeks.
  III. Move to open ground in two weeks.

It is not always necessary to move from the earliest time to the latest;
it may be equally appropriate to move from the latest to the earliest.
One could trace the history of rockets, gear shifts, or tariff policies
by starting with what we have now and moving back through those
that went before.

☐ **SPACE ORDER**

Space order divides or describes areas, places, or things to show
the physical relationship of the parts. In using space order, the
speaker moves from left to right, east to west, top to bottom, inside to
outside to show how the parts of a whole are related in space. Space
order is useful to the interior decorator describing a house room by
room. It is useful to the teacher or art critic describing a canvas or

a piece of sculpture. It is useful to the advertiser who sells his services by describing the layout of his copy. The student speaker certainly can use it for topics involving area or space, especially if his purpose is to inform. Such topics as "The United Nations Building" or "Our Fiftieth State" could easily be organized according to space. Here is a simple way of using space order to describe the air around us:

   I. The troposphere
  II. The stratosphere
 III. The ionosphere

When the speaker organizes these three space items in this order, he uses additional logic by going from that part of the atmosphere which is nearest the earth to that part which is farthest away.

RELATED-DIVISIONS ORDER

The related-divisions order is just what the words imply, a break-down of a topic into its branches or departments. Our government, for example, is in three related divisions: local, state, and national. The federal government is constitutionally divided into three branches: the Executive, the Legislative, and the Judicial. The United Nations is divided into the General Assembly and the Security Council. The workers in a wire mill are grouped as receivers, cleaners, drawers, galvanizers, and shippers. The outline below groups people on a college campus.

PERSONNEL ON A COLLEGE CAMPUS

    I. Students
   II. Faculty
  III. Administration
  IV. Service personnel

Such divisions are more than simply related; they are interrelated. That is to say, the functioning of one division depends in very large part on the functioning of another. It is immediately obvious that a faculty cannot function without students and that college administrators cannot function without a faculty or students. It is the same in a wire mill: the drawers cannot work with the steel until the cleaners have done their work, and, naturally, the cleaners cannot work unless the steel is received.

☐   **CAUSAL ORDER**

There are three major causal orders: (a) effect to cause, (b) cause to effect, and (c) causes and effects. Since the first two are similar, let us look at some detailed reasoning that illustrates them both.

A hotel burns to the ground. Several firemen suffer injury. A few people lose their lives in the fire, but most of the hotel's occupants are rescued. The financial loss in terms of personal property and real estate is great. The *effects* of the fire are disastrous. But what were the *causes?* How did the fire start? Someone says it was arson; another says it was faulty wiring; a third says it was a leaky gas line; a fourth says it was the explosion of a propane tank; a fifth says it was a faulty flue from the incinerator.

If we were to make a speech outline on the hotel fire with the information we now have, it would look like this:

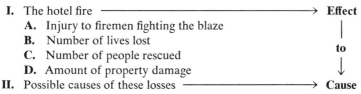

I. The hotel fire ⟶	**Effect**
A. Injury to firemen fighting the blaze	│
B. Number of lives lost	**to**
C. Number of people rescued	
D. Amount of property damage	↓
II. Possible causes of these losses ⟶	**Cause**
A. Arson	
B. Faulty wiring	
C. Leaky gas line	
D. Explosion of a propane tank	
E. Faulty incinerator flue	

The order is effect to cause.

Now we read in the newspapers that a thorough investigation of the possible causes of the fire is under way. The investigators finally decide, in the light of the evidence found in the ashes and rubble, that the cause of the fire was the explosion of a propane tank. We can now revise Part II of our speech outline accordingly.

But suppose we inquire into the *causes* of the propane tank explosion. We are now treating the explosion as an *effect*. Laboratory examination indicated that the tank was probably overloaded and that it had a defective valve. We could say that the man who loaded the tank or the man who installed the valve caused the explosion. A hotel custodian said that he had heard the tank "hissing" and had seen an open flame nearby. He did not immediately try to put out the fire but ran to inform the manager and get an extinguisher. The explosion occurred as he was doing so. Could we not call the custodian the cause of the explosion? Look at other possible causes for the "one cause" the investigators said started the fire:

1. The man who delivered and connected the propane tank.
2. The man responsible for the open flame near the tank.
3. The manager who ordered but did not check the tank.
4. The local Fire Marshal who failed to enforce a local ordinance.
5. The Mayor who did not see to it that ordinances were enforced.

We may conclude that instead of one cause there were many, all of them due to human fallibility. Part II of our outline now looks like this:

II. Propane tank explosion ————————————→ **Cause**
    A. Careless manufacturers and installers
    B. Careless hotel manager
    C. Irresponsible hotel custodian
    D. Slipshod city officials

A few days afterwards, the fire can be seen to have been the *cause* of many *effects*. In a speaker's outline they appear this way:

I. The hotel fire ————————————————→ **Cause**
    A. Firemen injured
    B. Lives lost
    C. Lives rescued   **to**
    D. Property damaged
II. Effects ————————————————————→ **Effects**
    A. Relatives of the deceased file suits
        1. against the manager

    2. against the hotel
    3. against the propane company
  B. Hotel owners file suits
    1. against the propane company
    2. against several insurance companies
  C. Propane company
    1. fires three employees
    2. sues an insurance company
  D. Municipal government takes action
    1. Mayor asks Fire Marshal to resign
    2. City Council passes new ordinances on use
    of propane in public buildings

Now the speaker's organization is *cause to effect*. The fire, once considered an effect, joins the ranks of cause, and new and unforeseen effects arise.

When a speech is organized by causes-*and*-effects order, the topic of the speech is, oddly enough, not discussed in the body of the speech. The topic's possible causes and effects become the subject and occupy the central part of the speech. For instance, if we organize a speech about World War I in causes-and-effects order, we talk about the war itself only briefly in the introduction and/or conclusion. We include in the body of the speech the causes — the development of international friction from, say, 1900 — and the effects until, say, the rise of Hitler. Following is a sketchy outline of the body of our speech:

  I. Causes
    A. Entangling alliances
    B. Developing imperialism
    C. Armament race
    D. Developing nationalism
  II. Effects
    A. Development of League of Nations and World Court
    B. Emergence of U. S. as world power
    C. Developing friendship of U. S., France, and Great Britain

You will note that (a) the causes came before the event, (b) the effects came after the event, and (c) the event itself — casualties,

injuries, devastation, loss of shipping, military strategy, weapons, etc.
— could only be discussed in the introduction or conclusion of the
speech. This type of causal order is best suited to an analysis of some
event already well known to a group of listeners.

From the discussion of the hotel fire and the preceding outline on
World War I, we may draw several conclusions. First, a speaker may
organize his ideas from effect to cause, from cause to effect, or around
causes and effects, depending on the purpose of his speech. Second,
causes or effects rarely exist in isolation; they occur in clusters. The
speaker who insists there is only one cause for a particular social
problem is almost certain to be wrong. Let us not forget that there
are causes of causes! Third, a cause is not a fact. We infer causes
from facts. A cause is a judgment, an opinion, a conclusion, an
inference. Because each person infers differently, opinions on causes
differ, too. Fourth, the soundness of the inference depends on how
well the evidence indicates a real and apparent relationship between
the cluster of causes and the cluster of effects.

☐   **PROBLEM-SOLUTION ORDER**

The problem-solution order combines aspects of related-divisions
and causal order. The speaker first describes the problem; then he
describes the solution and explains how this will effect a cure at some
time in the future. He predicts "before the facts" that such-and-such
a thing will happen.

This kind of reasoning occurs daily. The doctor, for example,
examines an ill patient. He records temperature, pulse, breathing, and
all evidence that will lead to a proper diagnosis of the illness. When
he is confident of his diagnosis (the problem), he prescribes a remedy
(the solution) and reasons that the patient, at some time in the future,
will be cured or improved. The legislator organizes his ideas in a
similar order as he works for measures that will improve or remove
the many problems facing our society. What should be done about
the problem of civil rights? What is the best solution to the medical
needs of the aged? Should personal income tax be increased? Should
we take action to decrease cigarette smoking? What about flood con-

trol, national defense, poverty, foreign aid, space research, price supports, slum clearance, or aid to education? The problems are many; the solutions offered are many more. A choice must be made, tried, and perhaps remade many times over. Discussion of such topics will almost inevitably be arranged in the problem-solution order. One traditional method of handling the problem-solution pattern is the three-step sequence of *need, desirability,* and *practicability.* The intercollegiate debater, who frequently builds his case on this sequence, reasons: There is (or is not) a *need* for change from our present status, and the proposed solution is (or is not) *desirable* and *practicable.* A city councilman could easily use this organization in advocating a clean-up campaign:

  I. There is a *need* for a city-wide clean-up campaign.
    A. Highway approaches to the city are marred by junk yards.
    B. Empty lots are littered with debris.
    C. Streets are littered with paper, etc.
 II. *Desirability:* A clean-up campaign would bring benefits beyond the solution of the problem.
    A. It would attract new industry.
    B. It would instill greater community pride.
III. *Practicability:* A clean-up campaign is workable.
    A. City and local truckers would provide trucks.
    B. Local advertisers would publicize the campaign.
    C. Unions and private citizens would volunteer help.

The *motivated sequence* is yet another arrangement for the problem-solution pattern and is particularly adaptable to persuasive speaking. Alan H. Monroe established its five steps in *Principles and Types of Speech*[2]:

I.	**Attention** —	the speaker attracts the interest of his audience
II.	**Need** —	the speaker describes the problem in terms of audience needs

[2] Alan H. Monroe, *Principles and Types of Speech,* 4th ed. Chicago: Scott, Foresman and Company, 1955, pp. 310ff.

III.	**Satisfaction** — the speaker presents the solution and indicates how it meets audience needs
IV.	**Visualization** — the speaker helps the audience to form a mental picture of the benefits of the solution
V.	**Action** — the speaker seeks to motivate his audience into action

Regardless of the precise form of the problem-solution pattern selected, the speaker should be careful to show the definite relationship between his solution and the problem. He should make certain that he can adequately describe the problem, that the problem is serious enough to deserve attention, and that he has a clear understanding of its causes. Furthermore, he should, whenever possible, propose a solution which counteracts the causes. His solution may be the better of two good possibilities, the best of many, or the lesser of two evils; but whatever the choice, it should lead to an improvement of the prevailing conditions. These admonitions may seem unnecessary, but they are often violated by speakers inside and outside the classroom. Students, for example, sometimes assert that to avoid cheating we should abolish examinations; to cut down on the divorce rate we should make divorce more difficult to obtain; to eliminate juvenile delinquency we should outlaw crime comics; to avoid "have-to" marriages we should "not allow" young people to go steady; or to save American prestige abroad we should "take the U. S. out of the U. N. and the U. N. out of the U. S." It would be a mistake to say that all these solutions are thoroughly bad, but at the same time we cannot call any of them good because they fail to get at the heart of the problems.

☐   **SPEECH PATTERNS COMBINED**

Though the speaker has acquired an understanding of the patterns of organization available to him, he is not free to select whichever one pleases him. Particular patterns are suited to particular speech units and to particular purposes. The first unit of a speech might be informative or descriptive and therefore best suited to time, space, or simple-list arrangement. Later units in the same speech might be logical or highly inferential and best suited to causal order. A hypothetical speech on the civil rights question is a case in point. To describe the problem the speaker might organize his ideas according to time by talking about the progress of civil rights since the Korean War. If it were more to his purpose to discuss the different attitudes existing in the various regions of the country, he would organize according to space by discussing attitudes in the South and the North. Or, if he chose, he might combine both time and space to discuss the brief history of change in each geographical area. Later the speaker might use causal order in analyzing the causes for the change or proposing a solution to make the change more rapid.

The effective speaker's first responsibility is to discover what he has to say and why he is saying it. Once this is done, he will find that there is a pattern especially well suited to his subject and purpose. The speaker who takes the first steps of careful analysis and the subsequent steps of skillful organization is more likely to achieve his purpose.

In this chapter we have dealt with the organization of ideas and materials in the *body* of a speech, but organizing the *introduction* and the *conclusion* is equally essential. This we shall discuss in detail in the next chapter.

SUMMARY

1. The most basic order of ideas in conversation, discussion, and public speaking is the speech unit — a statement and its development.
2. An acceptable outline observes certain conventions of symbols and margins. These conventions help the speaker to determine the accuracy, subordination, parallelism, and completeness of development.
3. The two kinds of outline are *topic* and *sentence*.
4. Careful outlining (a) helps the speaker arrange his ideas and supporting material in an orderly, logical sequence and thus achieve his specific purpose, (b) makes clear to the audience the relationships, progress, and direction of the ideas in the

speech, and (c) provides the notes the speaker will use during delivery.

5. Some of the most common patterns of organization are simple list, time, space, related divisions, causal, and problem-solution.

6. Patterns of organization are determined by content and purpose and are frequently used in combination.

EXERCISES

1. From a recent issue of *Vital Speeches,* copy a speech unit similar to the ones found in the first pages of this chapter. Is the statement of the unit clearly expressed? Is the development appropriate to the statement? What is the avowed purpose of the unit? Does the development help the speaker to achieve that purpose?

2. Prepare a brief but complete outline to write on the blackboard.

3. After three or four speeches have been delivered by each member of the class, your instructor will conduct a class discussion on types of speaking notes. Keep the notes you have used so that you will have something to contribute to the discussion.

4. As you listen to the series of speeches, prepare a topic outline of each. Are you able to distinguish between levels of importance? Can you distinguish between ideas and their development? Compare your listening outline with the one prepared by the student next to you or with the speaker's outline. If there are significant differences, how do you account for them?

5. Read the student speech below, then answer the questions that follow.

Staying Out of Politics

Let us suppose that the next time you go home you say to your parents, "Mom, Dad, I've been thinking it over and I've decided to go into politics." Just how would they react? Would they jump up and down with joy, or would they try to talk you out of it? If they are the typical parents, they would choose the latter. They would try to talk you out of it, and they would talk pretty fast. This is to me a tragic situation, and if it goes on unchecked it will pose a very serious threat to our political system.

The profession of politics has fallen to a dangerously low point on the prestige scale. I'm not alone in this opinion. President Kennedy has said that politics has become one of our most neglected, abused, and ignored professions. A few years ago, a Gallup Poll was taken and mothers across the country were asked two questions. First: Would you like for your son to become President? And almost 90 per cent said, "Yes," they'd like for Johnny to become President. The pollsters then asked the second question: Would you like for him to become a politician? Almost the same percentage said "No." They didn't want their son to become a politician. Somehow or other, they apparently figured their son could become President without any of the stigma of being a politician.

This attitude isn't restricted to mothers. Many of us have it. For example, what would you say if your minister announced from his pulpit next Sunday that he was going to enter a campaign — run for public office, become a politician? Some of us would think, "Well, he can't be a very religious man if he's going to get mixed up with that politics business." Maybe that's why the Senate of the 87th Congress didn't have a single senator who had previously been a minister, and maybe that's why there were only four former ministers in the entire House of Representatives. Ministers have learned that they are better off not to mix religion and politics.

Why do people have this attitude?

First, I would say corruption in politics has been widely publicized. We have all heard of Tammany Hall and the various political machines. We are acquainted with big city bosses, ballot stuffing, and all the scandals that arise every time there is an election. There always seems to be some kind of voting irregularity.

In the second place, I think all of us would agree that campaign tactics are not always aboveboard. Mud slinging has come to be an acceptable tactic; so we aren't surprised when a political campaign becomes a smear campaign. And the smear campaign has to hurt. It has to. The opponent has developed a thick skin; and if he is going to feel the pain he has to face some very strong charges. That's the way it is. Here in 1964, the vice-presidential candidates are throwing charges of smear and corruption and the accusations get more and more outrageous.

Then there is a third cause, and this may be the most important. The politician has become the national scapegoat. Mr. Jones doesn't have enough money so whom does he blame? He blames the politicians. They are the ones who create higher and higher taxes so they will have more money to squander away. And the temperance worker looks at all the drunkards in the south end of town. And who is to blame? The politician. After all, he had to promise something to win back the vote in 1932. This is the way we think. If something goes wrong, we accuse the politician. He's the one who becomes the goat.

So what are we going to do about it? How can we improve the status of the politician? While it isn't our purpose today to offer solutions, I think something should be suggested for quick consideration. Politics is not a dirty word. It deserves our respect. And while it may be often mismanaged by the quack or abused by the unscrupulous boss, it is also practiced decently. All of us need to claim our share in government. We should take an active part whenever possible. Who knows? With our help the prestige of politics might zoom to new heights.

QUESTIONS

a. Is the speaker's organization easy to follow?
b. What is the predominant pattern of organization?
c. Does the speaker at any time attempt to inform or to describe scientifically? Or does the scientific become informal in tone? Describe the probable effect.
d. Does the speech hang together or does it appear disjointed and loosely arranged? Why do you say this?
e. What changes would you have made?
f. What type of material impressed you most, the factual or the emotional?

6. *Speaking assignment.* Divide the class into six groups. Assign one of the six patterns of organization to each. Have each speaker deliver a four- to five-minute speech organized in the pattern assigned to his group.

CHAPTER 7

INTRODUCTIONS, CONCLUSIONS, AND TRANSITIONS

Most of the speaker's preparation time should be devoted to the body of his speech, the portion that reveals and develops his thesis. The body, however, is but the middle, and if the speech is to be complete, it must also have a beginning and an end. Of course, a speaker could leave the introduction and conclusion to chance, assuming that they will take care of themselves when he gets up to speak. Though this may sometimes be true, the experienced speaker will testify that it is wise to plan an introduction that will lead the audience into the subject and a conclusion that will bring the speech to a purposeful close.

■   **SPEECH INTRODUCTIONS**

Introductions serve four primary purposes: (1) to attract attention to the speaker and arouse interest in his subject, (2) to establish a tie between the speaker and his audience, (3) to state and/or clarify the thesis of the speech, and (4) to serve as a transition to the body of the speech. An introduction may perform more than one of these functions at the same time, but unless it performs at least one, the speech begins lamely and seems to lack direction.

At the beginning of nearly every speech there is an unseen barrier between the speaker and his audience which causes discomfort to both. Some speakers feel it immediately and make a conscientious effort to break through to gain the goodwill of the audience. Others simply flounder, knowing only that "Something was wrong. I never could get through to them." What raises the barrier? And what can the speaker do about it?

In the first place, the speaker himself may raise the barrier. His manner, his mode of speaking, even his appearance may make his audience defensive. Without knowing it, he may appear pompous, patronizing, or insincere. But the audience may raise barriers too: some of the listeners may have no interest in the topic and be present only to be seen by their friends; others with a mild interest in the topic may know nothing about the speaker and his qualifications; others may suspect or distrust the speaker and be actually hostile. Whatever the nature of the barrier — indifference, ignorance, or hostility — the speaker must do his best to tear it down. This is the prime function of the introduction — to create interest in the speaker and his subject and to persuade the audience to give him a fair hearing.

☐   SOME COMMON FAULTS OF INTRODUCTIONS

The abrupt beginning. It is wise, of course, to avoid wasting time, but time used to prepare an audience for what is to follow is not necessarily time wasted. In a decision meeting of members of a labor union, a speaker might very wisely begin with an abrupt announcement: "I would like to present my case for voting for a strike." The members of the union have gathered for the distinct purpose of hearing this issue debated. If the same labor leader were to speak on a college campus, however, he would need to lengthen his opening remarks in order to whet the interest of and create a favorable impression with his audience. In either instance, he must pre-judge the attitudes and emotions of his listeners. He must then adjust his introductory remarks in order to make allowances for differences of opinion and intensity of feelings for or against an issue.

Student speakers must approach their audiences the same way. It is not enough simply to announce: "Today I'm going to tell you about the cave dwellings in Mesa Verde National Park." Students may not have significant differences of opinion about a national park, but they do have significant differences in their willingness to listen. The speaker should be creative enough, interested enough in his audience, and concerned enough about the success of his speech to develop a favorable climate for his major ideas.

The stilted beginning. Some speakers begin their talks ostentatiously, as though putting their vocabulary and literary skill on public display:

> In our constant endeavor to maintain the machinery of international peace and security so that we might take effective and collective measures for the prevention or removal of the threats of aggression against the nations of the free world . . .

After four lines, the speaker still has not come to the subject or the verb of the opening sentence. An introductory sentence like this is tedious, complex, and virtually useless. It strives for literary excellence and achieves only pedantic confusion. It immediately drives a verbal wedge between the speaker and his audience.

The gimmicky beginning. According to the dictionary, a gimmick is a device or piece of machinery for dishonestly controlling gambling apparatus. It is also a secret device to help the magician do sleight-of-hand tricks. A public-speaking gimmick is similar in that it is a spurious device to control audiences, but it is usually easily exposed. A student, speaking on the subject of traffic deaths, began his speech this way:

> Bang! Crash!
> [He pounded the lectern with both hands, screamed like a siren, and blew a whistle.]
> "All right, you people, stand back. Let the ambulance in!"
> These are some of the sounds you will hear at the scene of an automobile accident. If you've ever been present at such a scene,

you know that things aren't very attractive. Today I want to tell you about some of the gory aspects of automobile accidents.

One student speaker wanted to begin his speech with the ringing of an alarm clock. Another brought the head of a cow which he had borrowed from a local packing company. Some have played the role of actors in television commercials. Others have been known to fire toy six-shooters or blanks in real six-shooters!

No doubt such gimmicks will get attention, but for the gimmick rather than the speaker or his subject. Gimmicks tend to embarrass an audience and make it difficult for them to know how to respond. They do not know whether to smile or laugh or jump out of their seats in fright. Whatever the response to the gimmick, it is usually inappropriate to the subject.

The apologetic beginning. Beginning a speech with an apology generally causes a speaker to appear weak: "Well, I plan to bore you a little more today. I'm going to talk about our planet earth, a pretty dry subject, ha ha ha." The speaker assumes that his audience is not interested in his subject, and the reaction to his apology will automatically be disinterest. The apologetic speaker is like the man who knocks on your front door and says, "You don't want to buy no firewood, do you?" The audience is tempted to say, "No, we don't want to buy your ideas." The apologetic beginning also suggests to an audience that the speaker himself is not enthusiastic about his subject, or that he is insecure about his material or delivery. His insecurity communicates itself to his audience and estranges them. If the speaker does not convince his audience from the outset that he has something enlightening, vital, and interesting to tell them, they will respond with inattention and boredom.

Modesty and humility may bring the speaker and his listeners closer together; under certain conditions, a brief, to-the-point apology may even win respect for the speaker or interest in his subject (see the Roger Hilsman introduction on page 173). But it is generally better to avoid the apologetic beginning, unless that kind of effect will make a particular point.

The inappropriate beginning. In classroom speaking a student sometimes begins: "I heard a funny joke just before class today and thought you might want to add it to your list. Why does an elephant lie on its back? Why, so he can trip canaries. Now, this doesn't have anything to do with my speech, but I thought you would appreciate it anyway." Of course, if the joke is funny, if it is fresh and well told, the audience laughs. Later, when the speaker says that he is going to talk "not about elephants or canaries but about IBM computers," there is another moment of laughter. But the irrelevance of the joke distracts both audience and speaker; it adds another brick to the natural barrier between speaker and audience and makes it harder than ever for the speaker to introduce his subject.

Another kind of inappropriateness is the rote use of habitual expressions. A speaker will begin with "Good morning" even if it is raining, or afternoon. He calls the person presiding "Mr. Chairman" even if it is a woman. The story is told of a rather timid governor who spoke to the inmates of a men's penitentiary. He began conventionally with "Ladies and . . .," but there was laughter before he could get out the word "gentlemen." After he recovered, he began a second time with "Fellow inmates," and again there was a burst of laughter. A moment later he blundered on with "Glad to see so many of you here." Undoubtedly, more planning should have gone into the governor's opening remarks to make them appropriate to his audience.

Words may also be inappropriate because they are trite or smack of obvious flattery. Look at the following introductions:

1. It is with genuine pleasure that I am permitted to speak on this auspicious occasion.
2. It gives me great pleasure to speak to so many public-spirited citizens on such a profound subject as . . .
3. It is always a thrill to address so many beautiful ladies and handsome men.
4. I am filled with a deep sense of personal inadequacy when I presume to speak authoritatively in the presence of so many knowledgeable men.
5. It is good to speak to the youth of our country. In youth is the hope of our nation. In youth is our greatest and most indestructible natural resource.

The beginning speaker might think these examples acceptable or even very good. With time and maturity, however, his ear and taste will become more discriminating; he will learn to recognize triteness and flattery and to replace them with originality and sincerity.

The extended beginning. The student whose introduction lasts for three minutes of his five-minute speech has lost his sense of proportion. He is like the jumper who dashes fifty yards to make a three-foot broad jump. Short jumps require short runs; likewise, short speeches require short introductions. Even with a longer speech of twenty to fifty minutes, a speaker can never afford to take more time than is absolutely essential to create a favorable atmosphere, to disclose whatever background information is necessary, and to lead into the body of the speech.

Precisely how long should an introduction be? How many minutes? Unfortunately, these questions have no mathematical answers. The length of the introduction will depend on the subject, the occasion, and the nature of the audience. Generally speaking, a simple subject, a friendly audience, or a pleasant and convivial occasion encourages a short introduction. A complex or highly controversial subject, a hostile or apathetic audience, or a problem-solving occasion permits or even demands a longer, more elaborate introduction. As a rule of thumb, no introduction should take more than one-tenth of the total speaking time. This much can be said with certainty: the speaker should strive for brevity rather than length. A long and tedious introduction smothers interest and stifles communication.

□   **SOME USEFUL BEGINNINGS**

A speaker may introduce his subject in innumerable ways. The ones most useful to the student are these: (1) rhetorical questions, (2) striking statements, (3) narratives, (4) references to the occasion, and (5) direct statements.

RHETORICAL QUESTIONS

"How would you feel if you had nothing to sleep on but a dirt floor in a mud hut?" "How would you react if you were turned out of a restaurant simply because your skin was not the right color?" "Do you realize how many hours of each day, each month, and each year you must work in order to pay your income tax?" These are rhetorical questions — questions designed to force an audience to think about the subject at hand. The speaker does not expect his audience to answer the questions, although this does happen occasionally. He usually answers them himself as he wants them answered. Such questions are most effective when they carry striking or even shocking visual images or generate strong emotions in the minds of an audience. They are especially impressive if they are delivered in a barrage:

> How would you feel if you were hungry but could find no restaurant?
> — if you wanted to sleep but could find no motel?
> — if you wanted to refresh yourself, but could find no washroom?
> — if you wanted to be entertained but could find no theatre?
> — if you wanted respect, but could find none — anywhere?

The rhetorical question does require certain precautions. First, the student should not overwork this kind of introduction. Of all the methods of beginning a speech, the rhetorical question is by far the most popular with college students. Over half the classroom speeches early in the term are likely to begin with a question. The student should explore other methods. Too many questions are taxing, if not trite. Second, the student should reserve the rhetorical question for the crucial or impressive idea. Questions like "Have you ever flunked a final examination?" or "Have you ever been caught in a traffic jam?" are so pointless that they provoke neither active thought nor strong feeling. Third, the student speaker should realize that the rhetorical question usually reveals his attitude toward the subject. If he is addressing an audience hostile to his ideas, he would do well to abandon the question in favor of a more subtle or implicative beginning.

STRIKING STATEMENTS

There are several ways to make a statement striking. The speaker may begin with a statement contrary to popular belief, such as "Learning is a dangerous thing," "Money is the root of all bliss," or "Hate is what makes the world go 'round." He may also begin with facts or statistics that are startling; with a verbal style that is impressive; or with an attention-getting quotation. Any appropriate, positive state-

ment short of the gimmick that jolts an audience into attentiveness
may qualify as striking.

Notice how a student speaker bids for attention in the following
introduction:

> The movie industry today is like a spoiled brat. It is like a pam-
> pered child that screams for our undivided attention. Most of these
> ravings reach us in the form of sexy sensationalisms. "Cape Fear"
> is the study of a sex criminal. "Solomon and Sheba," supposedly
> based on a Bible story, is one long orgy. "The Dark at the Top of
> the Stairs" headlines frigidity, and "The Mark" features child moles-
> tation. The industry is sick and badly in need of redirection.

In the simile that begins the passage, a measure of impressiveness is
achieved by the obvious incongruity between the movie industry and
a child. Following the simile, the speaker presents a few undeveloped
examples, each of them a modest shock.

A second student introduction begins with a very simple statement:

> Parents can be the cruelest people alive. A three-year-old is
> brought to the hospital with cigarette burns all over the body. An
> undernourished eight-year-old is kept chained to his bed for months.
> An eleven-year-old is kept for years locked up in a brooder house.
> And an infant has his skull crushed by a loving father. Yes, I know,
> you have reason to groan, but these examples are just the beginning
> of a long list of events you have read in your newspapers. There are
> other events so gruesome they can't even be printed in our local
> newspapers. What makes a mother or a father so neurotic? What
> causes them to develop the battered-child syndrome?

The beginning statement contradicts popular opinion. Parents usually
are thought to abound in love and affection for their children. By
using a striking contradictory statement, the speaker shocks the audience into thinking about parents in totally different terms — his terms
— and therefore creates in them strong emotional curiosity to find out
how he will answer his rhetorical questions.

A third example combines several methods into a single striking
introduction:

> This slip of green paper is a one-dollar bill. Ninety-six cents of
> this bill will be spent for national defense. Benjamin Franklin once

said, "If a man empties his purse into his head no man can take it away from him." If a man invests in learning, he has made the greatest investment. When we put practice and theory together, however, we come to an impossible contradiction. How can we as individuals or we as a nation invest in learning when the purse must be emptied into a strong right arm?

This example begins with a visual aid, continues with a statistic, leads into a striking informal quotation, and concludes with a rhetorical question which implies the main subject: how the rising costs of education and the demands of national defense compete for the tax dollar.

The striking statement in all its forms is, then, a vivid method of attracting attention to the speaker or his subject. The speaker who attempts to create interest with a striking statement should take particular care to avoid gimmicks. In an effort to be interesting he may become cute, precious, or excessively clever, in which case the attention of the audience will be drawn to his gimmick instead of his subject.

NARRATIVES

The narrative may be true or fictional, formal or informal, developed or undeveloped. It is used to establish in the listeners' minds the structure of the speech and the attitudes of the speaker. By using an introductory narrative, the speaker avoids having to say, "I'm now going to talk about this, this, and this." The audience infers from his narrative his subject and his opinions.

Jokes or anecdotes are common introductory narratives. Likely to "fall on its face" unless it is appropriate to the occasion and the audience, the joke or anecdote must be relevant to the speaker's subject and purpose. The hypothetical story is another kind of introductory narrative used to attract attention; it often begins, "Let's suppose . . . ." Myths from all cultures and Biblical stories also may be used in an introduction to draw attention to the speaker's theme. But the most common narrative introductions are fables, short stories, and detailed true stories.

Here is how one student used a fable:

Once upon a time there was a mouse that crawled out of the tall grass beside a river. As he approached to drink, he ran into the hoof of a great ox; and feeling particularly playful that morning, he gave the hoof as big a pinch as he could manage. Of course, the great ox turned his head and stared at the mouse and said, "Don't you know that is dangerous? Look at my large feet, my enormous body, and my terrible horns." But the little mouse only giggled and said, "Oh, you aren't so terrible. I'm not afraid of you." "Now, be careful. Do that again and I'll crush you with my great body." And again the mouse giggled, gave the ox a pinch, and scampered off into the grass. The ox to this day is still trying to figure it out. How can one so small defy one so great? And to this day there are still members of our State Department who are pondering the same question. How can a little nation with no military strength pinch the toe of a military giant and get by with it?

Many beginning speakers are reluctant to use the fable because they mistakenly believe that it is beneath their level of maturity. In reality, fables are ready-made moral parallels and are used in every conceivable situation and on any subject, and by very mature speakers. Notice how Senator Ervin of North Carolina used a familiar fable during a debate on a civil rights bill:

Mr. President, I have heard that argument made by other advocates of this bill; and it reminds me of Aesop's fable about the wolf and the lamb. The wolf was seeking an excuse to devour the lamb. So the wolf said to the lamb, "You are muddying the water in the stream from which I was drinking."

The lamb replied, "I don't see how I could be muddying your drinking water. You are drinking upstream and I am drinking downstream."

The wolf's reply was to gobble up the lamb.

The moral of the fable, as given by Aesop, was that any excuse will serve a tyrant.

I know the Senator from Pennsylvania is not a tyrant; but some of those who are seeking the enactment of this bill are seeking tyrannical power.[1]

And minutes later, Senator Clark of Pennsylvania, after an opening sentence praising Senator Ervin's debating skill, says:

[1] *Congressional Record,* March 14, 1964, p. 5097.

. . . the analogy which occurs to me is not that of the Aesop's fable. . . . Instead, I think of the story of Little Red Riding Hood and the big bad wolf.

All that we seek by means of this measure is to protect Little Red Riding Hood, so we can unmask the big bad wolf, and can let Little Red Riding Hood see who is her enemy in her search for justice — which probably will end up in the Supreme Court of the United States.[2]

A third example of the narrative beginning is an actual rather than fictional event:

Perhaps you read in yesterday's newspaper about the English teacher in Wisconsin who found himself in trouble. His only crime was encouraging his students to read, but apparently the community mothers and fathers objected. They said, "No, we don't want our daughter exposed to the vulgar language of *The Catcher in the Rye.*" "Those children are too young for *The Ugly American.*" "They must be protected from the sin in *The Scarlet Letter.*" "And no one — simply no one — should read *Brave New World.*"

How will this argument come out? Who will win? I doubt if we ever have the chance to find out, but we do know that the battles will continue. In communities all over the country parents will try to dominate the high school. This morning I would like to investigate this problem — call it the problem of education by the amateurs.

Even though the details are sketchy, there are enough to capture attention. The audience is lured into the subject by reference to a small item which most of them had read in their own newspaper.

All the preceding narrative forms can introduce a speech effectively, but the one that best attracts and holds the interest of the audience is the detailed true story. It is not necessary to narrate a long, complex story to gain attention. On the contrary, students who start their speeches with such statements as "I want to tell you about my visit to the grave of President Kennedy," "Let me tell you about the night my plane nearly crashed," or "I was scared spitless when I was hitchhiking near Kansas City and was picked up by two men with machine guns," are more likely to attract the immediate interest and attention of the audience.

[2] *Ibid.,* p. 5098.

REFERENCE TO THE OCCASION

Speakers often begin with a courteous and complimentary reference to the occasion and to the people assembled. For example, any of the following beginnings would be appropriate:

1. *Referring to the purpose of the occasion.* A speaker at a convention, at a dedication ceremony, at a commencement, or at any similar special event will often begin by relating the purpose of the occasion to the purpose of his speech. Even on the floor of the Senate the speaker will say, "It is our purpose at this time to consider the foreign aid bill." At the opening of a federal highway we hear, "Mr. President, we come to cut a ribbon." On the college campus we hear, "We meet on this occasion to graduate the eighty-first class of this institution." The speaker then develops his opening statement about the occasion, relating it to the subject of his speech.

2. *Referring to previous speakers.* If a speaker is one of several to speak on a particular occasion, he may refer to the speakers who have preceded him or to those who will follow. This is frequently practiced in a formal debate, for example, when the speaker says:

> I believe the last speaker, the eminent Senator from California, has introduced a serious point and a very practical one.

> *or*

> I endorse much of what the first affirmative speaker has said. There is not only a real problem in regard to the recognition of Red China, we must find a solution for this problem. We of the negative just are not in agreement with the solution proposed by the affirmative.

> *or*

> Mr. President, I assure the delegate from Montana that he has introduced a very vital issue in this debate.

In debate, whether it be senatorial or intercollegiate, it is imperative to refer to the previous speaker and to his significant lines of argument to provide coherence and continuity of thought. More often than not, though, debaters are consciously generous to their opponents, despite their many differences of opinion. Debaters respect the points of view of their opponents and consider it rude to ridicule differences of opinion.

All speakers should follow the same practice. A complimentary story about another speaker on the program builds good will toward both speakers. The audience likes to hear that one speaker is good and warms up to the generosity of the other; it respects a speaker who respects his competition. We may appreciate the fiery disposition and uncompromising determination of a man who knows what he wants and pursues it vigorously, but we appreciate fair play and respect even more. Oddly enough, fair play and respect on the speaker's platform beget fair play and respect in the audience.

3. *Referring to self and to the audience.* A speaker may emphasize the nature of an occasion by referring to his special qualifications for addressing that particular audience, or to his lack of qualifications. Notice how Mr. Roger Hilsman, the Assistant Secretary for Far Eastern Affairs, used the second technique in his speech to a group of political scientists in Australia:

> I find myself today in a curious role — an outsider to the problem of "Australia's strategic position," talking to men and women who have lived and breathed the topic all their lives. I was thoroughly delighted to be asked to come here; I was honored by your invitation. But I was puzzled by the assignment.
>
> How, I wondered, could an American advise you on your own national interests and strategy without sounding presumptuous? Why had you chosen me to attempt such advice? And — a more sinister thought — what form of planned entrapment awaited me in this topic?
>
> I concluded, however, that I was suffering the traditional diplomat's malady — of reading excessive deviousness into the actions of others. And I was reminded of Talleyrand's response at the interminable Congress of Vienna when one of his aged fellow negotiators died of natural causes: "I wonder," he mused, "what his motive could have been."
>
> In this case I suspect you simply hoped for the fresh perspective that a foreigner can sometimes bring to an old and familiar topic. So let me talk in candor about your strategic position as it appears to one American who shares your concern with international affairs.[3]

Mr. Hilsman began on a purely personal note by confessing a feeling of modest inadequacy. He developed the feeling into suspicious in-

[3] *Department of State Bulletin,* February 17, 1964, pp. 243–244.

feriority by a series of rhetorical questions and dramatized it by suggesting that the invitation was a "planned entrapment." Then he humorously ridiculed his feelings by recalling the Talleyrand quotation and turned to the seriousness of this assignment. In his final sentence he revealed the subject of his speech. Hilsman counteracted the weaknesses inherent in an apology with his own flair, good taste, and apparent sincerity.

DIRECT STATEMENT OF SUBJECT

Earlier in this chapter we learned that one of the common faults of an introduction was the abrupt beginning. There are occasions, however, when the speaker is perfectly justified in plunging into his subject without first attempting to create interest. When time is limited, when the audience is already well-informed and primed for thought, or when the atmosphere is pleasant and free from distraction, the speaker may begin with a simple statement of his purpose. Perhaps no introduction could be more straightforward than the one used by Mr. Jerome Jacobson in addressing the Coffee Association in Florida:

> 1963 was quite a year for coffee. Let's review briefly what happened.[4]

Mr. Jacobson's audience obviously was already interested in and informed about his subject, so he had no need for a longer introduction.

The theory behind the brief introduction is that serious and busy men and women have little time to waste on social amenities. Before the theory can be put into practice, however, the speaker must analyze his audience. Only to the interested and informed is the direct statement appropriate. To a phlegmatic or apathetic audience, the direct statement lacks the wit or humor to pique their interest. To a hostile audience, the direct statement is little more than a red flag inviting attack.

We may summarize our discussion of the introduction by repeating that its purpose is to arouse interest and to draw attention both to the speaker and to his subject. If the student speaker understands the main points of the body of his speech, if he thinks through the

---

[4] *Department of State Bulletin,* February 24, 1964, p. 260.

purpose he hopes to accomplish while standing before his classmates for a few minutes, and if he understands his audience, he should be able to choose wisely the type of introduction best suited to his listeners, his speech, and himself.

■   **SPEECH CONCLUSIONS**

The body of a speech presents the speaker's main thesis — his main ideas and relevant supporting material. The conclusion of a speech also serves a specific purpose: to summarize or underscore the main ideas in the speech, to appeal for action, to elicit sympathy or understanding, or to add a note of finality and climax. The precise nature and purpose of a conclusion depend on the speaker's overall purpose. The conclusion of a speech to entertain, for example, necessarily differs from the conclusion of a speech to persuade; and both differ from the conclusion of a speech to inform. The entertainer uses the final moment for one more story, one last joke. The advocate makes a final attempt to persuade his listeners to change their minds or to initiate some positive action. The speaker whose purpose is to inform summarizes his content, emphasizes the point of greatest importance, and/or appeals for a judicious understanding of the information presented. Though conclusions differ according to the purpose of the speech, all are alike in at least one essential respect: they unify, round out, wrap up a speech. They offer climax and release.

☐   **SOME COMMON FAULTS OF CONCLUSIONS**

1. *The abrupt conclusion.* One of the most common offenses in the final moment of a speech is the simple announcement: "And I guess that's all I have to say," or, "I think I have covered all that needs to be said at this time." In a very informal speaking situation where the audience is small or the communication is more business-like than a public speech, such a conclusion is appropriate. In the more formal situation, however, the conclusion must not be so short or curt that it catches the audience by surprise and offends its sense of artistic completeness.
2. *The extended conclusion.* A conclusion may be too long, as well as too short. The listener despises needless length. Once he has

been promised "a few concluding remarks," he expects them to come and go with all reasonable dispatch. What makes a conclusion too long? First, the speaker may become intoxicated with his success. He may realize that his listeners have enjoyed the speech: they have been entertained by his stories, charmed by his humor, and motivated by his persuasive reasoning. Such success is enough to flatter any speaker; to prolong the moment, he continues with "just one more" story, a detailed personal experience, or an elaborate emotional appeal for understanding and action. Second, the speaker may decide to introduce new ideas and arguments. By the time he reaches the conclusion of a complex and difficult speech, he may sense that he has not been clear, that he has not adequately developed two or three points. So he says:

> I would like to go back to my second point and develop it a little further, if I may. We still have a few minutes before our time is up, and I think I might be able in the remaining time to clarify one or two complexities.

As the speaker continues to clarify, he may repeat material already covered adequately, or he may introduce entirely new ideas, with the result that the conclusion becomes a second speech rather than an ending to the first. Third, the speaker may not have a speech plan. He may be speaking from hunch and intuition — allowing the inspiration of the moment to guide his voice and intellect. The sensitive and experienced speaker might be able to do this effectively, but the beginner will find it risky indeed. All speakers need an organization of some kind, in the mind or on paper, formal or informal, expressed or implied. And once the organization is planned, it should be adhered to unless some most unusual event takes place before or during the speech.

3. *The conclusion without purpose.* The greatest weakness that can appear in a conclusion is the absence of purpose. The purpose of a speech to entertain is made obvious by the tone, content, and style of delivery. But if a serious speech wavers between the informative and the persuasive, confusion of purpose is not only possible but likely. The conclusion is a speaker's last opportunity to produce the response he desires. If he fails at this moment to make his purpose clear, he may easily fail as a speaker.

There are times when a conclusion *sounds* good but does not survive careful scrutiny. A student speaker, for example, after a very good speech on the subject of civil rights, concluded with this remark:

> As we study the events of the last few years, we can have no doubt that a great deal of progress has been made. Should we have more and bigger peaceful demonstrations or should we leave it to Congress and the courts? Should we uphold our private rights or the rights of the public? These are serious questions and each person here must answer for himself.

In this conclusion the speaker dodged his responsibility. He clearly implied in his speech that he was pro civil rights. He further implied that all his listeners should agree with him. When he reached his conclusion, however, he confused his purpose and substituted questions for a declaration, seriously weakening his position. His speech had purpose, but his conclusion did not.

This weakness is demonstrated by such remarks as:

> I don't think we ought to take it upon ourselves to decide on the rightness or wrongness of this issue. We must leave it for history to judge.

or

> I have no right to tell you how to vote or what to believe.

or

> There is no right or wrong. It is relative, not black and white.

or

> There is right on both sides. We must study the evidence and weigh these matters very carefully before we can arrive at a decision.

Of course, these remarks would be appropriate to a discussion leader, for example, or a teacher who wants his students to think and decide for themselves. But when they are used in the final moments of a speech to persuade, they suggest that the speaker has not done his homework and really does not know where he stands. An audience likes to consider a speaker a leader; but if the leader cannot make up his mind which road to travel, no one is likely to follow.

☐   **SOME USEFUL CONCLUSIONS**

Just as there are many ways to begin a speech, there are many ways to end one. The speaker may end with a particularly apt quotation, a story, an example, or even with statistics. Any method is acceptable as long as it accomplishes the speaker's purpose and gives the audience the feeling that the speech has unity and completeness. At least one of three elements should appear within the conclusion of a speech: (1) an emphasis on the major idea or thesis, (2) a summary of the main points, and (3) an appeal for desired action.

EMPHASIS ON MAJOR IDEA OR THESIS

In the brief speech or in the longer speech with a single prevailing idea, the most useful conclusion will stress only the major idea. A student speaking on our need for the United Nations emphasized his controlling idea with a story and a familiar quotation:

> . . . it is no longer possible for a great nation to remain great without the help of others.
> The story is told of a little girl who wandered away from her home and into the weeds and brush. When she didn't return for her lunch, her parents became worried and ran about the neighborhood calling her name and asking everyone if they had seen her, but she couldn't be found. Soon the neighbors joined the search, then the police, then the firemen. Everyone ran wherever he chose until, finally, someone suggested a plan: "Let's form a line and walk over the fields toward the mountains." A long line, with every available person, was quickly formed; and together they walked through the grass. The little girl was found — exhausted and sound asleep — and taken home. The thought of "all joining hands" is usually reserved for a good old revival meeting or a country square dance, but it's time we think in terms of nations. "In union there is strength."

Senator Allott of Colorado, in a brief speech during the 1964 civil rights debate, ended with a list of parallel statements which reviewed the one major idea of his speech:

> . . . there is one facet of the question which I agree no legislation can ever touch. That facet pertains to what is actually in a man's heart or in his mind. We may be able to cure some of the educa-

tional disadvantages. We may be able to equalize rights before courts. We may be able to equalize the right to vote. We may be able to cure other inequities, if there are others. We may even be able to increase opportunities. But there is one thing we cannot do, and we might as well recognize it. We cannot change the hearts and minds of men. But certainly if by law we establish a precept, we may have reasonable hope that the hearts and minds of men will follow along.[5]

After the list of parallel statements there is one that is not parallel; by virtue of the contrast and its terminal position, the final statement is the one with greatest emphasis.

Hubert Humphrey, when he was a member of the Senate, spent an estimated forty-five minutes of Senate time describing and denouncing an anti-civil rights advertisement called "$100 Billion Blackjack"; then, in his brief conclusion, he condensed all his condemnations:

It seems to me that such advertising should be frowned on, should not be respected, and should be repudiated. It is my intention to challenge such outrageous distortions whenever I have an opportunity to do so.

Honest arguments based on differences of opinion can be made against the bill; but dishonest arguments have no place in this country.

I know that the advertisement does not represent thoughtful consideration by any Senator; no Senator would be a party to it. The advertisement is nothing less than muckraking at its worst. It is the cheapest kind of advertising. It convinces no one; but it insults many, and is a reflection on the intelligence of the American people.[6]

A conclusion of this kind is good not because of its literary charm, but because of its straightforwardness. It is clear, definite, and unadorned by figurative language. It goes right to the heart of the matter.

SUMMARY OF MAIN POINTS

Even though a speaker has a single controlling motive for presenting his speech, he will frequently summarize each of the major

[5] *Congressional Record,* March 19, 1964, p. 5517.
[6] *Congressional Record,* March 17, 1964, p. 5247.

subdivisions. Look at Abraham Lincoln's conclusion to his Second Inaugural Address, delivered on March 4, 1865:

> With malice toward none; with charity to all; with firmness in the right, as God gives us to see the right, let us strive on to finish the work we are in; to bind up the nation's wounds; to care for him who shall have borne the battle, and for his widow and his orphan — to do all which may achieve and cherish a just and lasting peace among ourselves and with all nations.

Mr. Lincoln combined a summary of his main points with an appeal to his listeners for compassion, belief, and future action.

Now examine a summary delivered by Senator Jordan of North Carolina:

> Mr. President, I have not made any attempt today to go into the specific merits of the bill which we are being asked to consider.
>
> I have merely tried to give some indication of two things:
>
> First. The atmosphere which has been prevailing in the state of North Carolina for some time; and
>
> Second. The reaction that has been expressed in just a few of the newspaper articles and editorials which have been published in my state.
>
> I hope the Senators will carefully consider my remarks and the thoughts and observations contained in these articles and editorials. If they will, especially against the background and history of my State and the progress we have made, we will have gone a long way toward reaching a better understanding of what we are being asked to do.[7]

In this speech, Senator Jordan was not primarily concerned with argumentation and persuasion; his chief purpose was description. He wanted to inform his fellow senators about the social turmoil in his home state. If its purpose is to inform or to persuade, the summary conclusion is especially useful; it ties together all the significant elements and etches them in the listener's memory.

In informative speaking the speaker imprints factual detail; in persuasive speaking, he imprints logical relationships. Notice, for example, the persuasive conclusion of a student debater:

[7] *Ibid.*, p. 5288.

Now what have we said?

First, there are thousands of talented high school graduates who are refused a college education because they haven't the money. Second, even if they had the money, they are frequently refused the school and training of their choice because of the crowded conditions in our institutions of higher education. Third, even if these many schools were able to accept all qualified students, they would not have the facilities — the teachers, the dormitories, the instructional equipment — to provide the calibre of education that will make the most of the students' potential.

In this example the repeated use of "even if" shows the logical relationship between the main points. It ties them together into a single coherent unit and conveys the impression of logical finality.

APPEAL FOR DESIRED ACTION

In informative speaking the speaker may appeal for an understanding of the subject being described. He may also ask his audience to focus its attention on an important but often ignored aspect of the subject. In persuasive speaking, he may appeal for a particular action. Notice how David Ross Locke does this in the following passage. Mr. Locke, a satirist known as "Petroleum V. Nasby," was concluding a speech entitled "In Search of the Man of Sin."

I at last found the man of sin. I was the man. I am now busily engaged in reforming, — not the world, but myself, and I hope I am succeeding. I succeeded in checking myself in time to save lies only yesterday; I am now correcting all errors in accounts that are in my favor; in short, by dint of hard work and careful watching, I have got to a point of excellence where it is perfectly safe to say that I am no longer distinctively "the man of sin." My hearers, all of you who try hard enough and watch closely enough may in the course of a great many years, if you are gifted and have patience, get to be as good as I am. I know you will shrink from a task so apparently hopeless, but I assure you the reward is great enough to justify the trial.

Mayor Willy Brandt of West Berlin, in the conclusion to his speech "All Sitting in the Same Boat," emphasized his controlling idea, summarized his principal points, and appealed for continued action in an analogy rather than in direct statement:

Regardless of which side of the Atlantic we live on, we are all sitting in the same boat. We should constantly check our course and our stroke. We must adjust to every weather and every rise of the waves. If the wind is against us, we shall have to tack, but we must also know that everyone is lost who leaves the boat. Alone no one can reach the shore for which we are headed.[8]

Before leaving the matter of the conclusion, we should consider two additional points. First, *the conclusion should unify the entire speech* by returning to the interest material of the introduction, relating it to the main points of the body, and drawing from these ideas the major conclusions and appeals for belief or action. The minister might say, "As the Good Samaritan helped the traveler with problems [the introduction story], so must we help the teen-age youth [first point] and extend our hand to the adult with antisocial leanings [second point]. You can do this by practicing your religion at the YMCA or YWCA, in your own neighborhood, at your children's school, and at the polling booth [appeal for action]. You can act as though saving a man is saving mankind [appeal for belief]."

Second, *the conclusion must grow logically out of the body of the speech and not be tacked on for a special, unrelated effect.* It must be appropriate, germane, and honest. In a final frenzy of determination, the wordmongers often hurl *freedom, democracy, liberty, dignity, brotherhood, humanity, equality, peace,* and *Christianity* into the air and hope the wholesale use of such words will make them speakers of great public conscience. *Freedom, democracy,* and *liberty* are good words and rouse in audiences appropriate emotions, but they are words to be respected and not to be flung from the speaker's platform like so many puffs of dust to blind an audience to the issues at hand. The same stimulating effect can be achieved by letting the conclusion grow honestly, naturally out of the speech itself.

When Oliver Wendell Holmes spoke at a Harvard Medical School commencement, he first talked with the graduating class as students and then as colleagues about the ethics of the physician. He concluded tersely but appropriately as he welcomed the young men as equals into his profession:

[8] Willy Brandt, "All Sitting in the Same Boat," *Vital Speeches,* Vol. XXVII, No. 12 (April 1, 1961), p. 384.

It is time to bring these hurried and crowded remarks to a close. Reject what in them is false, examine what is doubtful, remember what is true; and so, God bless you, Gentlemen, and Farewell!

He assumed that they did not have to be reminded of the Hippocratic oath or their duty to mankind. He also assumed that they were bright enough to evaluate his speech accurately.

■   **SPEECH TRANSITIONS**

A transition is a *going across* from one idea or unit to another. In a speech, transitions are paragraphs, sentences, phrases, or words that bridge and connect the divisions or subdivisions of thought. Transitions enable the speaker to hold the various parts of a speech together, to make them *cohere*. A speech is coherent only when the transitions are effective, when the listener can easily connect one point to another. When transitions are missing, the listeners are likely to say, as they said of Peter Quince, "His speech was like a tangled chain; nothing impaired, but all disordered."

But where precisely do transitions occur and how do they appear? To focus attention on the transition alone, look at the following diagram:

> INTRODUCTION

The statistics and examples I have just presented indicate that the problem is large enough to warrant deep concern. Charlie Brown has proposed one solution. He thinks we should . . .   **Transition**

> BROWN PROPOSAL

At first glance this appears to be a very good proposal, but in my judgment it has two weaknesses. First, . . .   **Transition**

FIRST WEAKNESS

If my analysis is correct, Mr. Brown's proposal will not raise enough money to do the work which needs to be done.
    The second weakness in his proposal is . . .

Transition

SECOND WEAKNESS

Apparently Mr. Brown's proposal will lead to *fewer* parks and *less* recreational opportunity for our community. But statements of this kind obviously need some further explanation. Let me show you what I mean.

Transition

EXAMPLE

    The same point was made by our mayor when he spoke to the City Council last week:

Transition

QUOTATION

    Though Mr. Brown's proposal appears good, it has two very significant weaknesses. First, it does not provide enough money to do what must be done. Second, it means that our park system will eventually regress instead of progress.

Transition

CONCLUSION

Such an outline should help clarify the function of transitions and point out where they are most needed. Specifically, transitions should be found

1. Between the introduction and the statement of the thesis or subject of the speech.
2. Between the statement of the thesis and the body of the speech.
3. Between major divisions of the body to show logical relationships.
4. Between items of evidence to point up the logical development.
5. Between the body and the conclusion to summarize the major points of the body.
6. At any point where momentary digression takes the speaker away from his principal line of thought.

Following are some transitions ordinarily used by college students to connect one idea with another:

1. This illustrates why I want to talk with you today about . . .
2. In addition to the burden of taxes, the business man must also . . .
3. So much for wind instruments. Another section of the orchestra is . . .
4. Consider next the . . .
5. I might stop here with the problem of poverty; but I also want you to know about . . .
6. But there is more.
7. And there is one more cause.
8. But what is the solution for this problem?
9. Let me summarize my three major causes before talking about the effects.
10. In conclusion I'd like to urge each of you to . . .

There are many more transitions — thousands of them. The appropriate kind to use between a pair of ideas will arise naturally from what the speaker wants to do with the ideas — whether he wishes to *stress* the second (or the first), *relate* the two, *contrast* them, *introduce* a fresh idea in a series, or *summarize* everything that has gone before.

The student should give careful attention to the transitions of his speech. They hold all the speech units together. They provide coherence by connecting what is past to what is yet to come. They link

logically arranged materials so that the speaker will not sound like
"a tangled chain."

SUMMARY

1. A good introduction will create interest in the speaker and in the
   subject of the speech.
2. An introduction is considered faulty if it is (1) abrupt, (2) gimmicky, (3) apologetic, (4) inappropriate, or (5) too long.
3. The methods most often used in the introduction to create interest
   are: (1) rhetorical questions, (2) striking statements, (3) narratives, (4) references to the occasion, and (5) direct statements.
4. A conclusion should emphasize, summarize, and/or appeal for a
   particular response. It should give a sense of wholeness or finality
   to the entire speech.
5. A conclusion is considered faulty if it is abrupt, too long, or purposeless.
6. Transitions help to provide coherence. They summarize, introduce, bridge over, and, in general, give the speech logical unity.

EXERCISES

1. From a recent issue of *Vital Speeches* choose two introductions,
   one of which you especially like. Be prepared in class discussion
   to defend your points of view.

2. Repeat the same exercise, but use two speech conclusions.

3. Divide the class into three groups. The speakers in Group I
   should prepare and deliver a speech introduction appropriate
   for a "believing" audience. Group II should prepare for a hostile
   audience and Group III for an apathetic audience. After the
   introductions have been delivered, decide whether the speaker
   met the challenge presented by the audience attitude. Did he
   create a favorable atmosphere? Could you tell what ideas he
   would have developed had he continued?

4. Deliver a speech introduction beginning with a joke. Make sure to follow through to the end of the transition following the joke and preceding the body.

5. Repeat the same assignment, but use a fable.

6. Repeat the same assignment using any method except the rhetorical question, the joke, or the fable. (Inasmuch as each "speech" of this kind takes less than a minute, two series of assignments can be completed in a single class period if class comments are withheld until the end of the hour.)

7. Prepare and deliver a conclusion in which you use a story or a quotation. This assignment should begin with the transition preceding the conclusion and continue to the very end of the speech. When the class discusses these conclusions, answer such questions as: Was the transition clearly presented? Did the speaker emphasize, summarize, or make an appeal?

8. Read the student speech below; then answer the questions that follow:

POLICY TOWARD UNDERDEVELOPED NATIONS

Plato once said: "Democracy is a fool's government." To a considerable extent we have proved this wrong; but you have to admit he had a point. Any American who is alive and breathing, who has enough concrete between his ears and enough "go" in his legs, can hold a public office. This happens to governments, and it applies to modern times as well as Plato's Athens.

Our government is not without its incompetency. Consider our foreign policy which is supposed to aid underdeveloped countries. It's very bad. To illustrate this I would like to use an example which I think you are all familiar with — the Laotian crisis of 1959. We put on the average of thirty-five million dollars a year, for five years, into Laos to build and support a twenty-five thousand man army and to raise the economy of the nation in order to help these people. And where did this money go? It was handed over in cash to the Laotian government for proper distribution. But instead of to the people or to the army, the greater part of it went into the Laotian officials' pockets for their power, their Cadillacs, their good times. And then came the war, the great crisis. We saw it in the papers, and all of us were getting ready for the Third World War. Trouble with this was, there was no war in Laos. There were a few small Laotian tribes arguing over a piece of pasture land. And the Laotian officials built this up as a Communist invasion to get more money out of the United States. Why didn't we know about this? Because during this whole three-month period there was not one official American observer in Laos. All the information we got and all we read in our newspapers came from these same corrupt Laotian officials. To top this off, not one single American newspaper, with the exception of the *New York Times*, printed any exposé of this mismanagement.

Unfortunately this is no isolated situation. Viet Nam, Formosa, Thailand, Korea, Cuba, and a host of others — a similar story could be told about each of these. And still we wonder why our foreign aid does no good.

But what is this leading to? We have seen it — a slow but steady rise of anti-Americanism in many countries. And why not? After all, consider the little man in Laos. He sees the prosperous American and he watches on the sidelines while his own officials deceive the American government. We just don't look like leaders. We are too easily deceived. So our inefficiency breeds distrust. The little man distrusts us and his government grows to distrust us even more. And eventually they will come to the point of refusing to accept American leadership altogether.

And the tax dollar is wasted. It's one thing for an American to see his money put to good use; but when it comes to light that his tax dollar is being chucked down a rat hole, that's something else again. I read in *Time* magazine last night that we had given Cambodia two hundred million dollars in the last seven years. During that same time, Russia built a five-hundred-bed hospital and an industrial plant. When I read this, I couldn't help wondering where our dollars finally went. I'm sure they did some good, but was it a good that could be seen by the people? Could they see our money as clearly as they could see a hospital? Or was the money simply wasted?

Of course, the biggest, and I suppose the saddest, effect of our foreign policy is that the people who really need our help don't get it. As a result, the underdeveloped nations continue to be underdeveloped; consequently they continue to hold out the old open palm for more and more handouts. We have a policy that has

created a vicious cycle of giving. Once we give, we have to give
again to make up for what we didn't give in the first place. It will
never stop.
Let me review my stand. I have said that our foreign policy toward underdeveloped nations is bad, and I have indicated three
effects of this policy. It causes us to lose our role as a leader, it
wastes our tax dollar, and it leaves the underdeveloped nation in
the same state of poverty. Now don't get me wrong on this point.
I'm a good democrat and I know we have to help out. But I do
believe that we need to reexamine our generosity and make sure that
it is doing the work we want it to do.

QUESTIONS

a. Evaluate the student's introduction. Was it appropriate for the
   subject, for the speaker, and for the speaking situation? Did the
   opening remarks create interest? Did they adequately prepare
   for the discussion that followed?
b. Evaluate the conclusion. How is it best described? What is the
   purpose of the final sentence? Does it weaken or strengthen the
   implied purpose of the speech?
c. Does the speaker use enough transitions? Do they hold the ideas
   together, summarize and introduce them? Indicate the major
   transitions and discuss their function.
d. What reactions do you have to:
   — the general organization of the speech?
   — the supporting evidence for the major ideas?
   — the scope of the topic for a public speaking class?

PART THREE

Presenting the Speech

USING LANGUAGE EFFECTIVELY

USING THE BODY EFFECTIVELY

USING THE VOICE EFFECTIVELY

ARTICULATION AND PRONUNCIATION

CHAPTER 8

USING LANGUAGE
EFFECTIVELY

An interesting, properly narrowed subject, adequate supporting material, and logical order guarantee neither a good speech nor an effective speaker. The range of a speaker's vocabulary, his choice of words, and his general fluency with language are just as vital to successful communication. The effective speaker does not simply hope to stumble onto the appropriate word, nor does he purposely show off an extensive vocabulary. He deliberately chooses the words that will convey his meaning accurately and forcefully. He must know how to use words when he thinks, reads, and listens, as well as when he speaks. Ideally, he must be a phrase-maker and sentence-builder so that he will be able to use language precisely to achieve a particular response.

■   THE LIMITATIONS OF WORDS

What is a word? A word is a *symbol*, the vocal or written representation of a thing. The word *book*, for example, stands for bound leaves of printed paper; the word *room* represents an enclosed space within a building; the word *justice* means fair play as prescribed by law and interpreted by our courts. An infant soon learns that *wawa* is a symbol for water; that *bye bye* is associated with leaving home; that *Mama spank* is a promise of pain.

These examples should not lead us to believe that symbols are always so easy to understand. Sometimes they are extremely difficult. They are slippery; their meanings change from time to time and place to place. Some distortion is inevitable even when we speak briefly and simply. Why is this so?

1. *Our words are not understood as we want them understood.* A word has little or no meaning in isolation; it has meaning only in terms of the experience of those who use it. It stands to reason, then, that as experiences differ, so the meanings given to words will differ too. To the poet a bird may be a symbol of inspiration; but to the City Council it may be a nuisance to be driven from the court house. To a young man from a farm a cow may be a friendly and lovable animal; but to the young man from the city a cow may be a frightening beast. To the hunter a dog may be a welcome companion; but to others it is little more than another mouth to feed. Just as we have various reactions to *things,* we have varying interpretations of the words which symbolize them.

When President Johnson announced his "War on Poverty," millions of Americans thought of more jobs, increased slum clearance, and a higher standard of living; but to the Iron Curtain countries it meant something altogether different. There, according to Senator Morse, it meant the failure of the free enterprise system and the mobilization of the youth of America to protect the nation from the anger of the starving masses. The sensitive reader will argue that this example is not simply a matter of words — that tradition, international politics, and emotion enter in, too. And that is precisely the point. The speaker and his audience are sometimes at variance because they have not had the same experiences. They have different educational, cultural, and vocational backgrounds, different emotional outlooks, and different prejudices. In view of such differences, it is not surprising that they interpret words differently as well.

2. *We do not say what we intend to say.* How many times have we qualified one of our own statements with, "No, that is not what I

meant. That is not it at all. Let me try to reword it," or "I'm afraid I'm giving you the wrong impression," or "Oh, if I only had words enough to tell you what I mean." The frequency with which a student uses the words "I mean" is an indication of his insecurity in using words clearly and precisely. Notice how often the phrase appears in the following:

> But does anybody really know what Communism is? I mean, what do we know about it? I mean, when I went to my Civics teacher in high school, she'd say, "Look it up! Look it up!" And I'd look it up in some magazine and find out that the Communists were going to bury us and that they didn't believe in love or marriage or maybe they had atomic bombs hidden in all the church basements. I mean, if we're supposed to know how to combat this thing, we really have to know what it is.

It may be argued that the student didn't need the "I mean," that he was using it more as a "starter," a way to get into another sentence. It can just as easily be argued, however, that somewhere in his education the student realized that he was not always clear and that he frequently had to restate and restate again before the listener could understand him.

Everyone, even the highly skilled, uses words inadequately and incorrectly at times. We read in the headlines, "Suspect Grilled in Cigarette Case." We read the classified ads, "For sale '64 Ford, low mileage, formerly owned by minister, clean inside and out." We read in the King James version of the Bible, "And he spake to his sons, saying, Saddle me the ass; and they saddled him." News reporters find it necessary to ask the State Department what it means by "self-determination," and one Senator must ask another what he means by "fractionalization." And Mrs. Malaprop, of course, will always be misunderstood with her "oracular tongue, and a nice derangement of epitaphs."

As we speak, then, some confusion is inevitable because our listeners do not understand our words as we want them understood and because we simply do not say what we intend to say. We may put the blame on *words* if we like, but a more satisfactory answer will be found in *us* and the way we use words. We are careless; we lose respect for clarity; we omit words; we choose the wrong ones; we jumble them; we are vague and ambiguous. In short, we fail to communicate. This picture has been made intentionally distressing so that we may all become more self-conscious in our use of language. Naturally, we should not be so self-conscious that we are satisfied with nothing but the "only" word. Nor should we agree with those who insist that words are so unreliable that we should either cast them out or retreat into silence. Words are our primary means of communication; we *must* use them to make ourselves understood. But we must make them serve us, not let them dominate us.

■   **GETTING HOLD OF WORDS**

The size of the vocabulary a speaker actually uses in a speech is governed by his subject and the occasion. Dr. Seuss, for example, can successfully entertain an audience of six-year-olds with a twenty-five-word vocabulary in *The Cat in the Hat.* When he writes for an older child or one with more verbal sophistication, he increases the size of the vocabulary in order to increase the complexity of his story. Public speakers operate on the same principle. On simple, familiar subjects, a student can speak quite successfully with a basic vocabulary of 500-800 words. On certain scientific or technical subjects, however, he will be handicapped — just as he will be handicapped in expressing subtle shades of feeling or meaning in relatively simple subjects. A student with an 8,000-word vocabulary — the estimated vocabulary of the average high school freshman — should have more success; and an adult with a vocabulary ranging upward to 80,000 words should have still more. In general, the more words one has at his disposal, the more likely he is to have the right word at the right time.

Each of us has several vocabularies. For everyday, impromptu conversations we have a relatively small vocabulary made up primarily of simple nouns and verbs tied together with a few helping words. For reading, studying, thinking we have a vocabulary of several thousand words. Many of the words that make perfectly good sense to us on a page we reject at the moment of speech. They may not be commonly known; they may not "sound" right; they may not roll easily off our tongue; they may not have the proper ring and rhythm. Between the conversational vocabulary and the reading vocabulary, there are others adjusted to different occasions. When the student delivers a classroom speech, he uses a larger vocabulary than when he converses casually. His vocabulary is larger still when he competes in intercollegiate debate, when he addresses the student body, a luncheon club, or a church group. The speaker must adapt his words to various shades of thought and feeling and to the nature of the speaking occasion, and his vocabulary must be large enough to make that flexibility possible.

There are three valuable ways of increasing the size of your vocabulary.

1. *Learn words by their use in context.* Many of the words which we presently use we learned with no help from a dictionary. Few people bother to check the meaning of *mother, brother, five, cold, sweet, run,* and *hurt.* We have lived with these words for years. We have spoken, read, and thought them almost daily. But think of another word — *innocuous,* for example. We hear someone say, "Oh, his proposal is *innocuous* enough — it will do no harm to try it." From the meaning of the simpler words which surround *innocuous,* we can assume that it means "harmless." When our assumption is confirmed by further use of the word in what we read and hear, we become confident that we know the meaning of the word and can use it sensibly when we talk.

Learning through context, however, is not always reliable. Suppose someone says, "I would appreciate a *candid* answer." There is nothing in the remark that gives a clue to the meaning of *candid.* Those who do not know the word may associate it with the television program *Candid Camera,* perhaps, and assume that it means "secret" or "hidden." Others may reason that because *candid* sounds like "candied," meaning "sweet," it must mean "polite" or "courteous." Many will use the word incorrectly for years until they accidentally bump into another word source that says candid means "frank." Obviously, we must always be aware of the shortcomings of the contextual method of building vocabulary and school ourselves to check meanings learned this way in a reputable dictionary.

2. *Use the dictionary regularly.* Most of us need to be deliberate and methodical in our vocabulary building. Naturally, we don't want to memorize a page a day from the dictionary, nor do we want to skim

its pages looking for the long and impressive words. These are the methods of pedants, not of those who would learn to speak well. A more sensible approach is to use the dictionary as a reference. When we see or hear a word that is unknown to us or known but used in an unfamiliar context, we should check its meaning. *Pedestrian,* for example, is a familiar noun defined as a person travelling on foot. But obviously that definition does not apply in the sentence, "That speaker has a *pedestrian* intellect!" We refer to the dictionary and find that as an adjective the word means "unimaginative." Thus, a *pedestrian* intellect is not an intellect on foot, but one that will make us bored and inattentive.

The dictionary is much more than a collection of definitions of unfamiliar words. It gives acceptable pronunciations. It explains the variety of meanings a word may have, especially its special meanings. It indicates the age and "respectability" of the word. It lists synonyms or equivalents. It gives the etymology or derivations of words. In fact, the dictionary gives us so much information about our language that no good student and no good speaker can afford to ignore it.

3. *Use recently learned words.* If a word is to have any value to the public speaker, he must make it his own. The egotistical Humpty Dumpty might ask: "Who is to be master — me or the word?" He made himself master by claiming that words meant precisely what he wanted them to mean. For the rest of us who want to play the game fairly, words cannot change by simple decree. Their meanings are relatively fixed. We encounter them in context and examine them in the dictionary; then we use them confidently and frequently. Only in this way can we become the master.

Here are a few to serve as a starter:

1. Is a *bucolic* man one who coughs excessively?
2. Is a *paramour* a female paragon?
3. Does an *allegory* rest on the banks of the Nile?
4. To what extent are *docile* students *ductile*?
5. Would a *dearth* of mirth make a happy home?

These are not unusual words. They are everyday words, words of the *egalitarians.* To become their master, we must find out what they mean and use them in our speaking and writing.

■ THE MEANING OF STYLE

Having a large vocabulary is not enough; choosing the correct word is equally important. Words have qualities that make them suited to certain occasions but unsuited to others. Some are pompous and some are frilly. Some are precise and others are general. Some are colorful and others are dull. Furthermore, words lend those qualities to the sentences in which they appear; the sentences, in turn, color the paragraphs or speech units into which they are combined. These qualities determine the *style* of a speaker and distinguish his language from the language of others. Oral style, then, is *the quality of language* manifested in the speaker's choice of words and the arrangement of words into sentences.

We talk about style on two levels, personal and imposed. First, all people have individual "styles" of speaking that are inherently theirs; they cannot be changed. The student who asks, "How can I learn to speak like David Brinkley?" must realize that he cannot. Brinkley's style is his own and nobody else's. However, the student can analyze the style of Brinkley and other speakers for attractive and unattractive qualities which he would like to adopt or reject. Although he cannot *change* his own style to simulate someone else's, he can take steps to *improve* it (see page 203).

The speaker imposes the other level of "style" on his personal style to suit the occasion or his subject. Though his individual style cannot basically change, he can impose on it an "academic" quality when he is talking to a group of professors about philosophy, or a "poetic" quality when he is talking about Dylan Thomas to a group of English majors. To the extent that he imposes qualities on his basic style, his style will *differ,* but it will not *change.*

■ STYLISTIC DIFFERENCES

The language we speak may be placed on a continuum of style. At one end is *formality,* at the other *informality.* Both styles are acceptable; both are commonly used; neither is necessarily better than the other. Just as there are social situations which call for formal attire, so there are situations which call for formal language, and *vice versa.*

The important point is to know when to wear a dinner jacket and when to wear blue jeans — when to speak formally and when to speak informally. It is necessary to be equally comfortable at both ends of the continuum and at the points in between in order to speak easily and appropriately.

☐   **FORMAL STYLE**

Formal style is reserved for formal occasions. The President of the United States speaks formally at his inauguration or in his State of the Union Address. The Secretary of State speaks formally when addressing a conference of foreign ministers. A speaker who wants to treat his subject seriously in a tightly reasoned discourse often uses a formal style.

Perhaps formality can be described best by example:

> The theory of books is noble. The scholar of the first age received unto him the world around; brooded thereon; gave it the new arrangement of his own mind, and uttered it again. It came into him life; it went out from him truth. It came to him short-lived actions; it went out from him mortal thoughts. It came to him business; it went from him poetry. It was dead fact; now it is quick thought. It can stand; and it can go. It now endures, it now flies, it now inspires. Precisely in proportion to the depth of mind from which it issued, so high does it soar, so long does it sing.[1]

This passage was taken from Emerson's "The American Scholar," an address delivered in 1837 to the Phi Beta Kappa Society at Harvard. The characteristics that make the style formal are these:

1. *The serious tone.* There is no joke-telling and no flippancy; the speaker treats his subject and his audience with dignity.

2. *The impersonal tone.* Emerson speaks of the impersonal and removed *him*, "the scholar of the first age." He does not use the *I, you, we, our, us* we hear so often in everyday conversation.

3. *The unusual stylistic devices.* Though the sentences are not long and complicated, a trait often present in formal style, there is

---

[1] Ralph Waldo Emerson, *Nature, Addresses, and Lectures.* Boston: Houghton Mifflin Company, 1876, p. 90.

frequent use of devices not common in informal conversation, such as inverted expression ("so high does it soar"), balanced sentences ("it can stand; and it can go"), and figures of speech, especially metaphor and personification. The words are generally simple and immediately understood, but in the second sentence we find words with special metaphorical overtones: the scholar "received unto him" and "brooded thereon." Both phrases are archaic or Biblical in tone, suggesting the near divinity of that "scholar of the first age." The point is that the formal speaker uses stylistic devices for special effects.

4. *The use of conventional grammar.* Emerson spoke according to all the "rules" of acceptable grammar. He did not permit himself a misplaced modifier, a sentence fragment, or even a contraction like *can't* or *doesn't.*

☐   **INFORMAL STYLE**

Informal style is not the opposite of formal; the two differ in degree rather than in kind. Most college textbooks are informal, as are most newspapers, magazines, and conversations. Indeed, the majority of our communication today is informal. Some of it is high-level informality bordering on the formal, while much of it is low-level bordering on the colloquial.

The following example is characteristic of the lower level; in tone and feeling, it is completely unlike the Emerson selection.

Oh, I had seen a roller coaster before but always at a distance — climbing and plunging and climbing again. I had heard the clatter of the wheels and the screams of the girls, and I knew it must be exciting. But I'm afraid I wasn't prepared for the sight of a track that goes right straight down. I sat there frozen, unable to get a scream out of my throat. And down we went — then a jerk and a twist and a climb and a turn. I can't remember ever being so scared.

Finally, after what seemed like a ride of three hours, we stopped. I opened one eye; then I stood up and tried to get out. It was all I could do to stand, let alone walk. I waltzed my way over to the rail and stood there while those other three idiots took another ride. Then I decided I'd take a real whizzer of a ride on the merry-go-round.

This is a portion of a speech delivered by a young lady to a class-room audience. Obviously, she was not addressing a Phi Beta Kappa society or another formal gathering; she was talking to a group of relaxed young people to meet the requirements of a very simple speaking assignment. What are the distinguishing characteristics of her speech?

1. *The light tone.* The speaker is concerned with no lofty topic, no serious purpose, and no dignified idea. The whole experience is handled with gay abandon. The language and style are as informal as the topic and the occasion.

2. *The personal tone.* The speaker is describing a personal experience. She uses the pronoun *I* thirteen times in two brief paragraphs. She does not refer to the "theory" of roller coasters or generalize about momentum or speed.

3. *The simple sentence structure.* While there is a modest variety in kinds of sentences, none of them is long or difficult to understand on first hearing or reading. The most frequently used is the simple sentence with a subject-verb-complement arrangement.

4. *The liberal interpretation of grammatical rules.* We can find no grammatical errors, but we can find several things that would not be appropriate in a formal speech. The contractions *I'd, I'm,* and *can't* are informal. So are such colloquialisms as *right straight down, let alone walk, other three idiots,* and *a real whizzer.*

5. *The simple words.* The speaker uses mostly familiar one-syllable words, and even the polysyllabic words are easily and immediately understood without the help of the dictionary.

Before leaving the subject of stylistic differences, we should emphasize three additional points. (1) *The line dividing the formal from the informal is not always sharp and clear.* Lincoln's remarkably simple "Gettysburg Address" is human and personal; but primarily because of its gravity and dignity, it is considered formal. (2) *Neither style is superior to the other.* The value of either is largely a matter of appropriateness. Emerson's style in "The American Scholar" is not better than the student's style merely because it is formal. As a matter of fact, few things would sound more ludicrous than a roller-coaster ride narrated in Emersonian rhetoric. (3) *The student must learn to use each style as the occasion demands* without getting the two confused.

■   **IMPROVING STYLE**

Regardless of the subject of a speech, the speaker must always give it certain stylistic qualities if it is to have maximum effect. The first is appropriateness, suiting the style to the subject, audience, and occasion. The second is immediate intelligibility, speaking so lucidly and logically that the audience will understand at once, without puzzlement or strain. The third is force or impressiveness, that quality of language which constantly tugs at the listener's attention and helps him understand and remember. The speaker attains these qualities through clarity, precision, and vividness.

□   **CLARITY OF LANGUAGE**

Many speakers ask their listeners to labor under the weight of strange and ponderous words. Students do not usually display this weakness, but classroom lecturers and other serious speakers are often guilty of it. Perhaps a professor uses a learned word because he wants his students to increase their vocabularies. Perhaps — though few would admit it — the speaker uses unusual words to win admiration, respect, or belief. He knows, let us say, that if he uses easily understood language, even the least sensitive in his audience will see the holes in his logic. He thinks more complex expression of thought and impressive words that glitter like baubles on a Christmas tree may dazzle his listeners into believing what he says. Unfortunately, he is mistaken. An audience usually recognizes glitter for glitter's sake and rejects it emphatically. As we noted in our first chapter, a speaker should try to make listening and understanding as easy as possible; he can do this to a great extent by using simple words that are immediately clear.

1. *Avoid polysyllabic words.* There is nothing wrong with the short word. *Try* is just as good as *endeavor, hopes* is as good as *aspirations,* and *use* is always better than *utilize.* Notice in the three examples below what happens to language when the speaker goes out of his way to use polysyllabic words:

   1. Labored: He was a man possessed of imperturbability.
       Simple: He was a calm man.

   2. Labored: This problematical predicament may be disen-
                   tangled by a tighter centralization of authority.
      Simple: This problem may be solved by central control.
   3. Labored: What we need is an innervation of volitional be-
                   havior!
      Simple: We need to get busy!

The polysyllabic word tends to push the speaker into longer, un-
necessarily cluttered sentences. The result is "over style," the mark
not of literary excellence but of pomposity.

A word of caution: do not *fear* the longer word or go out of your
way to avoid it *if* it is the better word for your purpose. If you need
veracity rather than *truth,* or *protuberance* instead of *bump,* use it.
Choose the word that expresses your meaning most clearly.

2. *Use foreign words and phrases sparingly.* There are a few
occasions when expressions like *in flagrante delicto, O tempora! O
mores!,* and *in medias res* are appropriate — in law, perhaps, in
medicine, or in literary criticism. But even in learned papers at
scholarly meetings foreign phrases generally sound exhibitionistic and
rarely clarify. In Greece one speaks Greek. In Germany one speaks
German. In America it is best to speak American.

3. *Avoid technical language when speaking to nontechnical listeners.* Professional jargon is meaningful only to those with special
interests or training. The average certified public accountant cannot
understand the technical language of the neurologist; the economist
might have difficulty talking with the bartender. Every skill or profession has its own special set of words. The teacher of speech talks
with his professional colleagues about *invention,* but he is thinking
of speech content rather than something which must be patented. The
federal legislator concerned about our overabundance of corn and
wheat speaks of *surplusage.* The investment advisor will use the
words *bull* and *bear* without thinking of animals. Even the golfer
has his special vocabulary — *divots, seven-iron, four-wood,* and *hook.*
When the speaker is talking with people acquainted with his special
vocabulary, such words are appropriate; but when his listeners are
strangers to the words, the speaker should rephrase his thoughts in
the language of the layman.

☐   **PRECISION OF LANGUAGE**

The precise word says exactly what the speaker intends it to say —
assuming, of course, that the speaker has something definite in mind.
Mr. Smith, for example, is angry because his neighbor's dog barks all
night long. He is definitely angry with the dog. His anger is specific.
As he speaks to others about his loss of sleep, however, his words
become less and less specific until they are unbelievably general.
First he speaks of the dog; then he condemns his neighbor; then he
berates the entire neighborhood; finally he concludes that "all
mankind is selfish and thoughtless." As his anger spreads from the
specific to the general, his language also changes. His words for
berating the dog are strong and precise; for berating mankind they
are weak and vague.

To achieve precision of language, the speaker should follow three
rules:

1. *Use "omnibus" words sparingly.* An "omnibus" word is a
catch-all word. It can mean almost anything but is likely to be so
general that it means nothing. Here are several examples from classroom speeches:

1. As soon as he could, he went back to the fire and saw the remains of the furniture and *everything.* He picked up *everything*
   he could and carried it out to the yard where the police and
   everybody could protect it.

2. Well, by this time, a regular mob had gathered. They were
   yelling and singing and *doing just about anything you could
   think of. They were just crazy.*

3. What with exams *and all* we thought we'd better get in early —
   you know what I mean — so we left.

4. It's a beautiful park. It has an artificial lake for swimming and
   a lot of rides, a pavilion for dancing, and *things like that.*

5. She was *real nice* to us girls — I mean, she asked how we were
   getting along in school and *everything.* She'd always smile as we
   went out; and if we got back late, she'd say, "Well, ten minutes
   early," or *something like that.*

Of all the italicized words in the above excerpts, the one most
frequently used is the word *thing,* probably the least specific word in

the English language. The five speakers never tell us what they specifically mean by the word *thing*. In the second example, the people "were doing just about anything you could think of." This covers the full range of human actions. In the fourth example, the park was described as having rides and a pavilion and "things like that." But we don't know whether the things are like the pavilion or the rides or, as we suspect, really quite different. In the fifth example, "she" asked the students how they "were doing in school and everything." *Everything* means so much that the listener suspects it means nothing at all. In these instances the precise meaning is never given. The surest way to avoid the error would be simply to delete the words *thing, something, anything,* and *everything*.

2. *Avoid hazy words.* Closely related to the "omnibus" word is the word that is hazy, vague, or ambiguous — *pretty good, cute, just wonderful, simply marvelous, divine, swell, grand, awful, sort of, kind of.* We all use them in informal conversation, and though they say little that is precise, they seem to create an atmosphere of warmth and informality. On the speaker's platform, however, where points of view must be expressed precisely, the hazy word is out of place. Notice how much of the haze can be removed from the fifth example above:

General:	She was real nice to us girls.
Less general:	She was considerate of the girls in the house.
Even less general:	She was a housemother in the real sense of the word — cheerful, friendly, and helpful to every girl in the sorority.

or

General:	How are you getting along in school?
Less general:	How are your studies going?
Even less general:	How do you stand in the calculus class?
Particular:	What was your grade on Kemp's last exam?

If the speaker's thinking is hazy, verbal haze is the probable result. On the other hand, if the speaker has a specific idea in mind, he should use specific words to express it.

3. *Avoid words that have become emotionally charged labels.* Other close relatives of the "omnibus" words are the emotional labels — *agitator, bureaucratic, Fascist, radical, Communist, un-American.*

The instant we hear them our emotions grow turbulent, our biases more firm, and our thinking more shackled — and all because we react to the label without examining the contents of the bottle. This metaphor may become clearer with the following example:

> Mr. Chairman, I shall always vote in opposition to any proposal so *radical*, so *un-American* as the one presently considered. I must question the originator's motives for introducing such a proposal. I certainly must express my regrets that he has been *duped* by the *wily subversives* who have *infiltrated the ranks of freedom*. Our *national honor* is at stake. Our *constitutional guarantee of liberty and equality* must remain *unviolated*.

The only point the speaker makes in the entire passage is that he will not vote for the proposal; he never says why. As we study the italicized words, we see the speaker's strategy. He is aware that Americans automatically oppose people or things labeled *radical, un-American,* and *subversive,* and just as automatically favor *national honor, constitutional guarantees, liberty,* and *equality.* He uses these labels deliberately to evoke public reaction against the bill and for his position, substituting "name calling" and a strong emotional tone for ideas clearly and specifically related to the content of the proposal and logical reasons for opposing it. Instead of presenting evidence against the proposal or challenging the evidence for it, the speaker expects to support his position with empty emotional generalities. It is doubtful, of course, that the speaker could remove these labels from his vocabulary; they have become too much a part of it. But he could use them sparingly and not attempt to persuade by name-calling alone.

☐   **VIVIDNESS OF LANGUAGE**

If a speaker is to win the attention of his audience, his language must be colorful, original, and energetic; it must have a sense of action and direction; it must further the progress of his speech with every sentence. These qualities are not easily acquired, but the speaker willing to take a few pains with his language will win surprising results.

1. *Avoid clichés — the overworked words and expressions.* The

overworked word or phrase is the one used so often that it has lost its vitality and much of its meaning. Within this category are: "I'd like to talk with you," "this leads me into my topic," "and in conclusion I'd like to say," "it goes without saying," "this calls for drastic action." And there are many more. The student who stays up late to study for an examination *burns the midnight oil* and *hits the books*. He earns a decent grade *by the sweat of his brow*. The good grade entitles him to a *sumptuous repast* if he has enough *filthy lucre*. After eating, he returns to the dorm where he *reigns supreme*. He is the *life of the party*. He *presides at the piano* before *a vast multitude* and wins their *tumultuous applause*. Then, in the *wee small hours,* he *wends his way* to his room where, *a bit the worse for wear,* he falls into the *arms of Morpheus* just as *Ole Sol* comes *winking o'er the brim*.

The inexperienced speaker may find choosing fresh words particularly difficult since what may impress him as fresh may impress his listeners as hackneyed and overworked. It is conceivable, for example, that he has never previously associated the word *tumultuous* with applause. It is also conceivable that he has never before been introduced to Morpheus, the god of sleep, or Sol, the sun. Reading and careful listening will help him develop a greater sensitivity to the style of our better writers and speakers and an awareness of overworked words.

Being original is further complicated by phrases that are overworked but, at the same time, particularly appropriate. The remark "I'd like to talk with you" is certainly commonplace, but it is difficult to find a remark as economical and straightforward. Some speakers avoid it by saying, "I'd like to *visit* with you" or "I've a few ideas I'd like to *share* with you," but these, despite the folksy tone, are weaker than the phrase the speaker is trying to avoid. Another overworked remark is "there's method in his madness," but again it is difficult, especially in the extemporaneous speech, to find an equally good substitute. "He's crazy, but you can be sure he has a reason" is wordy and sounds as if the speaker is straining to avoid the familiar. "He's crazy like a fox" simply substitutes one overworked expression for another. In this situation the speaker would do best to use the expression that is well known — even if he does run the risk of showing little originality at the moment.

Being original is difficult, too, because a speaker's bad language habits are established early in life; learning what they are and just what to do about them comes slowly. Certain phrases become pets and are used repeatedly. One student was victimized by the expression "down the drain." To him, anything wasted or changed or given up went "down the drain." On one occasion he reported: "At the end of my senior year all the girls and the hot rods and the rock-and-roll went down the drain." Obviously his pet phrase caused him to strain a metaphor and describe an impossible phenomenon.

The speaker must make the effort to be fresh and original in his choice of words, no matter how difficult it is. He must look first for words that are simple and precise and then work for originality. As he reads, he must try to evaluate what makes the successful writer's style fresh — the active verbs, the sensory images, or extraordinary treatment of ordinary ideas. He must also, alas, listen to speakers whose phrases have lost their value through endless repetition. In short, he must develop a sensitivity to the old and the new, the fresh and the stale.

2. *Use figurative language occasionally.* The figures of speech most commonly used by the public speaker are the metaphor and the simile. Both compare the familiar with the unfamiliar. Both attempt to turn the abstract into the concrete. We use them in our everyday speech to add color and vitality. We create a metaphor by stating that one object *is* something else: "Fullback Grabonski is a Sherman tank." A simile uses *like, as,* or *seems,* thus: "Fullback Grabonski is like a Sherman tank." Much of our conversation, especially about sports events, uses the implied metaphor. A quarterback *plows* through the line or *wheels* around left end. Our home team gets *smashed, swamped, inundated, slaughtered, trounced, run over,* and even *murdered.* The coach *throws a fit* (but that is not necessarily a metaphor), *blows his stack, flips his lid, hits the ceiling, reads the riot act, cans* the quarterback, and swears to have a thoroughgoing *shakedown.*

Using figurative language effectively entails observing certain commonsense rules. First, *the effective speaker uses the familiar to explain the unfamiliar.* If, for example, he wishes to show how wild, untamed, and savage some of our major cities are, he may refer to them as jungles. He does not need an elaborate or highly literary metaphor to make his point; in fact, the stark simplicity of *jungles* is more effective. In using figurative language, simplicity is the watchword. The speaker asks too much of his audience if he describes a man's head as "a sphere of purest Parian," but if he calls it "a piece of marble," he can be relatively sure every listener will understand what he means.

Second, *the effective speaker does not mix his metaphors.* One of the classic examples of the mixed metaphor is, "You have buttered your bread, now you must lie in it!" Stay either with the bread and butter or with the bed; when mixed, neither makes sense. Another classic example is the remark of the busy executive: "I'm fed up with all this double-dealing; from now on I'm going to take off my gloves and call them as I see them." He manages to imply four metaphors in one remark and ends up with gobbledygook.

Third, *the effective speaker uses a comparison that is not strained or inappropriate* — unless he is doing so for comic effect. Consider: "He rushed onto the Senate floor like a housewife about to attack a Monday morning wash." This simile compares the energy and vitality of the two parties, but there the comparison stops. The listeners are likely to find the image too far-fetched to be anything but funny. The community reformer produces the same humorous effect when he exhorts his audience to "Gird your loins and join the crusade for decent literature."

Fourth, *the effective speaker uses fresh figurative language.* Again we face the question: "Am I never at liberty to use old, familiar figures of speech?" The answer is, certainly — if they are appropriate to the occasion. But before settling for the "old, familiar figures," examine the following list.

> running all around Robin Hood's barn
> clearing the decks
> getting the gravy
> bringing home the bacon
> snapping at the bait
> champing at the bit
> playing second fiddle
> holding the purse strings

having his cake and eating it too
opening a can of worms
getting it in the neck
tightening our belts
shutting the barn door after the horse is out
putting the cart before the horse
letting the cat out of the bag
putting the shoe on the wrong foot
putting all his eggs in one basket
counting his chickens before they're hatched
putting his foot in his mouth
beating around the bush
passing the buck
resting on his laurels

Is any one of these figures of speech fresh? Does the listener get any new sense impressions? Does he see, feel, hear, or taste more acutely? Or is he so bored by the trite, hackneyed figures that he yawns or dozes? These and similar phrases have been used by speakers for decades if not centuries. Consequently, they have lost their cutting edge; they are worn smooth. All things considered, good ideas appear even better in vivid, *original* figures of speech.

3. *Use personal pronouns.* The personal pronouns — especially "we," "our," and "us," as opposed to "you" and "I" — establish personal contact between the speaker and his listeners. They suggest that the subject being discussed involves us all. The use of pronouns suggests still another idea — that anything worth talking about is closely related to people. Concern for disarmament, for example, can be generated only by showing how it is related directly to people — particularly the immediate audience. Any subject — marriage, divorce, law enforcement, safety, education, world peace, war — becomes vital to an audience only when they understand how it affects human beings — themselves.

4. *Vary the sentences.* Among inexperienced speakers, lack of variety in sentence structure is one of the most common faults. The simplest way to vary sentences is to change their length, structure, and rhythm. The short, simple sentence is especially appropriate for conveying liveliness, speed, and energy. The long compound-complex

sentence is often reserved for solemnity and stateliness. But neither should be used to the exclusion of the other. Examine the two examples below:

1. Dr. Barnard enters the classroom. He is a tall man. He combs his hair forward. He tries to cover his baldness. He glances over his class list. The bell rings. Everyone waits for him to call, "Mr. Adams."

2. Dr. Barnard enters the classroom, but he is in no hurry. He is a tall man, but his slouch makes him appear smaller than he really is. He combs his hair forward, but everyone knows he is trying to cover his baldness. He glances over his class list as the bell rings, and everyone waits for him to call, "Mr. Adams."

Both these examples are monotonously deadening. The first sounds like a first-grade primer; all the sentences are simple and of nearly the same length and rhythm. The second strings complete, simple sentences of the same length and rhythm into repetitive "and/but" compound sentences, and the whole passage sounds like someone straining to produce a sophisticated style. The first version is distractingly choppy, the second sticky and sluggish. In both examples, the second and third sentences intrude on the action. Neither succeeds in making the content of the passage vivid and interesting. Both examples need the dramatic effect of sentence variety.

Another way of varying sentences is to shift from a simple declaration to a command or a question. The speaker may say, "Think about that for a moment!" or "Give the problem your attention" or "Whatever you do, be certain to vote." Each of these is a modest command, direct and forceful. The question is especially good for transitions or for setting up alternate proposals or courses of action. For example,

But what precisely is the cause of dishonesty in the classroom? Is it the professor and his demand for high standards? Is it society and its demand for high grades as a mark of distinction? Or is it the student and his basic dishonesty?

Above all else, a speaker must think clearly. If his purpose, attitudes, or information are confused, he cannot hope to speak with variety and interest. On the other hand, if he has a clear command of his thoughts and is at home with the issues, he is far more likely to speak with exactness — to say precisely what he means in sentences that reflect in structure, length, and rhythm the thrust, urgency, and force of his ideas.

After having read this chapter, the reader may assume that a speech should be planned down to the last word. This, of course, would be true only of the manuscript speech. It is quite untrue of the extemporaneous speech, the kind presented with greatest frequency. To handpick every word, weigh it for its effect on an audience, then reject it or keep it would be tedious enough to turn the average speaker into a sullen psychopath. Much of the beauty of speech lies in its spontaneity. We must develop the skill of finding words and using them sensibly the instant we need them. That, of course, is forbiddingly difficult. The majority of students who read this chapter will already have studied the English language for over a decade without discovering this invaluable secret. Another year, five years, even ten — with gradual improvement here and there along the way — may make the search worthwhile.

SUMMARY

1. Words are symbols which frequently do not convey our meaning because (a) they are not understood as we want them understood, and (b) we do not say what we intend to say.
2. To increase the size of your vocabulary (a) learn new words by their use in context, (b) use the dictionary regularly, and (c) make frequent use of recently learned words.
3. The formal style is usually reserved for a manuscript speech delivered on a serious occasion. The advantage of formality lies in the precision with which ideas may be expressed. Its disadvantage lies in its impersonality and aloofness.
4. The informal style may be used in the manuscript speech as well as in the extemporaneous speech. Its chief value lies in its personal contact with the audience.
5. Regardless of the speaker's style, his language should be clear, precise, and vivid.
6. To be clear, the speaker should avoid (a) polysyllabic words

wherever possible, (b) most foreign words and phrases, and (c) technical language with nontechnical listeners.

7. To be precise, the speaker should (a) use omnibus words sparingly, (b) avoid hazy words, and (c) avoid words that have become emotionally charged labels.

8. To be vivid, the speaker should (a) avoid overworked words and expressions, (b) use figurative language, (c) use personal pronouns often, and (d) vary his sentence structure and rhythm.

EXERCISES

1. In a recent issue of *Vital Speeches*, locate one formal and one informal speech, and write a two-page paper in which you contrast the two styles. Use brief excerpts to support your conclusions.

2. In the near future record one of your extemporaneous classroom speeches; then prepare a written transcription. Revise the transcription until you are confident that your speech meets the criteria of clarity, precision, and vividness.

3. Below are a number of overworked expressions. Test your ability to recognize them by supplying the missing word:

age before _____	brown as a _____
all sorts and _____	busy as a _____
_____ of doom	cool as a _____
goes without _____	green as _____
last but not _____	innocent as a _____
one fell _____	mad as a _____
shadow of a _____	pale as a _____
slow but _____	quick as a _____
well-rounded _____	sick as a _____
wine, women, and _____	sly as a _____

4. Prepare a similar list of the pet words and phrases commonly used by members of your class. Lists may also be prepared for (a) grammatical errors, (b) improper use of words, and (c)

particularly effective stylistic devices, such as imaginative metaphors, parallel structures, sentence fragments effectively used, and the like.

5. A learning technique which was regularly practiced years ago but which now has fallen into disrepute is *imitation*. Choose a passage from a speech by Winston Churchill or John F. Kennedy and imitate it by constructing a similar passage on a different subject. This requires careful study of the model's structures. Its words, phrases, and sentences, and the orderly arrangement in which they appear should be recaptured with similar or equivalent words and phrases. Understand, too, that this is purely an exercise to help you understand the work of others.

6. Study the style of each of the three following excerpts from student speeches. What weakness of word usage is most apparent? How would you describe the tone or feeling? Choose the poorest and rephrase it effectively.

   a. From a speech on poverty in South America:

   I've often wondered why these miserable people from the mountains come to Lima and live in the slums, but they all say, "Well, at least here in Lima we have someone to beg off of." And this is true, because you find a lot of tourists and other rich people living in the cities of Peru. And there are many beggars. You walk down the street and shoeshine boys will come up — maybe you'll meet six in one block — and then there's always little kids, five or six years old. They say, "Mericano. Mawney, mawney." Always begging. And then, too, you go down the street you might find a legless man. He's blind, but he blows a little whistle, and he plays a tune on it, begging for money from the cars. And all these are typical scenes in Lima.

   b. From a speech on college tests:

   But the questions are always questions that make you beat around the bush, you might say, and some of them are really so bad that even the professor himself couldn't give an honest, straightforward answer. Too much emphasis

is put on a student's ability to read. I don't mean *read*.
Everyone ought to be able to read. I mean . . . well, it's
like the test is a puzzle almost and before you can write
the answer you have to solve the puzzle. And it seems like
I've always had trouble with puzzles. And to make matters
worse these tests are always timed so you always have
to rush to solve the problem so you can beat around the
bush and have time at the end to figure out if you've said
anything or not.

c. From a speech on the values of fraternity life:

Now what I mean is when you apply for a job. They will
look over your record and see what you've done in college.
If you've got a B average and another applicant has a B
average and you're both applying for the same job, he
wants to see what you've done besides study. He will
look at your manuscript and he'll see that you were an
active member of a fraternity and then he knows that
you can get along with people because you've not only
took the time to study but you've also had time to get
a well-rounded college life.

7. Read the student speech below; then answer the questions that
follow.

CAMPUS KIDS

Have any of you ever wondered as you walked across in the
morning or the afternoon about all the different types of kinds you
see walking across? Take for instance the "sleepy" kids, especially
if it's early in the morning. If it's a boy, he hasn't shaved, and if
it's a girl, she doesn't have any make-up on, and she's walking real
fast. They're both walking real fast, they keep looking at their
watches and they stop at the scramble-light just about ready to
jump up and down waiting for the light to change. And hand in
hand with the sleepy kid is the kid who is late. These kids get —
either they're running or rushing to class and you'd think they're
either late or they're out for track. And besides them there's the
kid who's cramming. Now these kids will go to class — they've
got their notebook open and studying as they walk down the side-
walk and run into people and everything else. All they're trying

to do is get five minutes cramming in before they get to class. And you know, they're either studying for a test and they have — uh — they have the test — other kids have had it, and they're trying to memorize it before they get to class. And besides them there's the day-dreamer. Did you ever notice the day-dreamer? He's got his head in the air and doesn't see anything — he's just walking. If you asked him what he saw, he wouldn't know. He's got a smile on his face thinkin' about what he did last night or what he's gonna do tonight or the good grade he got out of class or why he got a bad one. Then besides the day-dreamer there's the friendly kid. Ah, this kid, he's a good one. He says "hi" to everybody. He has got a big cheery smile all over his face and he looks so happy-go-lucky and that's the kind of guy you like to be — friendly guy. And then besides him there's the gangs. Ever notice the gangs? They're usually freshmen, freshmen girls as a matter of fact. There're usually about at least four of them. They all look alike — I mean not physically but they all got trench coats on. They all got tennis shoes on. They all got a dress or skirts on — only the two — one won't have slacks on and the other skirts or something. They all look pretty much alike and they all go the same place together. They plan the night before where they're going and what they're going to do and how they're going to get there and they'll all be together. And then besides them there's the inevitable lovers — always the lovers everplace on the campus especially this time of year. Hand in hand they go everwhere together and besides staying outside of class buildings where they have to part in about two minutes and it's about to drive them out of their minds. Their whole world is there. And you think, "How on earth can all these people fit together?" How can the crammer who's worried about his grades so and the kid who's late who doesn't seem to have anything on his mind if he can sleep like that and be late. How can they all fit together in one school? And, you know, because you know that you have played every one of these roles at one time and you'll play them again before you're out of school.

QUESTIONS

a. Judging from the style or tone of this speech, what kind of personality does the speaker have?
b. How does the speaker violate the principles in this chapter? Give examples.

    c. Is there anything of merit in the speech? Refer specifically to particular phrases.

    d. How does this style compare with that of the speeches delivered in your class?

8. Prepare a three-page manuscript speech in which you demonstrate good formal style. Practice its delivery often so that even though reading you may still establish contact with your audience.

9. Prepare a three-minute informal speech to entertain. Try especially to project a feeling of life and vitality by using any of the methods discussed in this chapter.

CHAPTER 9

USING THE BODY
EFFECTIVELY

Before the speaker says even his first words, he sends a message to his audience. He "speaks" with his appearance — the way he sits in his chair waiting for the chairman to introduce him, the hole in his shoe, his five o'clock shadow, a pair of shaggy brows. He communicates in the way he walks to the lectern, the way he nods his head to acknowledge the chairman's introduction, and the way he arranges his notes. As the speaker talks, the audience watches as well as listens. All viewers are quick to note visible signs of friendliness or hostility, sincerity or "phoniness," vitality or lethargy. The speaker's appearance — his dress, his posture, his movements, his gestures — is important to the proper reception of his ideas. Bodily action will either support or contradict the speaker's words.

■ DIRECTNESS

The first and most important principle of good bodily action is directness. An effective speaker communicates with his audience eye-to-eye, person-to-person, and intellect-to-intellect, as well as with the spoken word. An ineffective speaker delivers a soliloquy; he seems to forget his audience and retreat into a world of his own. All of us have experienced the warmth of contact in a spirited conversation among friends. We know that as long as we can meet one another in a face-to-face relationship, it is possible to have a rapid and easy exchange of ideas. We also know the feeling of distance when talking with a stranger or an excessively shy person whose eyes never meet ours directly; our ideas travel more slowly and with less confidence. Even in the speech classroom, where the atmosphere is informal enough to assure audience contact, many students are unable to speak directly to their classmates. Some look only at the instructor, as though he were the only one in the room. Others look only at their friends or stare at the rear wall, the windows, or their notes. Directness is, for many students, a very real problem.

□   **EYE-TO-EYE CONTACT**

In assuring a warm personal relationship with an audience nothing is so significant as eye contact. This is not to say that a speaker should never look at his notes or never look at the wall, the ceiling, or the floor. On the contrary, these are quite ordinary and human actions. But obviously, the speaker must not look at these things — these objects — exclusively. He must look at his audience and demonstrate his interest in them.

But how is a speaker to show an interest in everyone? It would be ridiculous to allocate a fair share of seconds to each pair of eyes and shift methodically up one row and down another. The speaker probably would not meet the eyes of everyone even if he tried. He *can* divide his audience into groups and speak momentarily to one group after another. As the speech progresses, he can distribute his time equally among the groups and thereby give the impression of speaking to everyone. But eye contact is more than a matter of simple direction. The eyes must *say* something. If his voice, for example, says, "This is important!" his eyes should agree and reinforce his statement. Especially in small and informal groups, the speaker should work for the same closeness and eye contact of active conversation. His eyes should clearly reveal his interest in his audience.

☐   **PERSON-TO-PERSON CONTACT**

To establish person-to-person contact, the speaker must cross the barriers that separate him from his audience. Sometimes the barriers are physical, sometimes spatial, and sometimes a combination.

Physical barriers include objects between the speaker and his audience, like lecterns or tables. Obviously, no speaker should hide behind his lectern as a refuge and bulwark; if he does, he gives the impression that he is afraid or really doesn't want to confront his audience. He should not think a lectern lends dignity or erudition to his ideas; some audiences regard it as a psychological obstruction to communication. At best, a lectern is only a piece of furniture for holding the speaker's notes, reference materials, and a glass of water. When a speaker finds himself separated from his audience by a table or lectern, he should, if he can, come out from behind it and speak to his audience from one side or in front of it. If the occasion prevents that, he should at least imply to the audience that he would like to come out from behind the barrier by leaning across it and strengthening his other means of personal contact.

Physical distractions are harder to cope with. An audience may become more engrossed in the potted palms behind the speaker, the other dignitaries on the stage, the flags, or the stage drapery than in the speaker's ideas. When physical distractions make close contact impossible, there is little the speaker can do. He cannot demand that the stage be cleared of all other people and decoration; he can only hope to make personal contact stronger through interesting material, well-timed movements and gestures, and an attractive voice.

When the barrier is space, the speaker should abandon his platform, if he can, and physically close the gap between himself and his audience. Of course, tradition and custom often require the speaker to stay in his pulpit or on his platform. The only way to cross the barrier then is by working doubly hard to project his own magnetism.

In combination, physical and spatial barriers can be formidable.

Sunday after Sunday, the minister must project his sermon over pulpit, altar or table, and rows of empty pews before he reaches the first pair of ears. A celebrated speaker spotlighted on a stage is distracted and blinded to the house beyond by the bright lights. The psychological barrier of the line where light and darkness meet separates him spatially from his audience; it is as if he were in one room, the audience in another; they can see him but he cannot see them. Whatever the combination of barriers, the speaker should try to avoid or overcome them and go forward to meet his audience, mentally and emotionally at all times, and physically when possible.

☐   **INTELLECT-TO-INTELLECT CONTACT**

Even though a speaker and his audience may be in personal contact, there will be no communication between them without "a meeting of the minds." The speaker's eyes and ears detect rapt attention, interest, and enlightenment, as well as boredom, restlessness, and incomprehension in the physical reactions of his audience. People sit still when they are interested, and their faces reflect their interest; they wiggle or cough when they are bored, and their eyes wander or even shut. They look puzzled when they do not understand. This reactive audience behavior is often referred to as feedback, and it is the speaker's only way of gauging whether he is communicating or not, and how. Feedback is never completely absent even in the most lethargic of audiences; it is always present, always expressing some kind of response to the speaker. It may be loud applause, unmuffled yawns, or any reaction in between; the speaker must train himself to be sensitive to even subtle reactions. When the audience laughs, applauds, or shows obvious interest, the speaker knows he is on the right track; but when feedback relays disinterest, the speaker must work for positive intellectual contact with more interest-building materials or a more active delivery.

A second way the speaker works for a meeting of the minds is through his own appearance, not only physical — the color of his necktie or the way he moves about on the platform — but also intellectual — the feelings, impressions, and even hunches he transmits to his audience. Intellectual "appearances" cannot be defined or measured precisely, but they do affect the listener. It is common to hear someone say, "I have great faith in that man, but I don't know why. It's just that he impresses me as being a fine person." And, of course, we have heard the opposite too: "No, I could never vote for him. He's too . . . too . . . well, he's just not the kind of man I vote for, that's all." When we hear such comments, we know there is something in the speaker's intellectual "appearance" that defies analysis. One speaker impresses his audience by appearing fair and logical. Another makes a good intellectual appearance with the clarity and simplicity of his language. Another creates a bad intellectual impression because his speech is poorly organized.

The speaker is powerless to channel all the individual judgments made by his audience. He has no control over their past experiences, or any foolproof means of making himself well-liked by everyone. If he is liberal, he will be disliked by the conservatives. If he is conservative, he will be disliked by the liberals. If he makes a passing attempt to be both liberal and conservative, he will be disliked by both. If he has an unruly shock of hair, a stern countenance, and a fiery disposition, some will be pleased, but others will be disappointed because he is not bald, benign, and placid. The speaker cannot hope to reshape all the prejudices and preferences of his listeners. At best, he can only hope to dispel them by using the resources of effective speaking: interesting material, clear organization, and appropriate language. When he has communicated these resources to the audience with his voice, posture, movement, gestures, and facial expression, he has done much to achieve a meeting of the minds.

■   **PHYSICAL APPEARANCE**

When the speaker first stands before his audience, his physical appearance gives them an early opportunity to develop some attitudes toward him as a speaker. They note his general stance, the way he carries his arms, the angle of his head and shoulders, the position of his feet. Any one part of the body might escape unnoticed, but when the parts are viewed together, they transmit a total picture. It is important that the speaker make the picture effective; it should support what he is to say later. Good posture, effective movement, meaningful gestures, and appropriate facial expressions all contribute to an impressive physical appearance.

□   **POSTURE**

Most of us have known the rules of good posture since our high school health class: "Stand erect, shoulders back, head up, and chin in. Distribute the weight evenly. Sit tall; stand tall; walk tall." Aside from these general rules of good posture, there is no *best* way for the speaker to stand. His posture should essentially convey poise and alertness. Perhaps a few specific "do's" will clarify the general rules:

1. *Stand still.* Avoid aimlessly shifting from foot to foot, swinging the hips from side to side, stamping the feet, rocking fore and aft, involuntarily dancing. Any movement should be appropriate, definite, and purposeful.

2. *Look human,* not like a ramrod or a robot. Military rigidity — feet together, shoulders back, chin in, and arms pulled tightly to the sides — may be momentarily effective, but it is tiring to maintain and to watch, and often gives the impression that the speaker is tense with stage fright. The "Colossus of Rhodes" posture or, as students call it, the "Mr. Clean" posture — head back, arms folded, feet planted firmly apart — gives the impression of arrogance. Both robot-postures should be relaxed, not into a droop or slouch but into an appearance of composure.

3. *Give your arms and hands something to do.* Restless, aimlessly moving arms and hands are distracting. The ill-at-ease speaker crosses his arms over his chest, clasps his hands at the small of his back, plunges them into his pockets, hikes up his trousers, plays with a pencil, rolls his notes into a paper spy glass, or fidgets with a piece of jewelry. If your hands and arms are not being used in a meaningful gesture, simply drop them to your side or rest them quietly on the lectern. If you use notes, hold them easily, not desperately, with both hands. If the occasion is casual, put a hand momentarily in a pocket. At all times, control your hands and arms so that you appear composed and comfortable.

4. *Stand up.* Avoid leaning on the lectern. In the classroom this problem is far more easily corrected than any of the others mentioned. It is usually enough for someone to say, "Don't lean." Leaning in itself is not necessarily bad. When an effective speaker wishes to emphasize a point, he often leans over his lectern toward his audience. He does not, however, use the lectern to support lazy weight; he knows that standing comfortably erect without the use of props suggests energy and vitality.

Before we leave the role posture plays in the speaker's appearance, we should acknowledge the fact that not all good speakers follow the rules. The student asks: "Why is it that my history professor is such a good speaker? He never makes eye contact; he stares at the ceiling or the windows, drapes himself over his lectern, wanders aimlessly around the room; he covers his mouth with his hand, constantly massages his face, scratches his head, and drums on his desk. Yet he is the best teacher I have ever had." One answer is that unorthodoxy can be effective. Unusual platform behavior does become the signature or trademark of many experienced speakers. This professor's rule-breaking was part of his personality, and it gave him color, casualness, and interest. He was all the more effective because he escaped the patterns of the neatly tailored, properly polished speaker.

The student will not be ready to imitate his professor for a good many years. His bearing is not yet sufficiently poised; his personality is not yet fixed; his style is not yet determined. When he strays too far from the norm of platform behavior, he appears cocky and flippant. Once he has learned the rules and can practice them successfully, he will know when, where, and even how to break them effectively. Now it is best for him to stay within the limits of the principle: *The effective speaker's posture suggests dignity, comfort, energy, and alertness.*

☐   **MOVEMENT**

The speaker recognizes that action is compelling. As we look at a broad landscape, our eyes are almost immediately attracted to a moving object. As we read an essay, our thought is attracted to those ideas which grow larger in significance. We are attracted by a story if things happen in it. We like language that is active. We shun monotony and are attracted to activity. Every good teacher has learned that he must ease the difficulties of listening, that he must occasionally provide relief from boredom. He has learned that he can probably rouse the young lady dozing in the third row by simply moving to another spot in the room. Every student has learned that it is considerably easier to listen to the active teacher than to the stationary teacher who perches behind the lectern and pecks away at his notes. Movement is just as essential in attracting attention to the public speaker; unless he is restricted by a microphone, he will rarely stay in one spot.

But a speaker does more than create interest when he moves. Interest is fundamental to movement, but there are other values to be recognized, too.

1. *Move to release tension.* Many student speakers refuse at first to move because they do not trust their legs. They say they are "too nervous" to move. With only a little experience, however, the student realizes that movement helps rather than hinders; he finds movement an outlet for pent-up, excess energy. For the frightened speaker, even aimless pacing is better than immobility; but if the pacing can be channeled into purposeful action, so much the better. He can walk forward to display a visual aid, move backward to draw a diagram on the blackboard, or simply change his speaking position from the right to the left of the lectern. All these movements serve the purposes of the speech, and they help to steady shaking knees and quiet the butterflies in his stomach as well.

2. *Move to emphasize a point.* Movement directed toward the audience carries greater impact than movement from side to side or front to back. The conversationalist, for example, often leans forward when he wants to get an important point across. He leans back in relaxation when he has finished. Similarly, the platform speaker reduces volume before an emphatic moment, saying, "Now there is one point I must make clear." At the same time he walks toward his audience. He gives us three clues to the importance of his next thought: lowered volume, verbal statement, and forward movement. In this instance the action suits the words; it is psychologically appropriate. It implies, "I must get closer to get the importance of this idea across."

3. *Move to indicate progress in thought.* In some respects the writer is in a more enviable position than the speaker because he communicates in sentences and paragraphs that can be seen and digested at varying rates of reading; sometimes key sentences are even numbered and underscored. If an idea escapes us momentarily, we can turn back and try again to pick up the thought. We are not so fortunate in listening to a speaker, however; once he has started, we must follow along as best as we can at his rate, for we have no opportunity to turn back. We must infer punctuation and paragraphs from his vocal force or inflection. The speaker must rely chiefly on his voice and on movement in transitional passages to tell us that he is making progress. As he says, "Now let's move to the third point," he may take a few steps to the right and momentarily relax eye contact. This subtle movement, reinforcing the spoken words, indicates that the speaker is preparing, and allowing his audience to prepare, for another step in his progression of thought.

4. *Move to establish anticipation of thought.* Immediately after the chairman has introduced the speaker, the members of an audience, even the most captive one, feel anticipation. They wonder how the speaker will walk and what his first words will be. They wonder about the sound of his voice, or the color of his humor. The good speaker recognizes the value of anticipation and continues to encourage it during the course of his speech. Movement helps a great deal in building expectancy. The speaker moves without saying a word to get attention; the reaction is "Why did he do that? What is he about to say?" Or as the speaker nears his conclusion he says, "What is to be done? Shall we pass more laws? Shall we send more letters to our Senators? Shall we hold that the only way to secure freedom is to buy it?" On each question he moves a little closer to his audience. By the time he asks the last one, he is at the point nearest his audience, and his audience anticipates a significant idea. This step-by-step approach is called prophetic movement.

5. *Move to reveal personality.* The speaker suggests his personality with every move he makes, voluntary and involuntary, as he approaches the lectern, moves during his speech, and returns again to his chair. A shuffle or heavy plod suggests low vitality and weak wit. An easy, coordinated, confident stride suggests poise and security.

Naturally, appearances can be deceiving; the speaker's personality may be altogether different from his walk. But because the walk is noticed first and because first impressions tend to influence later judgments, a speaker will do well to project a positive personality in the way he moves. He should let his audience "see" the most favorable qualities of his inner make-up. He should move actively, not lazily; definitely, not cautiously; and appropriately, not ostentatiously.

The five principles of bodily activity usually operate together, not independently, and are governed by a sixth: *Movement should be appropriate to the speaker, his material, and the occasion.* The effective speaker does not gallop and prance in making a two-minute announcement or in delivering a memorial address on a solemn occasion. Neither does he stand like a statue when speaking to an audience keyed up for action. At all times, he tries to make his actions spring up as a natural outgrowth of his thoughts.

□   **GESTURES**

Gestures usually mean movements of hands and arms, but a small movement of any part of the body could as easily be considered a gesture. A football coach might gesture with his foot; a boxer with his chin and shoulder; a dancer with her hips. But the platform speaker, unless he is playing a role or impersonating someone, gestures almost solely with the hands and arms. A gesture, in the full sense of the word, is always purposeful. Throwing out a hand for no reason at all, little flutterings with the fingers, gripping and regripping the lectern, fussing with watch bands, coat buttons, necklaces, belt buckles, fraternity keys, and engagement rings are not gestures. They occupy idle hands, but they add no meaning to the speaker's language, and they often detract from its significance.

Gestures, like gross physical movement, should be as natural and appropriate as they are in conversational speech. A stranger wants to know how to get to the administration building, and immediately, without planning, the person he asks stretches out his arm in the direction of the building. Perhaps a roommate wants to go bowling, and he gets a simple "no" and shake of the head in reply. Whenever two or three people engage in an informal but heated argument, fingers point, hands caution, palms slap, and fists pound. In all these examples, no gesture is planned. The hands act as spontaneously as the words are spoken. Every beginning speaker should try to capture this sense of freedom by throwing himself unabashedly into the ideas he talks about. When his enthusiasm is as unrestricted and spontaneous as it is in conversation, helpful and appropriate gestures will come to him naturally.

There are two types of gestures: *emphatic* and *demonstrative*. In a sense, all gestures are demonstrative and all are emphatic; but because they are usually more one than the other, it is useful to think of them separately.

EMPHATIC GESTURES

A good speaker emphasizes an idea in many ways. He may discuss it at length to set it apart from ideas mentioned in passing, or he may place it at the end of his speech to create the final and most lasting impression. He will always develop it with clear reason, sound evidence, vivid language, and a forceful voice.

Emphasis is enhanced by the size and vigor of gestures. For example, an orchestra playing a symphony grows louder and faster and rises to an emotional climax in response to the increasing size and emotion of the conductor's gestures. The orchestra becomes quiet and pastoral when the conductor's arms move with less haste and less decisive action. The conductor draws his hands and arms closer to his body, and his body itself appears to grow smaller. The members of the orchestra read and play the music before them, but in addition they read and react to the gestures of the conductor.

A good speaker, of course, is not a conductor. He is much less active, but he, too, uses visible signals to control his audience: small, in-close signals for quiet thoughts, and big, extended, or tense signals for important thoughts. This idea may be made clearer by examples from conversation. Two men, let us say, are quarrelling at fever pitch. Finally one of them shouts, "Get out!" and accompanies the words with a gesture: he points a stiff arm and forefinger to the nearest exit. If the speaker were a wife quarrelling with her husband, she would probably not only point but stamp her foot as well. If a little girl were fighting it out with her brother, she would shout the words, point to the door, jump up and down, open the door, and push him out! In each of these situations the emphatic gesture is quick, tense, graphic, and timed to coincide with the words and emotion.

The best known emphatic gesture of the platform speaker is the clenched fist — a gesture immediately associated with the great orators of the nineteenth century or with the brimstone evangelists of today, and widely used by speakers of all descriptions. The clenched fist implies vital importance: "This is something we *have* to do. In this *we must not fail!*" Of course, the fist does not come into great play in classroom speaking because feelings rarely grow that intense; but in the speeches of politicians, social leaders, ministers, and businessmen, this emphatic gesture is much in evidence. When used, the fist is almost never pounded on the lectern; it usually is shaken vehemently in front of the body, or less often, thrown with a smack into the other hand.

Speakers the world over use variations of the clenched-fist gesture for emphasis. Harry Truman chopped the air with his right hand like a hatchet. John F. Kennedy stabbed the air with a single finger or a cluster of fingers. The principle is obvious: virtually any gesture is emphatic (1) if it is big and intense, (2) if it is timed to coincide with the words, and (3) if it is appropriate to the speaker and his subject.

DEMONSTRATIVE GESTURES

The speaker gestures demonstratively when he illustrates a thought with his hands. Like an actor, he uses his hands to describe words or feelings. The speaker may show a given measurement by a distance between thumb and forefinger, between hands, between a hand and the floor, or between two places in the room. How thick is a history book? How long and tall is a great Dane? How wide is the front door at Monticello? Obviously, all these questions may be answered satisfactorily with words and figures; but the answers are more graphic, more easily visualized, when the speaker shows them with his hands.

Often the speaker wants to demonstrate a quantity which cannot be described mathematically. Othello, for example, says, "Look here, Iago, all my fond love thus do I blow to heaven." What does the actor *do* to demonstrate losing *all* his love? One will hold his arms wide and curved as though to reproduce a small world; another will fling his arms into space in despair; another will touch his fingers to his lips and literally blow his love to heaven. The third gesture is a bit too theatrical for the speaker, but the first two are appropriate. Such words as *all, entire, everywhere,* and *everything* are frequently accompanied by the free and open gesture of outstretched arms.

A third demonstrative gesture illustrates ideas set in opposition to each other. With both hands raised slightly above his waist, the speaker says, "This is the condition of the right and this of the left" or "On the one hand we see . . . while on the other we see . . . ." As the words are spoken, the hands, palms up, represent the two sides of the issue; they imply the balance of two ideas or movements. The free world, for example, is balanced with the slave, liberals are balanced with conservatives, the North with the South, or public rights with private rights. And when the speaker wishes to indicate that one side has more weight than the other, he lowers the hand that represents that side and raises the other.

An explanation of all gestures would be impossible and unwise. A century ago teachers of speech and writers of texts described and catalogued all acceptable gestures, but such speech-by-formula is now wisely out of vogue. There are no absolute rules to assure success. Today, teachers coach the student on the use of gesture with caution. They *generally* advise keeping the hands ready to gesture, out of the pockets, away from the back, off the buttons, out of the hair. But for a particular speaker in a particular situation, any of the so-called faults might prove quite human and effective. The speaker is not a machine designed to respond to push-button control; he is human. His gestures do not follow formulas. They arise freely and spontaneously to complement the idea or emotion of the moment.

☐   **FACIAL EXPRESSIONS**

Every face is said to reveal the construction of the mind behind it. Certainly we initially judge people on their facial expressions. When someone's face is slow to respond to a joke, we conclude, "He has no sense of humor" — meaning his mind is incapable of grasping the joke. When a person's face shows no concern for the children in a divorce case, we conclude, "He is callous" — meaning his sensibilities are not affected by the tragedy. Contrarily, a quick smile and a bright eye indicate to us a quick wit and a bright mind. We assume that a face which readily expresses changes in emotion conceals sensitivity and perception.

In the same way, an audience judges a speaker's appearance to a great extent on his facial expressions. They expect his face to reflect the construction of his thought. A speaker should recognize that facial expression does influence audiences; properly keyed facial expression will help them understand, believe, and act on the speaker's proposals.

A speaker may be beset with one of two problems: he may have trouble using his face expressively at all, or he may tend to exaggerate facial expressions to the point of absurdity. Both problems are difficult to combat because we cannot see our own faces when we talk. Without knowing it, our faces may unconsciously reflect misplaced tension, excitement, boredom, or tiredness in a grotesque grimace, or they may be registering no feeling at all. Exaggerated facial expression will alienate an audience; blankness will bore them. But what can we do? We watch for, notice, and correct an out-of-place gesture or bodily movement, but there is no visible or audible signal to tell us when a facial expression is appropriate or not.

The student speaker must depend on the criticism of his instructor and classmates to tell him if his facial expressions do not convey what his words say. When he is aware of his problem and has analyzed it, he can begin solving it. The student who has trouble expressing any emotion with his face will discover and break away from the habits or fears which restrict him; the student who is prone to grimacing will learn to discipline his facial muscles.

A good place to start attacking either problem is in five minutes' concentration on facial expression a day, in ordinary conversation outside the classroom and away from an audience. The student with lazy facial muscles should conscientiously try to reflect in his face the varying moods of the conversation as rapidly as they change. The student with hyperactive facial muscles should try to restrain them, reflecting in his face emotion and reaction appropriate to the conversation. Both students are well-advised to deliver their classroom speeches in front of a mirror before trying them on an audience. The expressionless student will watch for and concentrate on places in his speech where he needs to react facially; the active student will let the mirror tell him when he is going too far and will tone those expressions down. While delivering a speech before the classroom audience, both students should be alert and responsive to audience reaction. The faces of the audience often mirror the speaker's facial expressions. The speaker will be able to tell immediately and conclusively how his appearance is impressing them. Ideally, he will be flexible, adjusting his expressions to the minute-to-minute mood of the audience, the occasion, and the ideas he is presenting.

SUMMARY

1. Physical action should support the speaker's thoughts.
2. The effective speaker must appear direct. He communicates directness through eye-to-eye, person-to-person, and intellect-to-intellect contact.
3. The effective speaker's posture suggests dignity, comfort, energy, and alertness.
4. Movement is used primarily to secure attention and secondarily to: (a) release tension, (b) emphasize a point, (c) indicate progress in thought, (d) establish anticipation, and (e) reveal personality.
5. Gestures, whether emphatic or demonstrative, are used for reasons identical to the reasons for movement. All gestures should arise spontaneously to complement the speaker's ideas.
6. Facial expressions, like movement and gesture, are part of the total speech process and can help to stimulate a favorable audience response.

EXERCISES

1. Observe the physical behavior of other speakers and write a short paper on how action helps or hinders good communica-

tion. Restrict your discussion to any one of the following speaking situations.

    a. Action in conversational speaking. Notice especially how the participants use their hands and arms as well as their faces. Try to draw some valid generalizations.

    b. Action in classroom speaking. Examine the action of your instructors as well as your classmates. Prepare as long a list as possible of actions which are effective and actions which are distracting. Determine whether or not there is any relationship between good vocal action and good physical action.

    c. Action in speech delivered by a well-known lecturer. Study the appearance of the next guest speaker on your campus, or a local minister, priest, or rabbi. To what extent does formality of the speaking occasion change or restrict a speaker's behavior?

2. Observe your own appearance and behavior. Have you, for example, for any of your previous speeches, worn clothing that was not appropriate to your subject or to the classroom situation? Have you appeared without shaving? Without combing your hair? In a dirty shirt, a wrinkled blouse, or a twisted skirt? Do such things matter to your particular audience, or will anything go?

3. Practice your next speech in front of a full-length mirror. (Some speech departments, incidentally, are equipped with mirrored practice rooms so that the student can get a good look at himself, and some classrooms are equipped with a wall-to-wall mirror so that it is impossible for a student to speak unaware of his behavior.) In your room deliver your speech to a mirror. Forget the absurdity of trying to instruct or persuade your own image long enough to practice some strong action — positive, clear-cut movement and definite arm and hand gestures. Intentionally overdo it to help free your body.

4. Get acquainted with your face by standing in front of a mirror and talking to it. When you talk, run the gamut of emotional expression. Tell the image how disappointed you are in what he has accomplished in school; then tell him that he ought to be kicked out of school! Then repent, retract, become penitent, and express your love and admiration for one so erudite as the figure in the glass. Intentionally overwork the muscles in your face. Help yourself learn what your facial expression can say.

5. Practice any one of the following passages until you can enhance its meaning by motion and gesture; then deliver it to your classmates.

a. As we approached the intersection, we noticed a second car approaching from the left. We thought it would stop. The sign was there right before him; he was going slow; there was no reason to believe that he wouldn't stop. Then we noticed a third car coming in from the right. It was unbelievable! All three cars make for a spot in dead center of the intersection. Not one — not one of us — showed the least measure of caution.

b. The law on this point is very clear; there is no reason for confusion. No one can get his new license plates until he has paid his local taxes. The procedure is simple. You pay your tax and get a receipt. You take your receipt to the license bureau, say, "I want my new plates," show the clerk your receipt, and fill out the necessary papers. Nothing could be simpler.

c. Now I'll tell you how *I* feel about this. I'm waiting. I'm waiting until we get angry enough to do something about this. I'm waiting until our civic leaders over in the courthouse become disturbed. I'm waiting until our teachers from Central and Northside and Cathedral decide it's time to act. I'm waiting until the parents of this city become angry enough to *care* what happens to their children. Then we can move! And *all* of us — together — with a single concern will get something done!

d. When you sit in a chair, don't reach out and hang on to it. Don't hold to the sides and lower yourself into the seat. Simply walk over to it, make contact with the back of the leg, then without relying on your arms, sit.

6. In these days of inexpensive home cameras and other photographic equipment, a moving picture of your classroom behavior is not out of the question. Locate a camera; then after

making arrangements on sharing the costs and after deciding on exposure time for each speaker, get a visible record of each speaker's appearance. For those willing to make the effort to do this exercise, there is no better instructional device.

7. Prepare and deliver a four-minute demonstration speech requiring specific physical action. A golfer, for example, might demonstrate two or three principles of a good swing. Other topics might be signals from a baseball manager, a basketball or football official, or a traffic officer.

CHAPTER 10

USING THE VOICE EFFECTIVELY

Our voices normally reflect our feelings and dispositions. In the early morning, for example, before we are fully awake, our voices are often husky, flat, and unexciting. At noon on a day when things are going well, they have a note of lively optimism. Late in the evening, with fatigue setting in, they again grow lifeless and "scratchy." We all have made this observation in our casual study of personalities. Rightly or wrongly, we usually assume that the loud and boisterous man is a bully or an egotist, just as we assume that a soft-spoken and hesitant man is an introvert. Most of us think a speaker who rattles off words without a second's hesitation does not think very deeply, and a speaker who pauses too often and too awkwardly doesn't know what he really wants to say. We base our first impressions of a speaker largely on his voice. Most of us are sensible enough to realize that first judgments are not always correct, but unless a speaker forces us to change our first impressions of him during the course of his speech, we tend to stick to them. A good voice will not only make a good first impression of the speaker's personality, it will heighten the meaning of the speaker's words throughout his speech. There are, for example, many ways to say: "These are the times that try men's souls." An unskilled speaker may say it too fast to be understood, too slowly to be exciting, too highly pitched to be pleasant, or too flippantly to be serious; but the skilled speaker will suit his voice to the thought, giving the words appropriate meaning. He will express their significance by vocal nuance: a contrast in volume, a shift in speed, or a difference in emotional quality. With his voice he will bring the idea to life.

But what kind of voice makes this possible? An ideal speaking voice is forceful, vibrant, warm, rich, flexible, well-modulated, and always artfully controlled. We should all work toward this ideal voice, even though most of us will never achieve it because of our own physical limitations. A second description is more realistic: A good speaking voice reveals the speaker's thoughts and feelings for a particular purpose, as the occasion demands.

■   **THE SPEECH MECHANISM**

Speech, it is said, is an *overlaid function*. This is to say that man, in the process of evolution, superimposed his speech on organs designed primarily for other functions: (a) the entire respiratory system, whose first function is supplying the body with oxygen, and (b) the upper portion of the digestive system, the main functions of which are chewing, sucking, and swallowing. These two systems produce speech by respiration, phonation, resonation, and articulation.

☐   **RESPIRATION**

The air stream is the prime force of speech sounds. During inhalation, the diaphragm, assisted by smaller muscles of the chest and selected muscles of the neck, flattens, relieving its slight pressure on the lungs so that air is free to rush in. (Part of the oxygen is transferred from the air into the blood and on to the countless millions of body cells.) During exhalation, the muscles of the diaphragm and

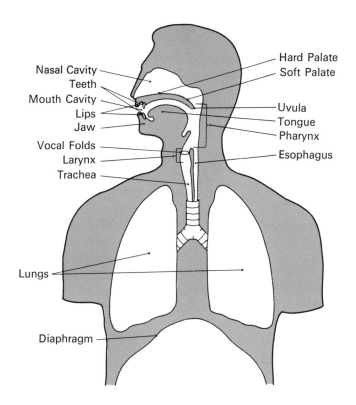

The Speech Mechanism

abdomen, assisted by selected muscles of the back, expand, compressing both the chest and the abdomen. This compression forces the "used" air from the lungs up the *trachea,* or windpipe, into the *larynx* where most voice sounds originate.

☐   **PHONATION**

When the air reaches the *larynx,* or voicebox, a noise or sound may — if we choose — be created. The larynx is a structure of cartilage, muscles, and mucous membrane protected by the "Adam's apple" or thyroid cartilage. At the center of the larynx are *vocal folds (vocal bands* or *vocal cords*), which are caused to vibrate by the exhaled air. It is the vibration of the vocal folds that is responsible for phonation. As we phonate, we contract the folds or cause them to grow tense. The more they are contracted, the thinner they become. The thinner they are, the higher the pitch. The thicker the folds are, the lower the pitch. If they are relaxed, they become widely separated so that only whispered sound is produced.

□   **RESONATION**

The human voice *within* the larynx is hardly recognizable. At this point, it is a noise without quality or identity. Immediately above the larynx, however, and extending as far upward as the nasal area is the *pharynx,* a system of cavities in which the sound resonates. When we engage in the classic *how-now-brown-cow* exercise, we attempt to open the pharynx and also to enlarge the mouth cavity to produce a rich tone. If the exercise is negatively repeated by deliberately constricting the throat and decreasing the oral cavity, the voice sounds "thin," "pinched," and colorless.

□   **ARTICULATION**

The final step in voice production is articulation, the act of shaping sound into recognizable word and idea symbols.

The movements of the soft palate, lower jaw, and especially the lips and tongue change the "hum" of the vocal bands into vowels and consonants. The lips part to form vowels, diphthongs, and such consonants as *d, g, h, k, l.* For consonants like *b* and *p,* the lips are brought together and quickly parted; for *w* and *wh,* for instance, they are brought almost together and then slowly parted; for *f, j, n, r, s, t, v,* they are brought *nearly* together; for *m* they are closed. The tongue is even more facile than the lips. As it moves inside the oral cavity, it constantly changes its shape. For some vowels it is flat in the floor of the mouth; for *ee* and *oo* humped toward the hard palate; for *k* and *g* arched up against the soft palate; for *l, d, n, t* it lightly touches the upper teeth or the alveolar ridge behind them; it is between the teeth for *th.* The soft palate with its uvula moves up slightly for most sounds to close the entrance to the nasal cavity; for the nasal sounds — *m, n, ng,* — the soft palate moves down so that the sound may enter the nasal passage.

The articulators are shapers of sound. They retard, interrupt, glide, blend, and fashion human sounds into word symbols. Effective speech consists of word symbols which are immediately clear, intelligible, and interesting.

The vocal mechanism is frequently compared with musical instruments. The comparison may help to explain the meaning of vibration, resonance, and quality, but it grossly oversimplifies the nature of the human voice. The vocal structure is unique and quite unlike any product of man's making. It is not composed of rubber, brass, and wood; it is composed of muscle, nerve, ligament, and membranous tissue. It is capable of changing its shape with tremendous speed at nearly every point of its structure. The lungs obviously expand and contract, the larynx moves up and down, and the vocal folds often change in less than a tenth of a second and a dozen or more times in a single word. The soft palate may move just as frequently. And when all these movements are added to the movements of the jaw, tongue, teeth, and lips, the total number of changes will reach the thousands in even a brief classroom speech.

■ FOUR CHARACTERISTICS OF VOICE

The human voice, like all other sounds, has four characteristics: loudness, pitch, time, and quality. *Loudness* is determined primarily by the openness of the mouth and throat and by the thrust of air released from the lungs. *Pitch* is the "highness" or "lowness" of sound and is controlled by the vibration of the vocal folds. *Time* is the rate at which the speaker utters words, his rhythm and phrasing, and his use of pauses. *Quality* is the vocal characteristic that makes individual voices recognizable. Many voices may be alike in loudness, pitch, and time, but very few are alike in quality.

It is important for the student to learn the meaning of these four words because they will enable him to be specific as he criticizes the speech of others and as he works for improvement in his own speech. "He sounds peculiar" means almost nothing. When we say, "His vocal quality is peculiar," we are more specific. We are more specific still when we say "The quality of his voice is nasal." We can speak of loudness, pitch, and time in the same way.

☐   **LOUDNESS**

Loudness refers to volume or force — the speaker's ability to make himself heard easily and effectively. We vary the volume of our voices continually. We speak casually to an audience of one person at the moderately quiet level of conversational speech; but as the number of listeners increases or as our emotion mounts, we almost automatically increase our volume. When we are in a small room with no distracting noise we speak quietly, but when we move into a larger room and wish to project our voices over a greater distance and through more distractions, we must, of course, speak louder.

In public speaking, we vary volume within a speech for three reasons. First, variation from the normal speaking volume, either loud or soft, emphasizes words and ideas. All words cannot have equal value. Transitional words that link one idea to another and "preparatory words" leading up to words of significance are generally delivered casually and moderately loud, important words with increased or decreased volume. Second, varying the volume helps to clarify meaning. Consider, for example, a simple word like *gentleman*. We know that the stress, or greatest volume, falls on the first syllable. To stress any other is confusing. In the same way, some words in a sentence are stressed to make a particular meaning apparent. Take the sentence *We must win the race*. In unexcited, unemotional situations we probably would stress the word *win,* because this is the strongest clue to the meaning of the sentence. If we wanted to be emphatic, however, we would grow louder on *we, must,* or *race.* Emphasis on any one of these words adds a note of compulsion to the literal meaning of the others. In very few instances would we stress the word *the,* for it is a simple word and relatively unimportant to the meaning of the sentence. Third, a variety of loudness is essential in maintaining interest. An audience will quickly tire of the speaker whose voice never changes in volume. To be always loud or always soft is to imply that all things are equal. It is important to learn that when everything is equal to everything else, nothing is equal to anything of importance.

LOUDNESS PROBLEMS

From the preceding brief analysis of loudness, we can recognize the obvious problems speakers must conquer to master volume control. In this section let us treat them more pointedly and discuss a few suggestions for improvement.

1. *The volume is too low.* A voice too low to be heard may be caused by poor breathing, poor habits of articulation, or an organic defect in the speech mechanism. If the student suspects the last cause, he should work with the campus speech clinic; but if either of the first two is at work, he can help himself. He can improve his breathing by consciously making sure he has taken plenty of air into his lungs before beginning to speak and by consciously controlling the amount of breath he uses for each word and sentence. He can improve articulation by consciously opening his throat and mouth and projecting words from the front of his mouth, not from his throat or nose.

The number of students whose volume is too low to be heard is small. Simply to be heard, however, is not enough. A speaker must be heard with ease. He must, in addition, have a reserve of volume so that he can raise it or lower it at will.

2. *The volume is too loud.* Loudness must be appropriate to the person speaking and especially to the room. We are stunned by a big, booming voice coming from a mere slip of a girl or by an enormous voice in a small room. Fortunately this problem is usually corrected without difficulty by heeding the reactions of the listeners.

3. *The volume is unvaried.* Unvaried volume is monotonously boring to an audience. In almost every classroom speech there is some variety of loudness, but often the variety is not great enough. Students speak very close to the volume of everyday conversation without ever venturing to the extremes of softness or loudness. This may seem appropriate to informal speaking until we recall that variety is essential to interest, emphasis, and even meaning. The speaker should not be afraid to experiment with variety. Experience and criticism will guide his progress.

4. *The volume is too varied.* A constant effort to adjust to rapid changes of volume can be as fatiguing to an audience as no changes at all. All of us have heard the child "recite" whose voice runs through all the extremes of change; the changes sound artificial, memorized, overly planned. Too frequent emphases in volume are as monotonous as none, and the audience loses the real emphasis. The greatest change should be reserved for the climax. The speaker should build up to it gradually, then raise or lower volume for contrast.

5. *The volume is patterned.* When volume is patterned, stress occurs at roughly the same place in every sentence. Attacking the first word of each sentence is a pattern. Letting the ends of sentences trail off into inaudibility is another. When the speaker's delivery is predictable, when the audience knows in advance at what points he will be loud or weak, he has a volume pattern. Once firmly established, any pattern of speech is difficult to correct. The first step is self-awareness: the speaker must hear the pattern and recognize the effect it has on his listeners. Then, with determination and the guidance of his instructors he can rid himself of the habit.

☐   **PITCH**

We all know that our singing voices will only reach a certain high note. Any note beyond it is out of our "singing range." Just as we have a singing range, varying up to four octaves depending on our skill, we also have a "speaking range" which varies at best only a little more than a single octave; most of us normally use an even narrower range in conversation. An habitually narrow and inflexible pitch range is unfortunate, because of all the characteristics of voice, variety of pitch is probably the most effective in maintaining interest and in revealing subtleties of thought and feeling. Moving easily from word to word, sliding or stepping appropriately from one pitch to another adds artistry, meaning, and feeling to words. This moving from one pitch to another is called inflection.

The downward inflection implies finality, the subtle suggestion that the thought has reached some emphatic conclusion.

My work is done.

It's up to you.

You be the judge.

The rising inflection implies a question, suggesting that the thought is quizzical, undetermined, undecided, *un*final rather than final.

Will it be Smith?

Brown?

Jones?

or Ferrill?

The double inflection or *circumflex* moves both up and down. It carries a feeling of mild surprise or perhaps of sarcasm and irony. It occasionally suggests that the speaker is opposed to some idea or act previously presented.

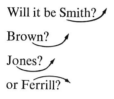

W---e---l---l

S---o

Now, now

A speaker, of course, cannot restrict himself by planning each of his inflections. He cannot afford the time or the awkwardness of asking himself at each sentence whether he needs a rising or falling inflection. Inflection usually follows naturally from the meaning of the words and the sentence.

PITCH PROBLEMS

It is important to be able first to recognize minor pitch problems and then to know how to work towards improvement.

1. *The pitch is too high.* The most useful generalization we can make about the pitch is that it should be appropriate to the speaker's

appearance. We are surprised when a young man sounds more feminine than masculine, or when a large, heavily built man or woman has a very high-pitched voice. Disparity between body size and pitch may be attributable to habit, a structural peculiarity of the larynx, a hormonal imbalance, or even a mother-fixation. If a student's pitch is "clinically" high for one of the last three reasons, he should seek the advice of a speech therapist. The student can correct poor habits in pitch if he can hear them and will consciously work to improve them.

2. *The pitch is too low.* Excessively low pitch can be as distracting as pitch that is too high. Lowness is often associated with a harsh or husky quality and with a generally low level of energy and enthusiasm. The cause may be habit or faulty musculature of the vocal mechanism. Or a speaker may simply be enamored of his lower register; he may think it sounds sexier or like the man from Marlboro country.

3. *The pitch is monotonous.* Pitch is monotonous when (1) the range of inflection is too narrow and unexciting to sustain interest, (2) the contrasts between high and low are not distinct or dramatic, or (3) the speaker's inflection follows a pattern. All of us are acquainted with the "singsong" inflections that frequently accompany the reading of poetry. Speakers often fall prey to this weakness in memorized and recited speeches, and even when the speaker's delivery is extemporaneous we frequently hear the pattern of the "dying" inflection, with each sentence trailing downward into mournfulness. To avoid monotony and increase the likelihood of interest, the speaker must increase contrasts in pitch change and avoid repeating inflectional patterns. Just as a speaker works for variety in all other aspects of speech, he should also work for a variety of inflections.

4. *The pitch is too varied.* Occasionally a speaker *over*-inflects: he uses more contrast than is typical of good speech or appropriate to good drama. The effect is youthful and artificial rather than mature and believable. It usually follows memorization or very careful and undirected rehearsal of speech delivery. Ideally, the speaker should simply expand and project the inflections of good conversation when speaking to a larger audience.

Some pitch problems are easily corrected, but others need special attention. Excessively high, low, or monotonous voices can be the result of psychological or organic causes. If the vocal folds of the larynx are too fleshy, too long, or too thin, or if lazy muscles have never learned to function properly, correction is difficult if not impossible; the student should be referred to his speech clinic where he can receive a thorough diagnosis and individual therapy. On the other hand, if the error is a result of habit or poor instruction it may be corrected by the student himself. He must first hear his error, then perform enough practice drills to correct it. He may need more than the guidance of his instructor; he may need a piano to help him discriminate between his present pitch and a desired pitch. With the help of both, he should certainly be able to solve his own problem.

□   **TIME**

In speech, time refers first to the speaker's *rate* — the number of words delivered per minute. The average rate for most speakers is between 125 and 180 words a minute. A typical speaker will speak at a slower rate when talking on grave or complex subjects. A funeral sermon, for example, is delivered slowly and solemnly, but a speech at a student pep rally is delivered rapidly. An inaugural address is slow and stately, but a campaign speech is full of rush and urgency. A sportscaster who reports the play-by-play action of a baseball game necessarily speaks more slowly than when he reports a blow-by-blow account of a championship boxing event. If the speaker is not typical, his speech is characterized by an extremely slow or fast rate. All of us have friends who are "fast talkers." As long as they speak of gay, exciting, and inconsequential matters, we find the rate appealing; but when they talk about matters of complexity, we wish they would slow down. We also have friends who are "slow talkers." They say everything *very* carefully. A simple "good morning" is uttered with such caution that we feel compelled to look out to see if it *is* a good morning. A good speaker is capable of speaking rapidly or slowly as the occasion and material demand. In a particular speech he might begin slowly in order to allow his audience to become attuned to his voice and personality. When he works into a narrative example, he quickens his rate because he knows that a story cannot drag. When he nears his thesis statement, he slows down again for emphasis. A good speaker adjusts his rate to his thought. He changes his pace often. And the change of pace conveys energy, interest, and emphasis.

The second consideration in the speaker's timing is his *rhythm* and *phrasing*. As we speak normally, our words fall into logical or reasonable groups. If we were to examine more carefully the words on this page, we could say, "Certain words seem to belong together. Here is a phrase, here a clause, and here a sentence." Then if we were to read them aloud, we would not permit a pause to break up the groups we had identified. By way of further example, consider this short sentence: "If you're tired, take a nap." The entire sentence is so short and the thought so casual that many would speak it without a pause at all. We may, for our purpose, call it a logical group of words. If we were to pause after *take,* we would interrupt the rhythm. If we were to pause after *tired,* we might have good rhythm, but we would add seriousness not justified by the words. Good rhythm, then, is an appropriate flow of logically grouped words. When we put these words together without inserting needless pauses, when we indicate the beginnings and endings of groups with brief pauses or inflections, we establish effective rhythm. On the other hand, when we break up those logical groups, they become choppy and difficult to follow. When we insist on hesitating between a verb and its subject, between a verb and its object, between a noun or verb and its modifiers, our speech becomes tedious and unrhythmical.

The third consideration in timing is the *pause.* A pause is not an interval of nothingness, a moment in which the speaker finds his place in his notes, clears his throat, and collects his wits, or a void that must be filled with *and uh's.* A pause is a silent punctuation mark indicating the beginning and ending of thought groups — the vocal equivalent of a comma, a period, an exclamation mark, a question mark, or even a dash. Try reading this paragraph aloud without benefit of pauses, and examine the results. First, it is difficult to do. Our minds want us to stop here and there in order to make the sense clear. Second, if we do succeed in getting through without pausing, we assume a monotone. We have to restrict the pitch and maintain a constant, unvaried volume. Third, and this is the most important observation for the speaker, the rhythm and swing of the language are lost, feeling is absent, and the meaning of the paragraph is much more difficult to grasp. Effective reading and speaking assume an intelligent use of the pause.

The pause is also used for emphasis. The speaker may say, "Now listen to this," and pause to let the audience collect itself before he continues with an emphatic statement. A pause may, of course, follow an emphatic statement or be placed between the statement and a restatement, as though to say, "Think about that. Take time for the idea to impress you." Naturally, the statement must deserve such emphasis. It must be significant enough to be set off by silence. If a speaker uses pauses excessively to make everything he says weighty and significant, he will soon become pedantic and boring.

Finally, the pause helps to create the impression that the speaker is capable of thinking on his feet. Some speakers are lost if they do not memorize a speech or if they do not have a manuscript before them. With the security of memory or manuscript, they never have to pause, never have to struggle for a word, and never have to adjust to audience reaction; but unfortunately they always lack spontaneity. An audience likes to feel that a speech is thought in process, not thoughts that occurred to the speaker when he was writing a manuscript. An audience likes to think that a speech is tailor-made for it on the spot, that the speaker is concerned about the reception of his ideas, and that he can respond to the needs of his listeners on the spur of the moment. The pause helps the speaker achieve this effect. Perhaps he suddenly stops and looks up at the ceiling, but the audience can tell he is trying to find a better way to make his point clear. Perhaps he holds the bridge of his nose with his thumb and forefinger, but the audience knows he is looking for the right word. A dozen similar postures are struck during the pause. They are not errors — or if they are, they are warmly human and forgivable ones, because the audience can see that the speaker is "thinking on his feet" for their benefit.

TIMING PROBLEMS

Inasmuch as the difficulties in timing have already been identified, a summary should be enough here:

1. The rate is too slow.
2. The rate is too rapid.

3. The rate is unvaried.
4. The rhythm is choppy.
5. The pauses have no meaning.

Assuming that all these weaknesses are bad habits, none is particularly difficult to correct. First, the speaker must hear and be able to identify his weakness. He must become convinced that his rate and rhythm, for example, are faulty and make listening more difficult. Second, he must be able to recognize effective rate, rhythm, and pause in the delivery of the accomplished speaker. And third, he must force himself to change accordingly. The difficulty comes in the third step, because few of us want to force ourselves to do anything. The student should try working on the weakness for very short intervals of time during daily conversation. Five or ten minutes a day may suffice. He should read aloud from informal prose to adjust his tongue to the rhythm of our language. He should use a tape recorder to determine if his efforts have been effective. And above all else, he should be well prepared for the classroom speech. Nothing does more to assure slow rate, choppy rhythm, and senseless pauses than poor preparation.

□   QUALITY

Voice quality is difficult to define. When two people sing a note of the same pitch and volume for the same length of time, we can tell two voices are singing. Because the three vocal characteristics of volume, pitch, and timing are constant, we know there must be another that allows us to distinguish between the two voices. That characteristic is called *quality*. We describe the quality of a voice as "pleasant" or "unpleasant," "rich" or "thin," "husky" or "nasal." Every person's voice has an immediately discernible quality that differs from anyone else's.

Quality, like the other vocal attributes, also varies according to the speaker's thought and emotion. He might say, for example, "His rank is second lieutenant" in his most neutral voice. When he says, "This is *rank* and *gross* in nature," his voice might become "darker" or "huskier." The speaker changes the quality of his voice to make the word "rank" and the thought ugly and objectionable. One can say *hate* with normal quality, or in a moment of hysteria he can distort and shout it. One can speak of love conventionally; or in a moment of ecstasy he can allow his voice to be "breathier" with a slight emotional quiver. In both these instances, the speaker changes the quality of his voice for interest and emphasis. Exaggerated contrasts in quality are usually reserved for the oral reader or the actor, but subtle use of theatre speech techniques by the public speaker can be very effective.

QUALITY PROBLEMS

We shall restrict our discussion of quality disorders to the two most common to untrained speakers, *nasality* and *huskiness*. Both are usually the result of poor speaking habits and are usually correctible with effort and practice.

1. *The quality is excessively nasal.* We have already learned from our discussion of speech physiology that the voice assumes its "color" from the structure of the larynx, the pharynx, the oral cavity, and the nasal cavity. We learned, too, that in American speech some nasality is essential in producing the *m, n,* and *ng* sounds. We may add here that even on the *non-nasal* sounds, a small amount of nasality is desirable.

Quality becomes excessively nasal when nasality is distracting, when the speaker sounds noticeably nasal on non-nasal sounds like "ow" as in *cow,* "eh" as in *bed,* "a" as in *cat,* and "i" as in *time.* Though the cause is sometimes traceable to physical problems, it is usually faulty habit. We often do not put enough energy into speech. We develop lazy, "closed" throats. Our lower jaws do not move enough. We have not been taught to hear differences in nasal and non-nasal speech. If the student is sure there is no partial paralysis and no nasal obstruction, he should work to correct nasality by developing a stronger air stream and a more open throat and mouth.

2. *The quality is harsh or husky.* When a speaker's voice is characterized by huskiness or hoarseness, we often say he has a "whiskey" or "gravel" voice. If huskiness is a result of "singer's nodes" (nodules or corns on the vocal ligaments), quality often cannot be improved until they are surgically removed. If the student's voice is chronically husky, he should consult someone at his speech clinic especially trained in speech disorders. If the huskiness is temporary, it is likely

to have been caused by excitement, tension, or vocal strain. When we cheer at an exciting ball game, we frequently "lose our voices." We may do the same after any period of prolonged yelling or at any time we express ourselves with marked intensity of feeling. We cannot remove the excitement or intense emotion from these situations, but we can work for vocal relaxation. It seems contradictory to be both excited and relaxed at the same moment, but this in effect is what a speaker must work for. He may be excited or tense delivering a speech, but the excitement must be controlled to permit good breathing and a composed larynx. He should breathe more deeply, forcing more air through the larynx, while working for clear tone and greater volume.

We may summarize our discussion of the four characteristics of voice by going back to our description of a "good" voice. Early in this chapter we defined a good voice as one used "as the occasion demands." Now that we have an understanding of the four vocal characteristics we can be more specific. *A speaker's voice is good when it is free of vocal faults and when it makes effective use of force, pitch, time, and quality to convey thought and feeling.*

SUMMARY

1. The speaker's voice reflects his personality; a good voice increases audience understanding of his words.
2. The four steps of voice production are: (1) *respiration,* which provides the necessary force; (2) *phonation,* which creates the sound; (3) *resonation,* which adds color and volume; (4) *articulation,* which shapes the sounds into recognizable words.
3. There are four characteristics of voice: *loudness, pitch, time,* and *quality.*
4. Loudness problems include weakness, too much loudness, lack of variation, excessive variation, and habitual patterns.
5. Pitch problems include tones that are too high, too low, monotonous, or extremely varied.
6. Time problems include too slow, too rapid, or unvaried rate; choppy rhythm; and meaningless pauses.

7. Quality disorders most likely to be found in a speech class are nasality and harshness.
8. To acquire a good speaking voice, the student should work to correct each of the problems discussed. Correction generally involves three steps: (1) developing auditory awareness, (2) personal analysis of vocal skill, (3) a planned and intensive program of improvement.

EXERCISES

(The exercises proposed here are not class assignments; they are suggested activities for the student to work on in his own time and at his own rate. His success will be measured by his subsequent classroom speeches.)

1. *Listen critically.*

   a. Examine first the vocal characteristics of conversational speech. Study voices and contrast them when conversation is dull and exciting.

   b. Listen carefully to discriminating speakers, a guest speaker on campus, perhaps, a college lecturer, or a fellow student in a public speaking class. Do they vary loudness, pitch, time, and quality? How is their speech different from yours?

   c. Listen especially to your own speech. Many of us are aware of our vocal errors. We can tell when the voice cracks, when the inflection is peculiar, and when our pitch is not suited to the thought. But we all have weaknesses we haven't detected. Perhaps we think we talk rapidly, but others tell us we are too slow. Perhaps we think our inflection is ideal, but others tell us it is patterned. It is easy to ignore another's personal judgment, but it is hard to ignore the evidence of a recording. Record your practice speeches often — record *every* speech. Listen to yourself objectively. Pat yourself on the back for work well done and get back to work on the obvious errors.

2. *Secure a vocal analysis.* Listening to the oral criticism of your instructor and classmates and using the tape recorder for self-analysis are a good start. On page 259 is a sheet for a written vocal analysis, as well. Distribute a copy to each person who is to analyze you. The results will give you a picture of how you impress others. Repeat the written analysis at a later date to learn whether or not you are improving.

3. *Practice regularly.* Practice is as essential for developing the voice as for any other skill. When you learn to play a violin or a French horn, you practice regularly and intensively. Without practice you would not progress beyond undisciplined squeaks and toots. Your voice needs the same regular attention if you wish to improve your speech.

    a. *Practice in conversation.* If you have a good analysis of your voice, you know what weaknesses to attack. Throw yourself into your conversation. Concentrate in five- or ten-minute periods on trying to vary the rate or widen your range of inflection. Give your weakness regular attention, but don't become a slave to it or so tense about it that you refuse to talk.

    b. *Practice in the classroom.* Naturally, you will practice in public-speaking class, but you can practice during discussions, reports, reviews, or debates in other classes, too. Always be well prepared, and don't be afraid of failing.

    c. *Read aloud every day.* There is no simpler and yet more beneficial exercise than reading aloud all types of material. If you need to improve timing, read aloud with rate, rhythm, and pauses in mind. If you need to increase your volume, read to the far corners of the room, or read above music coming from your radio. Read aloud from a weekly news magazine or from a novel. Read from your history assignment, a book of nursery rhymes, or the editorial page of your local newspaper. Adjust your voice to the meaning of the word and the strangeness of the phrase. And finally, out of respect for your roommate or the landlord, keep these daily sessions brief.

    d. *Speak into a tape recorder.* Use a recorder to measure your progress. Get into the habit of addressing the recorder as though it were an audience of apathetic listen-

VOCAL ANALYSIS

SPEAKER _____ LISTENER _____

TITLE OF SPEECH _____ DATE _____

LOUDNESS	No apparent weakness					Pronounced weakness	
1. Volume too weak	1	2	3	4	5	6	7
2. Volume too loud	1	2	3	4	5	6	7
3. Volume unvaried	1	2	3	4	5	6	7
4. Volume too varied	1	2	3	4	5	6	7
5. Volume varied but patterned	1	2	3	4	5	6	7

PITCH

1. Too high	1	2	3	4	5	6	7
2. Too low	1	2	3	4	5	6	7
3. Unvaried	1	2	3	4	5	6	7
4. Patterned	1	2	3	4	5	6	7
5. Excessively varied	1	2	3	4	5	6	7

TIME

1. Rate too slow	1	2	3	4	5	6	7
2. Rate too fast	1	2	3	4	5	6	7
3. Rate unvaried	1	2	3	4	5	6	7
4. Rhythm (phrasing) choppy	1	2	3	4	5	6	7
5. Pauses meaningless	1	2	3	4	5	6	7

QUALITY

1. Excessively nasal	1	2	3	4	5	6	7
2. Harsh or husky	1	2	3	4	5	6	7
3. Other: _____	1	2	3	4	5	6	7

ers; vary loudness, pitch, time, and quality enough to change apathy into interest. If your speech department has no recorder for student use, think seriously about buying one. Transistor models now sell for as little as twenty dollars; though they will not record your voice with life-like fidelity, they will give you evidence of your vocal variety.

4. *Gain control over your voice through vocal exercises.* On the following pages you will find three exercises for each of the four vocal characteristics. Each is designed to help you recognize your present skill and gain emphasis and variety. One word of warning: Don't work on every weakness at the same time. Follow this plan: (a) choose a single characteristic; (b) repeat the appropriate exercise three times; (c) limit your drill session to a brief but definite number of minutes; and (d) continue daily for three or four weeks.

☐   **EXERCISES FOR LOUDNESS**

1. Read each of the following sentences in a single breath and a firm voice.
   a. This is the house that Jack built.
   b. This is the malt that lay in the house that Jack built.
   c. This is the rat that ate the malt that lay in the house that Jack built.
   d. This is the cat that killed the rat that ate the malt that lay in the house that Jack built.
   e. This is the dog that worried the cat that killed the rat that ate the malt that lay in the house that Jack built.
   f. This is the cow with the crumpled horn that tossed the dog that worried the cat that killed the rat that ate the malt that lay in the house that Jack built.
   g. This is the maiden all forlorn that milked the cow with the crumpled horn that tossed the dog that worried the cat that killed the rat that ate the malt that lay in the house that Jack built.
   h. This is the farmer all tattered and torn that wooed the maiden all forlorn that milked the cow with the crumpled horn that tossed the dog that worried the cat that killed

the rat that ate the malt that lay in the house that Jack built.

i. This is the priest all shaven and shorn that married the farmer all tattered and torn that wooed the maiden all forlorn that milked the cow with the crumpled horn that tossed the dog that worried the cat that killed the rat that ate the malt that lay in the house that Jack built.

2. Stand erect, take a deep breath, then say "ah." Begin softly and gradually increase your volume as your breath is expelled. Repeat the same exercise with "aa," "ee," "o," and "oo."

3. Read the following statements aloud. Make your voice soft and tense on the italicized words, loud on the underlined, and moderate on all others. Repeat until you can do this with ease.

a. It was a perfectly normal evening of guard duty — or so I thought, but midway in my watch I heard something strange. *Something was moving — something out in the brush. I wheeled around to fire;* then I remembered — I was supposed to challenge. So I yelled out, "Who goes there?" And the answer came back, "It's me, and I've been here two hours trying to remember the password!"

b. Now I want to ask one very important question: *What has my opponent actually proposed?* I'll tell you: He has proposed nothing. He has said if the Communists do so and so; if we need to do so and so; if Congress votes so and so; if the people want so and so, then "I would seriously consider it." And that, my friends, is proposing exactly — *nothing.*

c. Now wait! Hold on! We get no place trying to talk through all this noise. (Pause) All right, you go ahead and yell. I'll talk to the front row. *Now, gentlemen of the press, let's begin again.*

☐ **EXERCISES FOR PITCH**

1. Try to discover your pitch range by singing the vowel sound "ah." While holding it, slide to your lowest note possible without straining and to your highest without getting into the

falsetto. Repeat the same exercise by saying (not singing) each of the following words: *Hay, he, high, hoe, who.*

2. Talk with the alphabet. By an appropriate inflection, capture the feeling indicated in parentheses.

    a. A B C   (A question.)
    b. D E F   (Please!)
    c. G H I   (Oh, why not?)
    d. J K L   (Are you quite sure?)
    e. M N   (So be it!)
    f. O   (So that's the way it is.)
    g. P Q R S T   (All right! Have it your way!)
    h. U V   (You think not?)
    i. W X Y Z   (I never want to see you again.)

3. By varying your inflection, read the following sentence in the manner indicated in parentheses.

    a. I couldn't get out of the room. (*Casually*)
    b. I couldn't get out of the room. (*That's why I wasn't here!*)
    c. I couldn't get out of the room. (*Exhausted*)
    d. I couldn't get out of the room. (*Fearfully*)
    e. I couldn't get out of the room. (*Big joke on me*)

☐   **EXERCISES FOR TIMING**

1. To show how rate influences meaning, read each of the following remarks rapidly, then slowly. In what situations would each be appropriate?

    a. I tried to open the window.
    b. Look out.
    c. Goodbye.
    d. Hand me a knife.
    e. Please read the book.
    f. He just crossed the border.
    g. He's an idiot.
    h. Just as I turned from the window, he came into the room.
    i. He took one quick glance about the room to see if I was alone; then he came to the fireplace where I stood.
    j. He stared at me with such intensity I could hardly breathe.

2. Read each of the following sentences several times, each time pausing after a different word. Notice how the meaning and emphasis change.

    a. If that is his answer, we have no hope.
    b. Surely you can see what this means.
    c. He is truly the greatest man alive.
    d. If she were to speak his name, I'd die.

3. Practice reading aloud a three-hundred-word passage from a story which has contrasting moments of excitement until you can demonstrate (a) good change of pace, (b) good phrasing, and (c) dramatic use of the pause.

☐   **EXERCISES FOR QUALITY**

1. Stand erect, take a deep breath, then say "ah." Begin softly and gradually increase your volume. Repeat the exercise several times while trying to relax all the muscles above your waist. As you repeat the "ah," relax and open your mouth and throat. The object is to produce a loud, rich tone free of nasality, thinness, and harshness.

2. Demonstrate the difference between good quality and poor by reading the following statements first in a nasal or harsh voice then in a rich, clear one.

    a. How, now, brown cow.
    b. Roll on, thou deep and dark blue Ocean, roll!
    c. Milton! thou shouldst be living at this hour!
    d. Alone, alone, all, all alone, alone on a wide, wide sea!
    e. Round the rugged rock the ragged rascals ran!

3. Read the following poem. Concentrate on giving richness and resonance to the vowel sounds.

THE "OLD, OLD SONG"

When all the world is young, lad,
And all the trees are green;
And every goose a swan, lad,

And every lass a queen;
Then hey for boot and horse, lad,
    And round the world away;
Young blood must have its course, lad,
    And every dog its day.

When all the world is old, lad,
    And all the trees are brown;
And all the sport is stale, lad,
    And all the wheels run down:
Creep home and take your place there,
    The spent and maim'd among:
God grant you find one face there
    You loved when all was young.

— *Charles Kingsley*

CHAPTER 11

ARTICULATION
AND PRONUNCIATION

Loudness, pitch, time, and quality are only four of the vocal tools for communicating effectively. Good articulation and pronunciation must finish and polish speech.

Articulation refers to the distinctness of speech sounds. If we slur our words, drop final consonants, omit medial sounds, or fail to produce any sound distinctly, we are guilty of misarticulation. *Pronunciation* is similar but somewhat broader in meaning. It refers to the sounds of syllables and to their stress or emphasis within a word. If we sound a syllable incorrectly or if we place the wrong stress on it, we are guilty of mispronunciation. In this chapter we shall use *pronunciation* to mean both articulation and pronunciation.

■ STANDARDS OF PRONUNCIATION

A dictionary is the final authority on pronunciation only if it is up-to-date on the changes in language, if it accurately records the pronunciation most commonly used by the speakers of the language, and if it is published by a reliable firm. A dictionary is not a book of laws; it is a book of observations. It does not legislate how all words *must* be pronounced; it merely records the way words *are* pronounced. When, over a period of years, a pronunciation changes, or when a "minority" pronunciation becomes a "majority" one, a good dictionary will record it as though to say, "This is the way the word is being pronounced at the present time." This is not to say that dictionary editors include only the pronunciation used by *most* people. They may report several pronunciations along with who uses the variants and when — some are used by the majority, some by the minority; some by the educated, some by the uneducated; some in the East, some in the South; some in formal situations, and some in informal or colloquial situations. Obviously, standards of pronunciation vary greatly and legitimately; there is no single standard.

☐   **1. THE STANDARD IMPOSED BY**
                                         GEOGRAPHICAL AREAS

Even the most casual observer of pronunciation has noticed that not all Americans sound alike. Some, probably the majority, pronounce the *r* in the word *park,* but in the East the word may become *pak* and in the South *pah-uk.* Some pronounce the word *fire* like *far,* some say *fi-uhr,* and some *fiuh.* A few pronounce the *t*'s in butter, but the majority say *budder* or *budda.* The students in a public speaking class have ample opportunity to train their ears to geographical speech differences. They usually come from a variety of regions, and of course the nature of the class encourages them to become amateur linguists sensitive to the sounds of words.

A professional linguist is meticulous and painstaking in his study of regional variations. He interviews natives of different localities: the older people whose formal education is limited, the teen-agers, as well as the college-educated cultural and professional leaders. When he has gathered his evidence and drawn his conclusions, he is able to map the dialects most predominant in an area. This kind of map is called a linguistic atlas. The areas of a linguistic atlas of the United States were at one time Standard Eastern, composed largely of the New England states; Standard Southern, including the states of the Confederacy; and General American, including all the remaining states. However, through the research and influence of Hans Kurath of Michigan, Claude Wise of Louisiana, and many others, speech areas are being redefined and renamed. Now some speak of such major dialect areas as Northern, Midland, and Southern, each beginning on the Atlantic seaboard and stretching to the Pacific Coast. Of course, the boundary lines separating these areas are neither straight nor always distinct. They curve northward or southward, ignoring state boundaries and allowing one area to blend or fuse with another. Within each of the three areas there are others — smaller regions and localities distinguished by the ways their people pronounce words.

Each geographical pronunciation standard is appropriate and correct in its own area; consequently, we cannot say that the pronunciation of Indiana is better than the pronunciation of New Jersey or Alabama. The question often arises: "Yes, but don't speech departments try to correct the pronunciation of a boy from Brooklyn or Baton Rouge to 'standard American' speech?" The answer is no. His pronunciation *is* a standard American pronunciation, and for the speaking he does while in college and will do in the immediately foreseeable future, it leads neither to confusion nor misunderstanding. Neither speech teachers nor Huntley or Brinkley themselves are final arbiters of all pronunciation. Furthermore, educating everyone to a single standard of pronunciation would be extremely time-consuming and virtually impossible.

The student from Baton Rouge sounds southern because that is the standard dialect of his region. He does not throw away his pronunciation to adopt the accent of the Bostonian; the student from Boston does not try to "sound better" by talking like George Wallace; nor does the student from Washington State try to sound like Everett Dirksen. Most of us realize that it is best to speak in the English that is natural to us. When we don't, we appear stilted and stuffy, affected and artificial.

☐   **2. THE STANDARD IMPOSED BY THE OCCASION**

Where we are, the people we are with, and what we are trying to accomplish at a given moment will greatly influence our speech. Even as we talk to a stranger at a bus stop (if we venture to speak at all) about a casual and inoffensive subject — the weather, for instance — we make our voices "safe," neutral, unlikely to offend. However, we do pay a certain amount of conscious attention to our pronunciation so that we will appear clear and sensible. In talking with an educated boss who believes in the value of good speech, we try even harder to make a good impression, especially to articulate and pronounce our words clearly. We may even defer to him in matters of pronunciation. The student reserves his best thought, his most polished language, and his clearest diction for the classroom, a teacher for professional meetings with his colleagues.

At home or among close friends, our pronunciation tends to be lazy. We are free of all social tension. We are relaxed and feel no pressure for "correctness," because we know our pronunciation will be neither misunderstood nor misjudged by the people who know us well. Perhaps this laziness is best illustrated by a fictional example. If you read it aloud, you will see that the phonetic spellings are not exaggerations of the way words are pronounced in relaxed situations. Two freshmen are having a conversation:

"Whaya say, Mel! Dgee chet?"
"Yeah. Wher' ya goin'?"
"No place."
"Jew go the dance?"
"Yeah. Jew?"
"Naw. Ya oughta knownat. I'da gone but I dint think mucha the band. Jew like it?"
"Tsaw right. Ass Norman, he went."
"Hey, how 'bout The Lil 500? Y' comin' er not?"
"I dunno."
"Well, seefya kin. I'm goin'. I ast Herman — sozee."
"Betche won't!"
"Betche will. He's gotta girl downair. Sgonna be great, man! Well, skitten late. I gotta go."
"See ya."

Many of us talk like this in conversational speech or in moments of haste. When no social penalty is at stake, we lower our guard, relax our standards, ignore the "pretentiousness" of good diction, and assume a lip-lazy speech. In all honesty we must say that there is *some* good in such pronunciation simply because it is unaffected. It is casual and free of artificiality and pedantry. Each speaker is immediately clear to the other. Both speak as the occasion demands in order to reveal their thoughts and feelings for a particular purpose. But danger lies in becoming so addicted to vocal laziness that we speak this way on all occasions. In the classroom, on the speaker's platform, and on all formal and near-formal occasions, lazy diction is considered crude if not barbarous. It calls attention to the speaker himself and detracts from the meaning of his words.

Though we must beware of slovenly diction, we must remember that it is temporal. Yesterday's slovenliness often becomes today's acceptability. Consider for a moment the word *hundred*. For years teachers of speech have been exhorting the student to pronounce the word exactly as it is written. There has been only one way to say it and that was the correct way — with a strong *d* in the middle followed by an *re,* not an *er.* And the teachers were "supported" by the dictionaries because they, too, listed only the one pronunciation. When we examine *Webster's Third,* however, we find four pronunciations, three of them acceptable in the opinion of the dictionary editors. They are: *hundred,* as the word is spelled; *hunderd,* with the *e* and the *r* reversed; and *hunerd,* with the medial *d* omitted. The fourth pronunciation — *hunert* — is the only one considered dialectal or substandard. Teachers of speech face the same problem with the word *business.* The one pronunciation — *biznes* — seems obvious. *Webster's Third,* however, also admits *bidnes* but indicates that this is said when in haste or in substandard pronunciation. Apparently, we are free to choose whether we want to be "hasty" or substandard. The dictionary is silent on the overly careful pronunciation of that word (*bizanes*) as well as on its very hasty pronunciation (*bines*). Even this limited evidence shows that the standard of acceptability changes. As prominent speakers use more dialectal or substandard pronunciations, as dictionaries begin to record the frequency of the usage, and as teachers follow accordingly, the one-time lazy and slovenly pronunciation may become standard.

Again the question arises, "Why can't we have one single standard for all occasions? Why don't we simply outlaw all substandard pronunciation?" This is easier said than done; it would be like insisting that every male wear a green four-in-hand and every female a hat with a feather in it. People naturally resist conformity.

One wants to have the freedom to wear no tie or a different hat. A speaker wants the chance to relax his diction in an informal situation; at another time, especially if he fears a penalty or has been promised a reward, he wants to be able to be impressive and communicative. He wants to be able to choose the occasions when he will use the slovenly and substandard and the occasions when he will use more formal "standardized" diction.

☐   3. THE STANDARD IMPOSED BY EDUCATION

Just as a speaker's pronunciation may vary according to his geographical area and the occasion on which he speaks, it will also vary according to his education. Here the word "education" means not only the number of years spent in school or degrees earned, but also the extent to which an individual remains conscious of his language when he is out of school: his reading habits, his fondness for sensible conversations with friends, and his general concern for being able to say things well. A speaker's formal education may have stopped with the eighth grade, but because he has worked actively in community affairs with other educated men or is a sensitive reader, he may be as knowledgeable about pronunciation as the man with a Ph.D.

A three-year-old may say, "I wanna quacker," but the five-year-old will say, "I wanna cracker." A four-year-old may run outside to play "Woy Wogers," but a five- or six-year-old will play "Roy Rogers." A child's articulation improves all the time. He is educated by other children and by adults to articulate clearly the words that are important to him. This education may continue for a lifetime, or it may stop at any point where the individual closes himself to learning, whether in or out of school. Language means little and pronunciation less to the student who is not challenged by his language, who dismisses all literature with "I don't get that stuff," reads with "one eye," or makes no attempt to experiment and increase the usefulness of his speech.

The pronunciation standard of the educated is probably closest to a national standard, the one we would consider ideal for everyone. It is usually clear and quickly understood. The educated Southerner, for example, regardless of his locality, is much easier to understand than the uneducated. This principle would prove equally true in

Boston, Brooklyn, or Chicago. Second, there is less variation among educated speakers than among the uneducated. Even the educated speaker has dialect peculiarities, but they are less sharp and less likely to call attention to themselves than the peculiarities of the uneducated. When the peculiarity does distract, the speaker's personality and his role of leadership usually command enough respect from the audience to make the distraction momentary. Third, the standard of the educated is desirable because the educated are most significantly responsible for changes in the old words of our language and for coining new scientific and conceptual terms. The educated, whose language figures very largely in their professional lives, constantly search for the right word, the right pronunciation to make their meaning immediately clear. Occasionally they even reach "down" for the one-time substandard word (*ain't,* for example), use it in the context of the clinically pure pronunciation, and give it a new sense of dignity.

Describing the pronunciation of the educated is troublesome. We could say that educated speakers sound cultured and refined, but this means very little. We could say that they pronounce their words so that they are immediately clear to all people in all localities and on all occasions. This is a reasonably sound generalization, but it is of little benefit to the student struggling to sound educated. We could say that educated speakers tend to (1) form open, clear, and pure vowel sounds; (2) avoid making vowels into diphthongs (combination of vowels) or diphthongs into vowels; (3) articulate consonants clearly; and (4) give "proper" stress to the "right" syllable within each word. Although useful and accurate, this description still leaves many questions unanswered. The problem of pronunciation is that the thousands of exceptions to pronunciation rules necessitate an almost rote learning of words. Each word has its unique pronunciation according to custom, tradition, and general usage. It stands to reason, then, that if one is to adopt the standard of the educated, he must himself *become* educated to the sounds of his language.

☐   **4. THE CORRECT STANDARD**

If the preceding discussion has made its point, we should understand that pronunciation is determined not by any *one* of the three

standards but by all of them combined. The college freshman from
Marietta, Georgia, who speaks unguardedly with his friends in an
informal situation, will sound quite different from the college senior
from St. Paul, Minnesota, who speaks in a formal situation. The two
speakers are different by virtue of their geographical area; they
speak in different social contexts; and they differ with respect to
education. We cannot say, however, that one is "correct" and the
other "incorrect." Both become incorrect *if they are inconsistent in
their speech* — if they (1) speak half the time with yankee pronunciation and the other half with southern; (2) if they are lip-lazy
in formal situations; or (3) if they lapse into barbarisms. There is
little this book can do about the first source of error other than to
admonish the student to be consistent in revealing his cultural background. The two remaining sources of error are discussed in the
section that follows.

■   **IMPROVING PRONUNCIATION**

In working to improve pronunciation, the student's responsibility
is to learn the proper sound and give it the proper stress, remembering
that the geographical area in which he lives determines propriety.

□   **1. AVOID LIP-LAZINESS**

The most common fault of any dialect area is lip-laziness —
mumbling and slurring speech sounds so that words are hardly recognizable. A careless student from New Albany, Indiana, for example,
might hastily introduce himself as "a graduate of *Njamnji* High
School." If the reader sounds out the word created by this strange
spelling, he will recognize several transformations of sounds. First,
the new word has become highly nasalized. Second, several sounds
have been omitted — the sounds of *u, l, b,* and *a*. Third, a four-
syllable combination has been changed to two syllables. Distortions
like these make the identity of the city a mystery to the student's
listeners.

Lip-laziness is not a matter of the lips alone. All the organs of articulation are involved. In the case of the New Albany student, the soft palate or velum was lazy and permitted the vowel sounds to rush up through his nose. His jaw remained fixed and refused to open as he approached the *aw* sound in Albany. Finally, neither his tongue nor his lips moved enough to give the words clarity. In short, all his organs of articulation were getting by with as little effort as possible. To correct this weakness, the student must overcome a habit which for years has characterized his speech. At least three steps of retraining may be required.

a. *Developing an awareness of English sounds.* Three kinds of sounds which characterize our speech are vowels, diphthongs, and consonants. The vowel, of course, is the greatest carrier of sound. It is initiated by vibration in the larynx and changed by the resonating chambers. When it is not combined with other vowels, it is emitted as a pure vowel sound. Examine and practice aloud each of the vowel sounds in the one-syllable words that follow. Pronounce each word; then go over the list several times, sounding out only the vowels.

1. bee	4. bad	7. tall
2. bit	5. bud	8. tube
3. bed	6. top	9. took

When we combine one vowel sound with another and pronounce them as a single sound, we create a diphthong. The word *fire,* for example, has only one vowel *letter* before the *r,* but it has a quick combination of vowel *sounds* called a diphthong. Pronounce each word in the following group of words and analyze the diphthong; then pronounce only the diphthong and in each instance determine which vowel sounds are combined.

1. boy, oil, coin, spoiled, voice.
2. pie, dine, guide, bright, alive.
3. cow, vowel, clown, towel, cloud.
4. so, bone, comb, hole, doze.
5. pay, rake, amaze, paste, awake.

The student will help himself get a "feel" for sounds if he ignores, insofar as possible, the spelling and concentrates on the sounds. Said slowly, the diphthong will become recognizable as two vowels *sounds* — *not* vowel letters. Said rapidly, the diphthongs in 4 and 5 might become pure vowel sounds.

The consonant sounds are created by an interruption of the air stream, deep in the throat, at the back of the tongue, the soft palate, the upper teeth ridge, the teeth, or the lips. When we create the sound *p,* for example, we block the air stream with closed lips, then force the air to explode through them. When we say *t,* we close off the air stream by touching the tongue to the upper teeth ridge, then push the air through. On some sounds the interruption is not a stop so much as a temporary slowing down of the air stream. In the word *five,* for example, we make the *f* and *v* by forcing air through the narrow space between nearly-closed lower lip and upper teeth.

A thorough examination of speech sounds would require a much more intensive study than is appropriate in a text for the public speaker. If the student is a speech major or expects to work with any of the world's languages professionally, he should be much more thorough and scientific in his study. At the very least, he should take a course in phonetics, the science of speech sound.

b. *Developing an awareness of the speech of the educated.* If a student becomes aware of the speech sounds of his language, the chances are he will simultaneously develop an awareness of how people talk. He will notice the substandard speech as well as the standard of his area. He will laugh at certain speech patterns, admire some, and imitate others. It is important to choose the right model for imitation. The advice usually given the student is to pattern his speech on that of the educated leaders in his community. But our society is highly mobile. A young man might attend grade school in Phoenix, boarding school in South Carolina, an undergraduate college in Boston, and a graduate school in Seattle. His years away from Phoenix are certain to have changed his speech, and retraining himself in his Phoenix dialect when he returns there to work would be both artificial and unnecessary. As we indicated earlier, the speech of the educated is widely if not universally understood and accepted — regardless of the home state of the speaker.

The student's first models will probably be his teachers. His second models could very easily be network radio and television announcers and news commentators. The third models will be the student's classmates. And fourth will come other business and professional people — the minister, the doctor, the druggist, and the lawyer. If the student has a critical ear — if he can listen and mentally record and compare the speech of others — he can do much to improve his pronunciation.

    c. *Developing an awareness of personal faults.* At home, the student talked as he pleased and seemed never to suffer. When he asked for something, it was given; when he expressed an opinion, it was understood. His small circle of friends — the people with whom he grew up — understood each other. In college, however, the student often recognizes a need to remove from his speech certain barbarisms established in an earlier day. First, he notices that his teachers sound different from the folks back home. Second, he notices that many of his classmates also sound different — a little sharper, more crisp perhaps, more energetic. Third, he listens to a recording of his speech while his instructor indicates how he distorts certain sounds and omits others, how he substitutes one sound for another or even inserts an extra sound. Such self-awareness is the first step in reaching up to the diction of the educated.

☐   **2. LEARN TO IDENTIFY THE MOST COMMON ERRORS**

    The errors most easily identified and corrected are: (a) substituting one sound for another, (b) omitting a sound, (c) adding a sound, (d) inverting two sounds, and (e) stressing the wrong syllable. Let us look at a few examples of each of these errors.

    a. *Substituting one sound for another.* Sound substitutions are common in the speech of the very young. A child may speak of a *widdle wabbit,* a *wawipop,* or *widdle wed widing hood. School* might be *tool, go* might be *doe,* and *car* might be *tar.* By the time the child reaches adulthood these obvious substitutions are corrected and more subtle ones take place. For example:

har	*for*	hire	kin	*for*	can
arn	*for*	iron	boosh	*for*	bush
aig	*for*	egg	yer	*for*	your
cain't	*for*	can't	pore	*for*	poor
git	*for*	get	excape	*for*	escape

b. *Omitting a sound.* Once we establish a rhythm in our speech, we quite naturally omit certain sounds. When we say "I want to buy a rat trap," the adjacent *t* sounds are assimilated into a single *t* by omitting the one in *want* and the one in *rat*. If we carefully put in every *t* we sound overly precise and unrhythmical. Our speech must move along gracefully without excesses of pedantry, but some elisions are considered substandard, as in the following examples:

bines	for	business	liberry	for	library
hunert	for	hundred	jogaphy	for	geography
fitty	for	fifty	sofmore	for	sophomore
rekanize	for	recognize	liss	for	lists
ass	for	ask	paticaler	for	particular

One has only to listen more carefully to see that these examples are not exaggerated; they and many other omissions will be recognized.

c. *Adding a sound.* A sound added to a word usually results in an extra syllable. Sometimes an addition is caused by faulty habit, sometimes by the desire to be precise. Among the unwanted additions are the underlined sounds in the following words.

idear	for	idea	eriudite	for	erudite
athalete	for	athlete	busaness	for	business
filum	for	film	evary	for	every
moderun	for	modern	corpse	for	corps
umberella	for	umbrella	grievious	for	grievous
medievial	for	medieval	stastistics	for	statistics

Similar errors occur in the effort to pronounce precisely the many words that are not pronounced as they are are spelled, such as *often, vehicle, subtle, victuals, viscount, forecastle, Worcestershire,* and *Wednesday.*

d. *Inverting two sounds.* A fourth common fault is pronouncing sounds in reverse order, as in hund*erd* rather than hund*red*.

prespire	for	perspire	revelant	for	relevant
childern	for	children	burgalry	for	burglary
calvary	for	cavalry	nucular	for	nuclear
larnyx	for	larynx	aggervate	for	aggravate
relator	for	realtor	asteriks	for	asterisk

e. *Stressing the wrong syllable.* The fifth error is caused by improper stress, as in *gar'age* rather than *garage'*. Though *gar'age* is definitely unacceptable in American English, other words are not so easily labeled because they have more than one stress possibility, for instance *research, harass, adult, cigarette,* and *detail.* Examples in which the stress is reasonably fixed in the speech of the educated — at least temporarily — are listed below with their errors.

the·A·ter	*for*	THE·a·ter	gen·u·INE	*for*	GEN·u·ine
GRIM·ace	*for*	gri·MACE	re·SPITE	*for*	RES·pite
PER·fume	*for*	per·FUME	ve·HE·ment	*for*	VE·he·ment
RYE·bald	*for*	RIB·ald	pre·FER·a·ble	*for*	PREF·er·a·ble
ob·STA·cle	*for*	OB·sta·cle	an·ti·THE·sis	*for*	an·TITH·e·sis

Because "acceptable" stress does change over a period of time, the student should check each pronunciation in the latest edition of a reliable dictionary. This advice is equally applicable to all the words selected to illustrate the errors of pronunciation.

☐   **3. USE THE DICTIONARY OFTEN**

Early in this chapter we stated that a dictionary is not a book of laws. The dictionary editors agree that their task is not to "prescribe" but to "describe." No matter how much and how often we emphasize this statement, however, the student will always consider a good dictionary too heavy, too thick, too scientific, and too comprehensive to be anything less than a final authority on pronunciation questions. Whether its editors intend it or not, the dictionary *does* "prescribe." It does give a "body of laws" to the student who is just beginning a study of his speech.

SUMMARY

1. Pronunciation refers to the sounds of our language and to the stress placed upon the syllables of a word.
2. Our pronunciation is determined by (a) our geographical areas, (b) the occasion on which we speak, and (c) the extent of our education.

3. Good pronunciation is that used by the educated speaker who speaks in a manner consistent with his dialect area and with the occasion.
4. To improve his pronunciation, the student should (a) avoid lip-laziness, (b) learn to identify the common pronunciation errors, and (c) make frequent use of the dictionary.
5. To avoid lip-laziness the student should (a) develop an awareness of English sounds, (b) become acquainted with the speech of the educated, and (c) become aware of his personal speech faults.
6. The most common pronunciation faults are substitution, omission, addition, inversion, and misplaced stress.

EXERCISES

1. The following sentences were constructed to help you analyze your ability to articulate each consonant. The first sentence, for example, gives special attention to the *p* sound, the second to *b*, the third to *m*, and so on through the entire list of consonant sounds. As you work over the list, you will also discover the presence of all vowel and diphthong sounds. These sounds, too, should be tested. Finally, you will note that many of the sentences are tongue twisters which should give you the kind of articulation exercise that aids clarity and distinctness. Read each sentence aloud and repeat the exercise once a day for several days. If you meet with a difficulty you cannot correct, consult your instructor.

   a. Please pick a stopping spot.
   b. It is best to bury his noble robe.
   c. Mount the mule and smite the same.
   d. Meanwhile, the white whale whipped like a whirling pinwheel.
   e. We twisted windward and awaited the work of warring weather.
   f. Fickle fate and ruffled pheasants forced a laugh at half my golf.

g. The evil of voodoo vanished from vogue for it gave the slave the raving hives.

h. Thirty-three thirsty atheists drank the worth of the fiftieth fifth.

i. Therefore, neither father nor mother can tithe for brother.

j. It takes ten tea bags to attempt to detect their taste.

k. Deep in depth, I took my spade to dig my hidden hoard.

l. I seldom sleep soundly when I'm missing your kiss.

m. With no zest for zinnias, he raises daisies and tries to please.

n. She shocked the blushing English with a shameful flash of passion.

o. To get a corsage is a measure of pleasure,

p. Charles choked the chirpy chicken in the kitchen just for lunch.

q. Jason staged a wager against the rajah's legions and won the gems and jewels.

r. He had a neat knack for feigning brawn.

s. A pearl from an earl and a palace of gold will lead a lithe lass to leap to the fold.

t. Run with alarm from rude rhyme and crude art.

u. The speaker could hardly talk after eating baked turkey and smoked cod.

v. Gladys gave Gus a granite gargoyle and a big eagle egg.

w. The gang sang to the hanging songbird.

x. The young stallion refused to yield to the usual yoke.

y. He and his handsome cohort hid behind the hunter's hut.

2. Many speakers have difficulty articulating certain combinations of consonants. Practice the following:

a. The soldier's shoulders
b. The longest lists
c. Which white witch
d. Amidst the mists
e. Brisk desk tasks
f. Scribble scrappy scripts
g. The asp's grasps
h. Pests infest feasts
i. Catching much cash
j. Try tree trunks
k. Clean clown cloth
l. Some sing along

3. What error of pronunciation is most likely to be committed in each of the following familiar words? When you are in doubt as to correct pronunciation, use your dictionary.

apron	entered	Mary	room
cache	fish	merry	smile
catch	forgot	picture	spoil
child	height	poem	such
choir	herbs	poor	sure
chimney	indict	power	ten
column	interest	pretty	thyme
coup	length	quay	tired
down	marry	rinse	wash

4. Polysyllabic words are often mispronounced because of improper stress. Check *Webster's Third* to determine stress in the following ten words; then check the same words in *Webster's New World Dictionary*. How do you account for the differences between the two dictionaries?

diminution	infamous
formidable	irrefutable
incomparable	irreparable
indefatigable	oregano
inexplicably	superfluous

5. Listen carefully for an hour or two to conversational speech. Notice the number of sounds which are assimilated or omitted for rhythm or easy articulation. Prepare a list of all those phrases which impress you as being slovenly and substandard. The list might begin with:

"Wanna coke?"	*for*	Want a coke?
"I gotta go."	*for*	I've got to go.
"Lemme lone."	*for*	Let me alone.

6. Prepare a list of words which you commonly hear mispronounced in the speeches delivered in class. What words are most frequently mispronounced? What kind of error, of the five discussed in this chapter, is the most frequent? Which is the most distracting to your audience?

PART FOUR

The Speaker and His Audience

THE ROLE OF THE LISTENER

HELPING THE LISTENER

CHAPTER 12

THE ROLE OF
THE LISTENER

In the preceding chapters we have considered speech from the standpoint of the speaker. We shift our attention now to the listener. A responsible citizen is obliged to listen. He knows that all communication involves a receiver as well as a sender. A writer, for example, must have his readers. A sculptor must have his viewers. And an orchestra or a speaker must have listeners. Without someone to receive the message there is no communication.

■   **THE LISTENING PROCESS**

One kind of listening may be defined simply as *hearing*. We walk down the street and off in the distance we hear a siren. In less than a second we hear an automobile horn. Soon we are overtaken by two young men who apparently are discussing economics. We pass a café and hear the clatter of dishes and the music from a juke box. Later we hear a truck, a cardinal, and a barking dog. We hear all these things but without any specific intent on our part. If the sound is soft, unimpressive, or unassociated with our immediate task, we hear it at a low level of consciousness and soon forget it. If, on the other hand, the sound is sharp, impressive, or closely associated with what we are doing at the moment, we react quickly and remember it perhaps for a lifetime.

A soldier, for instance, *hears* many of his instructors' words in his combat training. Though they are important to his well-being and to the safety of his fellow troops, he hears at a low level of consciousness. The instructors realize this; so to make the lesson impressive, they run him over a combat course, where the lessons take on meaning. There is no mistake about the sound of the machine gun, no error in the soldier's awareness of a land mine, and no doubt about the sounds of diving planes. He learns to react correctly to real sounds. When he finally goes into combat, the lessons stay with him. Obviously, mere verbal training, only partially assimilated, would not have been enough to save his life on the battlefield.

Listening is hearing with intent to interpret. A word or noise heard and forgotten is nothing; but a word or noise heard and interpreted by the listener is meaningful. What is meant by this word *meaningful?* After all, aren't our emotions, prejudices, and biases likely to distort our interpretation? Whose meaning are we talking about — the listener's or the speaker's? We are, of course, talking about both. This is the very nature of communication: (1) the speaker's words reach our ears; (2) we listen first for simple understanding; (3) we evaluate that understanding — our ideas and attitudes in opposition to the speaker's; and (4) we finally react — maybe in silent boredom or maybe in wild applause. The speaker is solely responsible for the first step, but in the remaining steps the speaker and the listener have a joint responsibility.

□   **SOME CAUSES OF POOR LISTENING**

Most people listen to a speaker for the "right" reasons. They generally do not go to hear a lecture or a panel discussion unless they want to; the student usually genuinely wants to learn from his instructors. When listeners are interested to begin with, they need to make no undue effort to listen carefully, and unless they accidentally misinterpret something the speaker says, they generally end up with a fair appraisal of the speaker's meaning. Good listeners have a genuine desire to "tune in" with the speaker; they want to understand him correctly, then accept or reject or hold reservations on his ideas.

But in spite of our efforts to listen and interpret accurately, communication breakdowns often occur. The reason may be a poor speech or a poor speaker, but if the speaker is good and his material well presented, the breakdowns are probably caused by one or more characteristics in the listening habits of the audience.

1. *The listener may be present for the wrong reason,* and his preconceptions may therefore prevent him from listening carefully and interpreting accurately. The listener may be present for social reasons, merely to "see and be seen." He may have found himself trapped into going; perhaps a friend persuaded him against his better judgment. The listener may be expecting entertainment and pleasure rather than mental stimulation and automatically "turn off" when he finds he will have to work at listening and understanding. Each of these poorly motivated, uninterested listeners is likely to receive, interpret, and react to the speaker's message incorrectly. His own inattention and lack of commitment will probably cause a breakdown in communication.

2. *Listeners retain little of the speech content.* Ralph Nichols and others who have investigated the characteristics of listening indicate that even very good listeners cannot retain all that has been spoken. They report that when listeners make a serious effort, they retain about 50 per cent of a speaker's remarks immediately after hearing them and about 25 per cent after a few weeks. No researcher has satisfactorily explained the reason for this. It seems not to be laziness or stupidity, for energetic and bright listeners have been known to miss the point or fail to retain it. If good listeners retain little, poor listeners will obviously retain even less. This, of course, is unfortunate, because if real communication is to take place, the listener should not only hear and react but also retain what he hears. College students, for example, ought to be able to retain instruction beyond the final examination.

3. *Listeners have particular difficulty retaining ideas presented in a brief period of time.* A fleeting remark or a brief speech made "on the run" is much harder to understand than one made more slowly and with more time for reflection. Poor listening is obviously compounded when the listener is expected to retain many ideas presented very quickly and not fully developed. Brief announcements are, therefore, often repeated or followed with the words "Do you understand? Are there any questions?" In the military services, the brief "speech" is preceded by "Now hear this!"

4. *Listeners have difficulty understanding an idea that is implied.* Suggestion and implication are more artistic than direct and explicit remarks, but they are also more elusive. The painter, the musician, and the poet imply in metaphors a certain observation about life. The public speaker, however, is primarily nonmetaphorical and nonsuggestive. When he does choose to suggest or imply, he must be aware of the difficulty for his listeners. And the listeners, on their part, should develop the skill of listening "between the lines" in order to discern the speaker's meaning.

5. *Listeners often have difficulty separating the significant from the insignificant.* Consult any college instructor who has tried to help the failing student or who has examined his student's lecture notes. Instructors are amazed by the substance of their lectures as revealed in the notes of the poor listener. Major points are confused with minor ones, and minor points are confused with the instructor's humorous interludes. The relevant and the irrelevant become confused. In many instances, this difficulty might be corrected by better lectures and improved notetaking, but very often the need is for better listening.

6. *Listeners often have difficulty distinguishing between a principal assertion and its support.* If we turn again to the college student, we may find him outstanding at remembering supporting examples but poor at recalling the assertion for which the examples were supplied. He might remember a joke but forget what the joke illustrated. A prime responsibility for any listener is to record, whether mentally or in writing, the principal statements of the speaker. Once these are identified, their support should fit easily within the speech units (see Chapter 5).

7. *Listeners often fail to distinguish between (a) factual description and nonfactual inference, (b) logical and illogical reasoning, and (c) acceptable and unacceptable evidence.* When both speaker and listener are guilty of these errors, a breakdown in communication is inevitable.

These seven characteristics of poor listening are probably the major ones, although there are many others. *Some audience members,* for example, *deliberately do not pay attention.* They look out the window, chat with their neighbors, read an Ian Fleming thriller, or fall asleep. Their behavior is disturbing and childish but not, perhaps, as serious a problem as the weaknesses of those who *want* to listen well but do so only with difficulty.

One additional symptom has been reserved for the final position in this section, because it is a characteristic of all listeners — good or bad. The listener's attention span is short. As a matter of fact, if we try to concentrate on *any* stimulus, we find our minds darting from it in a very brief period of time. Psychologists estimate average concentration time to be about thirty seconds. Try for a few minutes to concentrate — to think very deeply — about this one word: LEARNING. It is difficult under any circumstances and especially difficult when we are poorly motivated. Our attention wanders; our eyes run on to other words; our intellects say, "How foolish to study a word!"; the word reminds us of other things — perhaps of schoolwork that has to be completed. Attention does not stay fixed on a concept or on a speaker; it wavers and slips into daydreams. This thought lends itself to illustration:

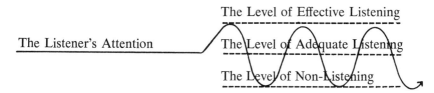

This picture of a normal listener's behavior implies that the speaker should help his audience remove all the dips below the level of adequate listening (one of the major topics in the following chapter). The implication for the listener should be equally apparent. Realizing that his attention is likely to wander, he should make a concerted effort to remove the dips, substantially reduce their number, or avoid dipping so low that he is outside the sphere of communication. To say it more simply, he needs to improve his listening.

■   **IMPROVING LISTENING**

No one can say for certain when poor listening habits are ingrained. No doubt some would insist they are developed very early, perhaps even before the child enters the first grade. Others might insist they are developed slowly throughout the child's education in the public schools. Still others contend that use of the word "habit" in association with the words "poor listening" is an unfortunate choice, implying that the listener *never* listens. This simply is not true; everyone is good at listening to something. The point at issue here is improving listening to the public speaker, or, if we must use the word "habit," *developing* the habit of listening critically to the public speaker. Three suggestions are offered: The listener should (1) *prepare* to listen, (2) listen for *ideas,* and (3) listen to *evaluate.*

☐   **THE LISTENER SHOULD PREPARE TO LISTEN**

We usually assume that the act of preparation belongs to the speaker. He must determine his purpose, gather and arrange his material, and finally deliver it to his audience. But the listener, too, must prepare for effective communication.

1. *By developing wide interests.* Since we listen more easily to things we are interested in, it seems likely that our listening will improve as our interests broaden. But how does one listen interestedly to a critical analysis of *Macbeth* when he "can't stand" Shakespeare? And how can he become engrossed in a lecture on modern art, classical music, or current events if he has disliked these things all his life? If we knew the answers, most of the problems of education would be solved, and the number of college drop-outs would be markedly lowered. We realize that it is impossible to find a listener who considers everything interesting, but no one can afford to be so narrowly selective that he turns a deaf ear to all serious speech. Perhaps it will help to remember that subjects considered boring or uninteresting

may, after all, be matters of great importance. They should be given their chance. Though it takes energy to cast aside long-established dislikes, by the time the listener has become an adult he should be willing to make the effort. He should widen his interests in discussions with his friends, at concerts, lectures, and exhibits, and in his reading.

2. *By conquering inattention.* As indicated earlier, all of us at times are inattentive. All of us have allowed our minds to wander. Maybe the speaker was dull. Perhaps we objected to his point of view or his foreign accent. Maybe we were too tired or too hot to concentrate. Even so, if we are to hear, understand, and remember, we must harden ourselves to a few discomforts and distractions. No one can evaluate a speech sensibly if he has not heard large portions of it. When daydreaming begins, the listener must redouble his efforts to concentrate, to engage his mind again. An occasional review of the main points of the speech, anticipating the speaker's direction, or associating the speaker's ideas with those heard or read elsewhere can help concentration, especially when the speaker is dull and the subject dry. A proving ground for testing these techniques can be found in the classroom, in the large campus auditorium, on radio and television — indeed wherever sobering topics are discussed without the benefit of song and dance.

3. *By understanding that physical effort is necessary.* Too often we make the mistake of assuming that certain activities involve only the head. We assume that seeing, smelling, talking, tasting, hearing, and thinking are head activities, and we concern ourselves little with the rest of the body. But good head activity often depends on physical effort and conditioning. We do not read well, for example, when our body is exhausted and needs sleep. We do not eat well when our body is ill. Likewise we do not listen well when we are hungry or sleepy. The good listener needs to understand and foster the conditions under which he listens best. If he continually falls asleep in his eight o'clock class, he should either avoid eight o'clock classes or get to bed earlier the night before. If he falls asleep when his chin is propped by the heel of his hand or becomes groggy when he slumps in his chair, he needs to adjust his body posture to a position that makes his brain more alert and responsive to the speaker. The effective listener is physically prepared to listen.

☐   **THE LISTENER SHOULD LISTEN FOR IDEAS**

It seems unnecessary to advise the listener to listen for the speaker's ideas, but in the course of communication so many variables are present that ideas may be ignored. Sometimes we listen or refuse to listen to a speaker because of his reputation. We are likely to believe the "good" man even though we do not have a complete understanding of what he says; we turn a deaf ear to the "bad" man. There are times, too, when the speaker's language interferes with grasping an idea. The salesman may "sweet talk" us into buying before we have investigated his assertions or the merits of his product. The highly emotional speaker may alienate us with wild gesticulations and language. Many things in a speaking situation may trigger our long-established prejudices and cause us to refuse to listen.

In our complex society, with many kinds of speakers daily discussing many different problems in many different ways, it is essential for the listener to exercise patience. He must learn to remain composed when the speaker's idea is fired with combustible language or is contrary to his own. Unless the idea is heard and understood, there can be no communication; conversely, when the idea is heard and when communication does take place, something important happens between speaker and listener. There is an exchange of ideas, a modification of ideas, or in certain rare instances, even a reversal of ideas.

But let us assume now that we have schooled ourselves to hear the speaker out in order to receive and understand his ideas. How are we to tell which ones are significant?

1. *Listen for explicitly stated ideas.* Explicitly stated ideas usually come (a) within the first sentence or two of the introduction, (b) immediately after transitions, and (c) are restated in the conclusion. Many speakers will reveal their central ideas early in the speech without reference to interest materials or to the commonplace joke: "Today, class, we shall continue our consideration of the fall of the Roman Empire." Assuming that the speaker is one who sticks to the subject, there should be little doubt as to what kind of material will follow. The speaker will precede explicit statements in the body of the speech with transitions: "Now, we have considered three causes for the Roman decline. Let us finish the hour with the fourth."

Transitions are clues not only to explicit ideas but also to the basic idea and the kind of organization used. They help the listener arrange his thoughts and be prepared for the restatement in the conclusion: "Now, class, we should have a better understanding of the fall of the Roman Empire." The listener should listen for idea guideposts in the introduction, in transitions, and in the conclusion as warnings of explicitly stated ideas.

2. *Listen for implicitly stated ideas.* Not all speakers state their ideas explicitly. Many speakers, in an effort to avoid the cut-and-dried, will *imply* an attitude or idea in a parable or fable (The Prodigal Son, The Lost Sheep, The Fox and the Grapes, for example), in their tone of voice, in a gesture or a movement. Not all effective speakers will restate the idea explicitly in order to increase clarity or avoid the chance of being misunderstood. Consequently, the listener must train his mind to hear beyond and between words if he is to be fully sensitive to the ideas expressed.

3. *Distinguish ideas from significant details.* The listener often needs to ask himself: "What is the speaker's assertion?" or "What is he now trying to prove?" Let us assume that a student speaker states that "final examinations should be abolished." As he continues, he asserts: "Finals are not a satisfactory basis for grading student work." And still later we hear an interesting example of how "a Phi Beta Kappa flunked a final sociology exam" and how "statistical study *proved* that final examinations are unreliable indices of student work." As we look at these isolated bits of the speech in print, the main idea appears clearly separate from the detail which supports it. But if we were *listening* to this speaker, would it appear equally clear? Would we leave the classroom with the impression that the student's basic idea was that examinations don't tell a teacher anything, or that he told a funny story about a straight-A student who flunked an exam? Or are we attentive and discerning enough to realize that the principal assertion was that "final examinations should be abolished"? All the material provided by the speaker in this instance was significant to the development of this point of view, but the listener had to hear all the items in context and conscientiously establish their relationships in his own mind in order to distinguish the principal idea from its significant details.

☐   **THE LISTENER SHOULD LISTEN TO EVALUATE**

As we have indicated, the task of the listeners is very difficult. They must remain awake and alert. They must isolate the precise ideas. Finally and most important, they must *evaluate* to distinguish the charlatan from the expert. To do this the listener must make judgments — often on the spur of the moment.

1. *Listen to evaluate the authority of the speaker.* Who is this speaker? Does he know what he is talking about? Is he better prepared than we? Why is he saying all this? Is there a chance he has some ulterior motive? Does he stand to gain personally from the position he has taken? Is his point of view consistent with the one we heard presented before or with that authoritative book we read last week? These are some of the questions we must answer in evaluating the authority of the speaker.

The reliable authority on any subject is the professional, the specialist, the expert who has studied his subject intensively over a long period of time. If we want to hear a lecture on the first battle at Bull Run, we go to the Civil War historian. If we want to learn about baroque music, we go to the expert in seventeenth century music, and so on. In time, of course, we learn that some "experts" are more reliable than others. We learn that their colleagues have given them awards for outstanding achievements, that their work is widely recognized and highly respected by laymen as well as experts. The acknowledged authority is the speaker most likely to receive our highest evaluation. Not everyone, however, can be an acknowledged authority. The student speaker, for example, has not established a national reputation; so he, like the majority, must borrow supporting material from the recognized authority. And the listener must acknowledge the acceptability of the borrowing.

2. *Listen to evaluate the reasoning of the speaker.* Again there are questions the listener must answer. Does the speaker reason or merely assert that such and such is the case? Is the speaker's reasoning acceptable? Does he stack the cards, indulge in name-calling, resort to glittering generalities, quote half-truths, distort accepted opinion, or oversimplify? Are his examples pertinent? Is he objective and fair in his causal analysis? By way of example, consider the following excerpt:

Do not get the idea that because you earn twenty or twenty-two dollars a day you have graduated from the class of the common man to that of the millionaire. You enjoy this unusual prosperity because of our benign and liberal administration. You do not want to lose the things you have. You do not want to give up your good job. You do not want your children to be unable to go to school. You do not want to give up your home or that wonderful little nest egg you have saved for a rainy day. You want to keep all of these things.

The "reasoning" is not difficult to spot, but we quickly recognize it as nonsense. The main idea is not explicitly stated; it is implied. It seems to say: "You must reelect the present administration, because if you don't you will lose your twenty dollars a day, your good job, your schools, your home, and your savings." The speaker's party is the party of "good times" while the opponent's party is the party of the "bad."

Such errors in reasoning may often occur — sometimes unintentionally and sometimes intentionally — because the speaker is so desperate to accomplish his purpose; consequently, it is necessary for the listener to recognize them. In the following discussion seven common errors in reasoning are identified.

INCONSISTENCY. A speaker is, of course, inconsistent if he presents two contradictory or clashing assertions. For example: "All of us are quite aware that money isn't everything. . . . Now, gentlemen, here is an opportunity to double your present income." The majority of inconsistencies are not this apparent; they are usually disguised or hidden within the complexities of the speech. For this very reason members of the audience must listen closely and critically. They must isolate the speaker's ideas and during the speech periodically reexamine them in relationship to other ideas in order to check the speaker's consistency.

BEGGING THE QUESTION. This fallacy assumes that an assertion has already been proved. For example: "My topic for this morning is how to avoid the evils of Federal aid to education." This remark assumes that Federal aid to education has evils that *should* be avoided. If the speaker knows he is speaking to people who believe as he does, he may be justified in leaving certain assertions unproved. But if the listener does not agree with the truth of that first premise, he should necessarily reject all reasoning based on it.

IGNORING THE QUESTION. Ignoring the question is digressing from the principal argument. One of the most common fallacies is shifting from the argument to a man, thus being guilty of *name-calling*. For example, "I'm against Federal aid to education because it is dangerous. It is one of those power-grab provisions dreamed up by Washingtonian bureaucrats who want to strip the states of all their rights." This statement shifts from the subject "Federal aid to education" to "bureaucrats." The argument is similarly ignored in this statement: "I'm against Federal aid to education because it is expensive. I challenge the proponents of this bill to prove that *any* Federal program is less expensive than state programs." In this instance, the speaker ignores the question by turning it over to someone else. He *shifts the burden of proof.* Some speakers ignore the question without intending to; however, others probably feel there is more to be gained by avoiding the argument than by meeting it head on. Regardless of the reason, the listener must recognize when the real question is not being discussed.

EITHER-OR. Reasoning is often considered unfair or fallacious if a complex of assertions is reduced to a single "either-or" statement. For example: "Now what does all this international hassle boil down to? Just one thing: Either the United States will stand up to any nation in the world, or she won't"! Pronounced with profundity, the statement has the ring of unfaltering patriotism; but, unfortunately, it is a gross oversimplification. The listener should develop the practice of looking with suspicion on any problem or solution reduced to the simple choice of black or white. Between "either" and "or" are the many shades and intensities of gray, the other choices that deserve consideration.

FAULTY ANALOGY. An analogy is considered faulty if it draws conclusions from a comparison of unlike things. For example: "Admiral Dewey, a popular American after the Spanish American War, couldn't make the presidency; so why should we expect Governor Thomas E. Dewey to make it?" The speaker implies without proof that the two Deweys are alike and, therefore, must be alike in their chances of becoming president. The fault is obvious: not all popular Deweys are comparable.

FAULTY CAUSE-EFFECT. There are many possible errors associated with causal reasoning. The speaker may have isolated the wrong cause; he may have discussed the least forceful ones; or he may have failed to establish a relationship between the causes and effects. This last error leads us to a fallacy called *post hoc, ergo propter hoc,* "after this, therefore because of this." For example: "We elected Herbert Hoover president in 1928 and the following year the stock market crashed." The implication is that Hoover *caused* the crash; but history and common sense deny it.

FAULTY GENERALIZATION. A generalization is faulty if there is not enough evidence to support it. This is often called a hasty generalization. For example: "Our next door neighbors bought an electric toothbrush. I tell you, Americans seem to grow lazier every year." It is doubtful that what is true of the neighbors is true of all Americans, and it is equally doubtful that purchase of an electric toothbrush constitutes laziness.

3. *Listen to evaluate the speaker's evidence.* All of us appreciate the speaker who says, "Now let's look at the facts. Let the record speak for itself." We have been taught that the speaker must "prove" his point and that the only way to do so is by sound reasoning supported by forceful evidence. But how shall we test the evidence? How can we guide our judgments? One good way is to ask these questions:

   a. Does the evidence support the speaker's assertion, or is the evidence beside the point?
   b. Is the evidence quoted in full, or has the speaker been very careful to use only those fragments favorable to his point of view?
   c. Does the evidence come from a stated source? Is the source reliable? Or, by contrast, are all sources ignored?
   d. Is the evidence consistent, or is it self-contradictory? Does it contradict common sense or simple human experience? Does it contradict commonly accepted facts?
   e. Can the evidence be further substantiated? Would the evidence hold up if we were to subject it to further tests? Would the evidence hold up if we compared it with evidence from other studies conducted by other experts?

The listener's responsibility in communication is obviously substantial, but he cannot consciously apply all the tests suggested and still be courteous and objective. Listening should not become all exercise and no communication. Some mercy toward the speaker is in order. In time, with experience and maturity, the student listener will learn to analyze and evaluate with relative ease, fairness, and accuracy.

SUMMARY

1. Listening is hearing with intent to interpret. The effective listener receives the words, understands them, evaluates them, and responds to them.
2. Characteristics of poor listening are (1) poor motivation, (2) inability to retain speech content, (3) inability to retain ideas stated briefly, (4) inability to understand implied ideas, (5) inability to distinguish between the significant and the insignificant, (6) difficulty in distinguishing between an assertion and its support, and (7) difficulty in making critical judgments.
3. The listener should prepare to listen (1) by developing wide interests, (2) by conquering inattention, and (3) by exerting some physical effort.
4. The listener should listen for ideas (1) explicitly stated, (2) implied, and (3) as distinguished from supporting details.
5. The listener should listen to evaluate (1) the authority of the speaker, (2) the speaker's reasoning, and (3) the speaker's evidence.

EXERCISES

1. Attend a campus lecture. While you are waiting for the speaker to begin, select a listener to observe during the speech. Make a note of his posture, the number of times he looks away from the speaker, the number of times he talks with the person seated next to him, or perhaps the number of times he yawns. On the basis of his overt behavior try to determine and report on the effectiveness of his listening.

2. Go to hear a guest speaker. Isolate each idea as it is introduced; review the speaker's ideas periodically; and review them again at the conclusion. An hour later, prepare a written outline and compare it with another student outline written after the same instruction.

3. Test your ability to listen by preparing a brief written outline of every student speech for the next assignment. Compare your outlines with the speakers' outlines and with those written by other listeners.

4. Conduct a brief class discussion on the various kinds or classifications of distractions in a public speaking situation. After establishing the major classifications, determine by class vote which classification is worst. Discuss some of the more reasonable ways to avoid that distraction.

5. In each of the following passages there is an error in reasoning. Identify the error and decide how to correct it.

   a. Oh yes, I know. Medical care for the aged sounds good, but look at me! Seventy-six years young, hale, hearty, and without a whimper. I have my own insurance, my own doctor, my own hospital, and I make my future the way every American is supposed to — by free choice and self-reliance.

   b. The most forceful argument for lowering the voting age to eighteen is implied by the provisions of the Selective Service. At eighteen a young man is believed to be man enough to defend his country on the battlefield. He is old enough to risk his life, old enough to kill, and old enough to be entrusted with the safety and well-being of those who remain at home. If he is old enough to do these things he is old enough to make wise and discerning judgments in a voting booth.

   c. Teenagers usually bear the brunt of criticism when it comes to the rising number of automobile accidents, but for the past few weeks I have kept records of the ages of drivers involved in accidents in Delaware County. During this time only 34 per cent of the drivers were under twenty, but 46 per cent were forty or older. This is a difference of 12 per cent. In view of local evidence we must conclude that old drivers are more responsible for accidents than teenagers.

d. I am against the President's program of urban renewal on the simple grounds that it is a waste of money. After spending hundreds of millions to remove the slums and possibly relocate those who live in slums, we will in a few years find new slums. The slum dwellers will go right to their new homes, ignore all housing regulations, ignore all sanitation laws, and rebuild their slums. This is their way of life. The only way to correct slums is to rebuild the people, to help them through education to learn the good way of life, and to effect some kind of change in the heart and mind.

e. Girls are much brighter than boys. Every class valedictorian for the past five years has been a girl. But! A word of caution: Don't drive behind one on the highway.

6. Read the classroom speech below; then answer the questions that follow.

THE EFFECTS OF POVERTY

Most of the world's population are living today under conditions which the average American cannot comprehend. Let me try to picture for you the extreme poverty of one of the world's poor men. His home is a shack or a hut some place in Cambodia or perhaps in Peru. He sleeps and eats with the other members of his large family on a dirt floor. His clothes are little more than rags, and he wears all that he owns. He has no shoes. His water supply is a nearby stream. This is where he bathes and washes his clothes, and this is where he gets his drinking water. He owns no land. He has no work. His diet is, to say the least, poor — a bit of rice or grain, perhaps a fish. He may have heard of a man called a doctor, but it isn't very often that he gets to see one. He is a man who is illiterate, but there are some things that he knows very well. He knows poverty, hunger, and sickness. And he knows that tomorrow or the day after or the day after that, he or one of his family will die of starvation or get lost in an epidemic.

But I don't think I need to elaborate. I think we will all agree that conditions like these do exist; so I'd like to spend the rest of my time in talking about the effect — especially the effect it will have on the remainder of the world.

Just in passing, let me run over one little effect. I call it little, not because it is in reality little, but because the American people tend to make it little. We act so unconcerned about world poverty. This problem doesn't seem to affect many of us in the least. We say, "Keep American dollars in America. We've done enough for the other fellow; now let him help himself. If he is starving, he has nobody to blame but himself." Arguments like these are disturbing to me. I don't see how we Americans can ever live with a peace of mind or a sense of dignity until we reach out to give man as much help as we can.

But if poverty has no effect on our personal conscience it should affect our sense of fear. Communism thrives on the underprivileged. It makes its gains among people who are down and out, hungry and oppressed. And it continues today — in Africa and South America especially. This isn't difficult to understand. These people are looking for a way out. They want a brand new way to live. Oh, we could go in and make pretty speeches about the beauty of democracy, but a speech won't fill an empty stomach. It takes bread and butter. If they have this they'll swear allegiance to any system of government — especially to the government that promises them more and more.

If Communism succeeds in South America, we'll find ourselves in an extremely dangerous situation. To illustrate my reason for alarm, I would like to quote Lenin. Please keep in mind that at the time this was written, Communism existed only in Russia. He wrote: "First we shall conquer Western Europe, then Asia, and then South America. Having done this we will have completed the encirclement of that last bastion of capitalism, the United States of America. We will not have to attack. She will fall like an over-ripe fruit into our hands." Does it sound incredible? Think about it for a moment. Step number one, Western Europe. How about East Germany? Poland? Czechoslovakia? Hungary? Rumania? Bulgaria? All these nations have gone over to Communism since Lenin made his statement. Step number two, Asia. How about China with all her people? North Korea? And how about Laos and North Viet Nam — and possibly South Viet Nam. Now, step number three, the last step in the encirclement of the United States. And we think immediately of Cuba — a base for communizing the countries of South America.

Will this happen? Will South America go, too? The signs are alarming. Student riots against American actions are common. Communist-led mobs feel free to hurl insults at an American vice-

president. The sentiment is there and the potential is there — and
the potential is poverty.

We do have a definite responsibility. We have a moral responsibility to help these people to a better way of life. But we also have
a responsibility to ourselves and our own defense. Poverty is everybody's concern.

QUESTIONS

a. Write a half-page outline of the speaker's ideas.
b. Was the speaker guilty of any error of reasoning?
c. How would you evaluate him as an authority on the subject?
In what ways does he help or hinder his authority?
d. How would you evaluate the speaker's evidence?
e. If you had listened to the speech rather than read it, what would
be your probable reaction?

CHAPTER 13

HELPING
THE LISTENER

   In the preceding chapter the emphasis was on the listener and how he might help himself in the communication process. This chapter is concerned with how the speaker can help the listener. This is not a new idea in this book; on the contrary, it is one of the principal recurring themes. As early as the first chapter we indicated that a breakdown in communication is likely to occur whenever the speaker forgets that it is difficult to listen. And with each succeeding chapter we looked for ways to overcome the difficulty — a clearly determined purpose, a carefully selected subject, and good organization, language, and delivery. Though these do not in themselves assure good listening, they do make listening less difficult. The speaker may further help by adjusting all these speech elements to the disposition of his audience. In this chapter we shall study the listeners from the point of view of the speaker — who they are and what he can do to make them listen.

■   AUDIENCE ANALYSIS

Who are the listeners? The sociologist, the social psychologist, the advertiser, the market analyst, the publicity agent, the propagandist, the leaders of the press, cinema, radio, and television — all are looking for the answer. They resort to many different techniques — individual and group interviews, word association, sentence completion, ink blot tests, role playing, questionnaires, psychoanalysis, hypnosis, and even the lie detector. Likewise, the speaker wants to know his audience; while he has neither the time nor the opportunity to make a scientific analysis, he does have access to audience information that should be useful during speech preparation and delivery. This information should include the general nature of the audience and, more important, the attitudes of the audience toward the speaker and his subject. If the speaker knows these things, he can adapt to them and make listening easier.

☐   THE NATURE OF THE AUDIENCE

Among the most easily acquired pieces of information about an audience are the occasion and location of the speech and the educational level of the audience. In most instances the person who gets in touch with the speaker will be able to give him this information. If he should be inaccurate or misleading — and that does happen — the speaker's only course is to make further adaptations when he arrives on the scene.

1. *Occasion.* Is the meeting celebrating a particular day or event? Is it a regular meeting for a sponsoring organization, or is it special? Is the level of audience interest and enthusiasm likely to be low, or are the members of the audience keyed-up and excited about the possibilities of getting something done? On annual ceremonial occasions and at regular weekly or monthly organizational meetings, interest is usually only moderately high. Whether it ever becomes high or not depends on the speaker. At special or "called" meetings, however, the opposite is usually true. The City Council, for example, may consist of extremely interested citizens who meet regularly to discuss and solve problems of city government. Much of their work

is routine. On selected occasions, however, council members give particular attention to special problems. Perhaps the city has just been inundated by particularly heavy spring rains, and citizens are angered by the water in their basements. They clamor, "Why don't we have storm sewers to carry away the water?" To let the people know why no storm sewers exist and how much it would cost to install them, the council calls an open meeting. On an occasion like this interest is keen; the issue is vital and the meeting unusual. The council does not have to work to get attention.

The implications for the speaker should be apparent. When speaking on regular and routine occasions, the speaker may anticipate courtesy but only moderate interest or even boredom. His task is to jar the listener from his apathy and heighten his enthusiasm. When the occasion is characterized by a high level of excitement, the speaker must either channel that excitement into constructive action or present the audience with the sobering realities that make hasty action impossible.

2. *Location.* Where is the speech to be delivered? In the community auditorium, a church basement, or the private dining room of a hotel? How large is the room? Is it likely to be filled? What about the acoustics? How are the seats arranged? One speaker was asked to address an audience of a high school honor society and their parents. Visualizing an audience of five hundred enthusiastic listeners crowded into the school auditorium, he prepared a finely phrased manuscript on the role of the educated person in modern society. When he arrived, he found the honor students sharing the stage with him and twenty-four parents, brothers, and sisters in the audience. He had to face the auditorium but address his remarks to the students on stage. Undoubtedly, the location had been unwisely selected and the arrangements poorly designed, but there was nothing he could do then to change them or his speech. He would have been better prepared if he had asked about the anticipated attendance and the plan for seating the honored guests.

Another man was asked to be the lay speaker for a July Sunday morning church service. When the day arrived, he was told that the congregation would meet in the basement. There he found the windows open to the traffic noise from the adjoining highway intersection. He learned that he was to stand on a small platform decorated with potted ferns and gold drapery. The listeners were divided into three groups by the steel posts which supported the floor above. Though the speaker had quite naturally anticipated a serious congregation in a quiet sanctuary, the atmosphere was distinctly informal and folksy. His only solution was to surrender to the prevailing mood, come down from the platform, amend the formality of his address as best he could, raise his voice to fight the traffic noise, and try to reach his audience through and around the supporting posts.

3. *Educational level.* By *education* we refer not only to years of schooling and degrees earned but also to the audience's knowledge of the subject. How well are the listeners prepared to grapple with the subject? Some audiences will have the same general level of training and experience. Others will be made up of listeners with varying degrees of competence. Obviously, they present two different kinds of challenge to the speaker.

In speaking to a homogeneous audience, the speaker must adapt to the one apparent educational level. He does not address the American Association of University Professors as though its members were high school sophomores; neither does he speak to the sophomores as though they were professors. In both instances the speaker adjusts his subject, material, and delivery to the audience. He must try not to exceed either limit. If he wishes to appear learned, he may accidentally speak "over their heads." On the other hand, if he underestimates the educational level, he may "talk down" to the audience. Either mistake is almost as bad as making no adaptation at all.

When the audience is heterogeneous, the speaker's problem becomes more complex. If he adapts to the level of the uninformed, he offends the informed by his rehash of old material; if he speaks primarily to the informed, he bewilders the uninformed; if he speaks sometimes to the informed, sometimes to the uninformed, he confuses himself. Theoretically, this seems like an impossible kind of audience. But the speaker can defend any of three philosophical positions: he can speak to the educated, reasoning that they are the ones who "get things done"; he can address himself to the uninformed, hoping, perhaps, to give them material for thought, and reasoning that the informed will take care of themselves; he can strike for the middle, reasoning that the purpose of communication is to make the greatest sense to the greatest number. The course the speaker finally chooses will probably depend on his purpose; he will speak most directly to those who are best able to help him achieve his goal.

☐   **AUDIENCE ATTITUDES**

The word *attitude* refers to the feeling or disposition the listener may have toward the speaker and his subject. Members of an audience may like or dislike a speaker because of something he has said or done on a previous occasion. They may like or dislike the subject because of lifelong biases or preconceptions. From these reactions we may distinguish five basic attitudes, any one of which might characterize the majority of the listeners in the audience.

1. *Apathy.* Every speaker should recognize at the outset of his speech training that he will often be confronted by a disinterested, inattentive, or bored audience. Even the speech class, a normally lively group, will have the blues once in awhile. Audience apathy has many causes: poor hearing, low mentality, fatigue, immaturity, or lack of knowledge vital to the subject being discussed. Even if the audience is not apathetic to begin with, it may become so during the speech if the speaker has not adapted his material to its interests and concerns. A speaker may want to excuse himself with, "It is my business to talk and if they don't choose to listen, that is their loss." This reaction is natural and in part justified. Certainly, the listener should make an effort, but the speaker has his responsibilities, too — among them the obligation to be clear and interesting. If the speaker has a justifiable purpose in speaking, he must change apathy into interest if he hopes to secure a response.

2. *Belief.* The members of a believing audience will convey, "Yes, I'm with you. I've always agreed with you." The listener may believe because he grew up in a society which believes. He may believe because it has been profitable for him to believe, or because he has investigated the matter and arrived at belief rationally. Recognizing belief is important but not so important as knowing what to do when confronted with it. When the speaker attempts to inform an already informed audience, the outcome is likely to be apathy; so he must try to strengthen belief with new information. If the speaker's purpose

is to persuade, he must use logical arguments and skills of delivery that will turn belief into positive action.

3. *Knowledge.* Members of a learned audience not only believe, they know. They have studied and thought about the subject over a long period of time. They know the subject so well that they know where they agree and disagree with one another. Herein lies the challenge to the speaker. He knows that these experts are firmly committed to their own scholarship and that they will yield only with the greatest reluctance. They will tolerate neither ignorance nor presumption in a speaker. The speaker, then, must be just as well prepared as his audience but tactful about displaying his knowledge. He can hardly run the risk of being laughed off the platform for an error, or changing courtesy into hostility with an insult to his audience's knowledge.

4. *Doubt.* The doubter is the pessimist who says, "It's a good idea, but I don't think it'll work." The doubter may be attentive, informed, or interested and still doubt. He may have faith that world peace will one day be a reality but doubt that the UN can accomplish it. He may believe in compulsory health insurance but doubt that Senate Bill X will effect it. When speaking to a group of doubting listeners, the speaker must do his best to determine the nature or cause of the doubt. If the doubt seems to be caused by insufficient knowledge of the subject, the speaker must provide the essential information. On the other hand, if the doubt is well supported by sound information and reasonable logic, the speaker must present sounder and more logical refutation. He should reconstruct the issues and indicate where agreement exists between him and his audience; then he should discuss the areas of disagreement. The speaker may not succeed in changing doubt into belief, but he may make it easier for the next speaker to be heard objectively.

5. *Hostility.* Like the other attitudes briefly described here, hostility has many degrees and kinds. It may be quiet, unspoken, and unactivated; it may be sullen or savage; it may be outspokenly raucous and rowdy. Hostility is not restricted to the political arena or the milling picket line; it is found with even greater frequency at home, in the college classroom, and in the boss's office. The hostile person

presents a particularly difficult challenge because he is actively fighting accepting ideas and courses of action different from his own. The immediate objective for the speaker confronted by a hostile audience is to win a hearing — not necessarily a critical listening but a courteous and quiet hearing. He may have to appeal to their sense of fair play; he may have to rely on humor, even a joke at his own expense; or he may simply have to "wait it out." Once a hearing is secured, the speaker should dwell on areas of agreement so that he and his audience, at least for the moment, can stand on common ground. His objective is not hypocritical likableness; he should not try to ingratiate himself with his audience at any cost. These methods are too easily recognized and too likely to generate even more hostility. It is better for the speaker to acknowledge openly and without apology that honest differences do exist and that his purpose is to discuss them.

As the speaker attempts to analyze each of these audience attitudes, he should bear in mind that there is no such thing as a group mind. Just as people vary in basal metabolism and blood pressure, so they vary in their attitudes. The speaker must recognize that every audience is a mixture of abilities, interests, and attitudes. Among poets there is an expert in insurance. Among novelists there are exceptional mariners. Among musicians there is a superb locksmith. Among audiences of older people there may be young people, and *vice versa*. The speaker deals in probabilities of audience makeup, not certainties. His responsibility is to determine the predominant attitude of his audience and use its implications to help him link his speech to their immediate interests.

☐   **AUDIENCE MOTIVES**

A third way to help the listener is by adapting speech content to audience *motives*. Motives are the drives, needs, and wants which determine human behavior. They vary from person to person, generation to generation, and culture to culture. Though dozens of motives have been identified, undoubtedly many are still not known. For the purposes of the speaker, we shall describe here only a few of the more recognizable ones as they fall into two categories, biological and cultural. The motives within these groups are not mutually exclusive; they overlap and depend on each other.

Biological motives seem to be basic to all people in all times, cultures, and locations. The basic drive of human beings is *self-preservation,* and through it, *perpetuation* of the species. All other drives contribute to this end. Among the lesser biological drives are *eating, drinking, sleeping, protecting ourselves* from pain, danger, and extremes of heat and cold, and *mating* (subsidiary to this are *loving* and *being loved*).

Cultural motives, on the other hand, are learned only after satisfaction of the basic biological needs is assured. We must be educated by the people who make up our immediate society to consider them as needs. We are free to reject or accept them as basic to us as individuals; consequently, not all people in a given culture at a given time consider the same "cultural motives" needs.

Nonetheless, generalizations can be drawn about the motives of most of the people of one culture. Most Americans, for instance, seem to share a hierarchy of cultural motives. An American first wants *freedom* for himself and his neighbor; he believes in his individualism, his rights to dissent, protest, excel, worship, and speak out. When he has freedom, he goes to work for *security;* he believes in maintaining and improving his financial, physiological, emotional, and mental stability. But being secure isn't enough. The American then wants private and public *status;* he is ambitious to be "the best" at something as a way to self-confidence, the approval of his peers, and the reward of tangible luxuries. Achieving status means making *progress:* job advancement, education, social development — even change for change's sake. When his own security, status, and right to progress are ensured, he turns his *sympathy* to the underdog; he works on committees and gives money to help others help themselves.

From these basic cultural motives, we develop a sophisticated and theoretical value system. Americans tend to supplement the six cultural motives above with the needs for rational and moral justifications for action; with a belief in pleasure and laughter; with respect for power and responsibility; and with faith in research into and pursuit of the unknown.

Appealing to motives obviously is the quickest way for any speaker to interest his listeners.   An audience will naturally respond with belief, support, and action if a speaker gives or promises satisfaction of one of their wants.   Look at the five everyday examples below:

1. The saleswoman in the dress department says:

   You look stunning in every dress you've tried on, but that sheath shows off your figure particularly well.

2. The professor in speech class says:

   Good speech is not a social frill; it has very practical value. It will always serve you — help to free you from your frustrations, help to gather the learning you need, help you to earn professional advancement, and help you to serve your society.

3. The legislator says:

   We are not debating wheat and cotton; we are debating jobs for Americans.   We are concerned about income for Americans.   We are concerned with homes, with food, with financial security, with the chance to grow and prosper in a growing and prospering nation.

4. The shop foreman says:

   We had a serious accident in the shop last Friday — and all because a press operator thought shop rules didn't apply to him.   Now don't get careless!   You know the rules!   Stick to them, if not for yourself, then for your kids!

5. The scientist says:

   Following a great deal of formalized observation, we develop what we refer to as a theory.   A theory is a probable explanation of the phenomena we have observed and supported by recorded data.

Four of these examples appeal to human desires and needs.   Only the fifth appeals to no motive at all.   In the first example, the saleswoman appeals through vanity to the customer's sex drive, the need to be attractive to men.   In the second example, the direct appeal is to security with an implied appeal to status; in the third, the legislator appeals to the needs for security, progress, and freedom; the direct appeal in the fourth is to the basic biological motive of self-protection, with an appeal to sympathy for the unprotected thrown in. In the fifth example, the speaker is talking about a theory unrelated to the motives of people. It helps us understand why it is difficult to be interesting when speaking solely to inform, and why most informative speakers work some kind of motive appeal into their speeches.

Many factors will influence the speaker's choice of motive appeal; most of them ought to be obvious. Naturally, a minister in church will not appeal to mercenary motives (he may even deny them); he will appeal to spiritual or sympathy motives instead. A speaker advocating the restoration of a 1740 house will appeal to the security or cultural values motive rather than the progress motive if his audience is a society for preserving historical landmarks. A politician will not appeal to the security motive when he speaks against a bill to standardize a product. He might appeal to the freedom motive instead: standardization means conformity, loss of individuality, no opportunity to choose. Even in the choice of motive appeals, appropriateness to speaker, subject, audience, and occasion is the test.

Reality, honesty, and sincerity are the speaker's criteria in using motive appeals. Threats, obvious flattery, and sentimentality have no place in them and are quickly recognized and rejected by a mature audience. A union leader urging a wage increase can honestly appeal to the progress, security, and sympathy motives of both management and labor if he does not use generalized invective. Management, in its reply, can appeal to the work motive of the employees if it does not threaten an unjustified layoff. A lawyer defending a murderer on the grounds of insanity can legitimately appeal to the freedom and sympathy motives of the jury, if insanity has been reliably and conclusively proven. At no time, however, should the speaker allow himself to be carried away by his appeals. They will serve him only if he is discreet.

■   **WINNING AUDIENCE ATTENTION**

Up to this point we have suggested that the speaker can help the listener by adapting his speech to the general nature of the audience, their attitudes, and their motives. A fourth way to make listening more effective is by winning audience attention through the use of vivid stimuli. *Effective listening varies correspondingly with the strength of the stimulus.* We tend to listen to the louder of two noises. Given two foods to taste, one common and familiar and the other pleasingly different, we choose the new one. There may, of course, be noticeable exceptions to the law, but in general it holds true. Consider the speaker at a weekly luncheon meeting of his service club. As he speaks he is in competition with numerous audible stimuli — the clinking of dishes, the scraping of chairs on the floor, and the rattling of pots and pans in the adjoining kitchen. In addition there are competing visible stimuli — the attractive waitress hurrying from table to table, the club president whispering to the vice-president, and the pigeons strutting outside on the window ledge. Which of these stimuli will command attention? If the speaker is alert to his competition — the noise, the waitress, the pigeons — and properly responsive to the challenge, he will win.

The effective speaker provides a vivid enough stimulus to win attention through all the elements of his speech — material, organization, language, and delivery. Each of these has been discussed at length, of course, in its respective chapter, but let us quickly review them from the standpoint of increasing the interest of the listener.

☐   **ATTENTION THROUGH MATERIAL**

As we have already learned, interesting speeches contain motive appeals; but we run the risks of shallowness and sentimentality if we always refer to freedom, security, status, and the glory of good hard work. There are other elements which can be worked into speeches to bid for the attention of the listener.

1. *Human experience.* It is possible to talk of almost anything scientifically and technically. An atomic scientist, for example, could present theory after theory and be very dull to the layman. His theory does not take on interest until he relates it to the experiences of people, particularly those of his audience. If he illustrates the power of a bomb by the number of deaths one explosion could cause, or atomic energy by the electric power it can generate, or radioactive isotopes by their uses in agriculture and medicine — if, in short, he

can show how atomic research affects people, he will be considerably more interesting.

The student speaker in the classroom often makes the error of speaking only theoretically. He may speak of the United Nations as an abstraction. Or he may speak of surfing as a textbook skill. A good speaker will bring the United Nations to life by showing how it has benefited its member nations or, better yet, how it affects the lives of particular people. Likewise, a speech on surfing attracts more attention if it is illustrated by pictures, live demonstration, or stories from personal experience.

2. *Significance.* How many times do we ask: "Is this material significant? Is it really vital? Does it really matter *to the people who are listening?*" A student speaks of what she hopes to accomplish during a semester of college. Another speaks in the same class on the wisdom of raising the minimum age for a driver's license. The first speaker listed her goals: finishing the research and outline for her thesis, passing the graduate record exam, and improving her cumulative average. The second speaker, however, pointed out that raising the minimum age might decrease accidents, deaths, and insurance rates. Obviously, the significance of the second speech was greater than the first. The first speaker did not relate her material to the well-being of her listeners. The second speaker showed how his proposal would vitally affect his audience.

3. *Conflict and suspense.* In most novels and short stories there is an element of conflict, and we usually find that as the conflict increases, so does suspense; as suspense builds, our attention grows correspondingly greater. When the conflict is great in a sporting event, we become all the more interested in the outcome; but if the opposing forces are poorly matched, conflict is missing and our attention lags.

There is a useful principle here for the speaker. In choosing his subject, he will do well to settle on a controversial issue rather than one on which there is universal agreement. He might also choose a long-established and unchallenged tradition and disagree with it (if he does not disagree merely to attract attention or for the sake of disagreement). If the speaker wishes to review a controversial issue, he can do so most interestingly by showing how the opposing lines of argument clash and come to no clear resolution. And finally, the speaker can almost always support his topic with a dramatic example or anecdote that makes the audience attentive to the outcome.

4. *Novelty.* A novelty is any marked departure from the ordinary. An eight-foot man is a novelty; so is a four-hundred-pound woman. In a speech, an unusual joke, anecdote, example, or twist on an old idea is a novelty. The purpose of novelty is to attract attention to an idea in an original, clever way. Because novelties are fresh and interesting to begin with, they are often adopted by all and sundry and quickly become clichés. Churchill's "blood, toil, tears, and sweat" was a succinct and moving expression in 1940 of what a people at war should expect, but it has been so overworked since that it is no longer novel. Will Rogers' powerful contradictions to established beliefs ("All I know is just what I read in the papers") were sometimes even shockingly irreverent in their day, but they are too universally known and accepted today to be novel. A speaker should stay away from clichéd styles, quotations, examples, and metaphors, unless he can recast them in a novel way. He should be sure that the novel joke, phrase, or example he uses is relevant, appropriate, and indeed new. Novelty for novelty's sake or a joke everyone has heard before will kill interest rather than create it.

5. *Familiarity.* Common points of reference attract audience attention. Listeners like to hear that a speaker knows something about their everyday lives. A speaker could establish rapport with his audience by relating an idea in his speech to a community problem or project, or an experience he has had in their city: a walk down Main Street, a ride on a city bus, or a cup of coffee at a lunch counter.

But certain precautions are in order. A speaker may be "familiar, but by no means vulgar," petty, or trite. He should not use deceit or chicanery to establish a commonality with his audience. Most important, he should remember that reference to the familiar is best used to make the unfamiliar clear and interesting.

☐   **ATTENTION THROUGH ORGANIZATION**

If the speaker's organization is functional, appropriate, and clear, he should have no trouble holding the attention of his audience. A word should be said, however, about "climactic order." Whenever possible, the speaker should organize his materials to begin with his least impressive idea and build up to the most impressive. In this way he injects a small element of suspense — not, of course, the suspense of the theatrical thriller, but suspense enough to make the listener curious about where the speaker's thought is leading.

☐   **ATTENTION THROUGH LANGUAGE**

Language is vivid if it implies action rather than inaction, if it is specific rather than general, colorful rather than drab, and personal rather than impersonal. Dull language is pedantic, overly theoretical, and abstract. It develops one precept or assertion with another, and rarely relies on personal and human experience. Vivid language, however, uses the immediately clear word in a novel way. Vivid language, like vivid material, is charged with conflict, irony, suspense, and humor. Recall for a moment the language of a sportscaster describing an evenly matched boxing event. Almost every word and every sentence tend to heighten the conflict so that those hearing the words over the radio lean forward in their chairs and slug it out with the fighters. Only after the final bell can the listener sit back and relax. The speaker naturally will not use the language of the sportscaster, but he will make his language just as active and colorful.

☐   **ATTENTION THROUGH DELIVERY**

All of us are able to describe uninteresting delivery. Most of us are able to describe adequate, run-of-the-mill delivery. But how can we characterize impressive delivery? Though detailed responses to this question vary, all who write on the subject agree that the details add up to one necessary ingredient — enthusiasm. A speaker *sounds* enthusiastic when he actively varies his loudness, pitch, and rate. A speaker *appears* enthusiastic when he actively moves, gestures, and uses facial expressions to capture the mood and emotion of his words. In short, he plans and cultivates energetic and discriminating use of his voice and body in order to convey the enthusiasm he feels for his subject and to arouse audience interest in it.

SUMMARY

1. To help the listener the speaker should increase interest by (1) adapting his speech to the audience and their attitudes, (2) appealing to motives, and (3) using vivid stimuli.
2. The speaker analyzes the general nature of the audience — the occasion, the location, and the educational level — and adapts his ideas and material to it.
3. The speaker analyzes the audience's attitudes toward himself and his subject and adapts to them. Audience attitudes may be classified as (1) apathetic, (2) believing, (3) learned, (4) doubting, and (5) hostile.
4. The speaker may increase interest by appealing to basic biological and cultural drives. American cultural drives include freedom, security, status, progress, work, and sympathy.
5. The speaker's material may attract audience attention with (1) human experience, (2) significance, (3) conflict and suspense, (4) novelty, and (5) familiarity.
6. The speaker himself may attract attention through (1) clear organization, (2) vivid language, and (3) enthusiastic delivery.

EXERCISES

1. Prepare a two-page written analysis of an audience of which you were a member. If possible, choose a special meeting rather than a regular meeting of a class or organization. In your analysis comment on the location, the distractions, and the probable attitude and makeup of the audience. Comment finally on how the speaker adapted to these circumstances.

2. From a recent issue of *Vital Speeches* choose one speech which you consider dull and a second which you consider interesting. Compare the two in a brief report.

3. Advertisers frequently rely on the motive appeals discussed in this chapter. Select five full-page magazine advertisements and analyze the basic appeals in them in a two-minute speech. When

all these short speeches have been delivered, determine the appeals most frequently used.

4. Prepare a list of motive appeals which you believe are at work in the academic and social behavior of college students.

5. Divide the class into three groups. The speakers of one group should address the audience as though it were apathetic. Speakers of the second group should speak to learned listeners and the third group to hostile listeners.

6. Read the following student speech and answer the questions at the end.

EDUCATION IN THE SMALL SCHOOL

Three days ago we heard a speech on the merits of the small county school. At that time we were asked to believe that small classes resulted in more intensive education. We were told that there was more attention to the individual, more free discussion, and more opportunity to exhaust an idea. My apologies, but I'm afraid I have to disagree. I don't want to be considered narrow-minded on the subject; so let me say first, especially to Miss Arnold, that I know there are — there must be — some very good small schools. But these, if my experience means anything, are the exceptions rather than the rule. The rule, in my opinion, is that small schools are not doing their job; and as a result, hundreds of thousands of students across the country are being deprived of a good high school education. This is the problem I want to talk about this morning.

Maybe you've already guessed that I come from a small school. I graduated in a class of thirteen. So far I haven't found anyone whose graduating class was smaller, and I'm not exactly proud of this distinction. When I came to college I was not prepared. I had never written a theme, never been introduced to the meaning of a term paper. When I got into English 232, I discovered that most of the students had already read *Oedipus, The Odyssey* and *The Scarlet Letter,* but I'd never heard of a single one of them. When I was a high school junior I had the same teacher for history and government. He was absent almost the entire year. When he was

there, he would talk about basketball during the class period. When
he was absent the principal would step in or he would appoint a
class member to preside. I got very little out of this kind of instruction.

I majored in vocational agriculture, and I think it's safe to say
that in my last two years we didn't refer to our books over a dozen
times. Most of the time the instructor would come to class, take attendance, and leave. Of course, he stayed long enough to divide us
into three small groups and tell us to sit in the corners and have
buzz sessions or discussions about agricultural problems. But, as you
might easily imagine, our minds were pretty far from agriculture.

So you probably think, "But this is just one example. This doesn't
make a rule." True. My experience only goes to show how bad a
school *can* get. I realized I needed more evidence; so I went through
some of the educational periodicals over in the library to see what
some of the experts had to say on the subject. I found what I was
looking for. Just listen to some of this evidence. The White House
Conference on Education says that an efficient high school needs a
minimum of three hundred pupils with seventy-five in each grade.
And this is supported by the Commission on School District Re-
organization of the American Association of School Administrators.
They say that a high school needs to have a graduating class of at
least one hundred students if it is to provide satisfactory education
for all. Now keep this in mind: To provide satisfactory education
we need a minimum of three to four hundred students. Do you
know how many schools in the nation are under this figure? According to the most recent figures, more than half of all our high
schools have less than two hundred students. But this isn't all. This
isn't the alarming part. There are approximately two thousand
schools that have fewer than fifty students. As one administrator
summed up the meaning of these figures, one out of every three
students attends a school in which the chances are slim that he can
get a satisfactory education.

This is the status of small schools. We know that there are many
of them and we know that they cannot offer a satisfactory education. But why? Why is the small school inadequate? I'm sure you
realize how foolish it is to try to discuss all the factors of population
and taxation and school finance; so I'll try only to refer to those
things that come into direct contact with the student. These are the
things he knows most about.

In the first place, the curriculum is nothing more than a skeleton.

There is a very limited number of courses offered. Most of these small schools — probably for reasons of finance — offer only the state requirements. In my school there was not a single elective — not even one foreign language taught. And, as you might have guessed earlier, when the courses are offered the instructional facilities are poor. There are no science labs; and libraries, which should be the backbone of any educational institution, are in the same sad state. The library in my school consisted of two sets of encyclopedias and a half dozen reference books. That was it.

In the second place — and this I think is the main thing — most small schools have unqualified teachers. This may not be a fair statement; but as a general rule they simply can't offer enough money to attract the better teachers. As a consequence, the school hires older teachers or beginning teachers who use the small school as a stepping stone to better jobs. The faculty is always fluid, forever changing, and never permanent enough to develop any long-term goals.

But there is a third factor and this also applies to the teachers. Maybe you can tell that I believe the teacher is most to blame. I believe that a truly good teacher can accomplish wonders, and I believe he can do it without much help from laboratories or movie projectors. But he has to have some skill and he has to have the right attitude. As I look back on my teachers I have to admit that some were well qualified, but I can't forget their attitude. They seemed to be saying, "Oh what's the use. Nothing really matters." Then they would appear to go through the motions of teaching in order to work up to the day the Township Trustee would bring the checks around. You could almost hear the faculty saying, "Well, here's a bunch of country kids. They'll never go to college. Why spend any extra effort on them?" I think this is a very sad thing.

So far I have tried to describe the status of education in the small school and, secondly, I have taken a quick glance at some of the causes. Now let's talk about the effects.

Think about the obvious effect on the student. How can anyone estimate the extent of his loss? Oh, there are the obvious things: He won't get a good job; he'll be an unskilled worker; he might become a drop-out; he won't earn as much money; he won't do well in college and so forth. These are the obvious things. I feel that if a student isn't given an adequate education — or better yet, a good education — he will never find out who he is. He will never be challenged to discover his own potential, to learn what he could accomplish if he had been given the chance. And the effect poor education has on society is just as important. We are living in a world which is full of problems. Many of us in this class say we can't find enough good problems to satisfy the instructor, but if there is anything we have too much of, it's problems. And when society looks around for a solution, it will find it most easily through education. It takes a well-educated man to preside over a court or to run a city or determine the affairs of state. When we are without the educational system which will give us an educated citizenry, we cheat ourselves and cheapen our society.

I'd like, in closing, to make a special appeal this morning and I make it because all of us are very deeply involved in this problem. In two or three years some of you will begin teaching. There is a strong possibility that you will begin in a small school; and if so, I would ask you to keep this in mind: That little country kid needs your help. He goes to a small school with a poor curriculum and poor facilities. No one can afford to give him a poor teacher.

QUESTIONS

a. Is it apparent that the speaker had analyzed his classroom audience?

b. What indications can you find that the speaker was adapting to his audience?

c. What motive appeals are apparent in his content?

d. Would you consider the content, organization, and language vivid? In what respects does the speaker fail and succeed?

e. Analyze the speech from the standpoint of attention-getting content. Which of the five techniques discussed in this chapter are used most extensively?

PART FIVE

Speaking in Groups

GROUP DISCUSSIONS

INTRODUCTION TO PARLIAMENTARY PROCEDURE

CHAPTER 14

GROUP
DISCUSSIONS

In almost every American classroom, conference of American business and industry, or important meeting of American labor, sooner or later someone will raise a hand as though to say, "Wait a minute, I have something that needs to be heard." Such action introduces us to a kind of communication which captivated the great teachers of ancient Athens and continues to fascinate us today — *discussion*. In this speech situation, we want to know what the listener feels, what he needs, and what he knows. We want to share our best thinking so that we may arrive at conclusions which are mutually satisfactory to the majority concerned. To accomplish this we must encourage the listener to become a talker. We must meet with him in deliberative and cooperative groups so that we may reason and talk together in order to inform, persuade, and even entertain.

The types of group speaking we shall treat in this chapter are (1) informal discussion, (2) panel, (3) symposium, (4) debate, and (5) forum. A sixth form, parliamentary procedure, we shall reserve for the last chapter.

■   INFORMAL DISCUSSION

Whenever a small group of four to eight or ten people meet to reason and talk with one another under the direction of a leader, we have what is called informal discussion. Such groups are numerous in our college communities. They frequently take the shape of special committees appointed by fraternities and sororities, study groups or policy groups within the student governing board, the religious council, or the staff of the campus newspaper. We surely have met in small groups with "the Prof," who directed our thinking and talking on other subjects.

Anyone who has ever participated in such group discussion has, at some time or other, declared the outcome a failure. What makes a discussion fruitful or a waste of time?

☐   DISCUSSIONS: FAILURES AND REMEDIES

1. *Informal discussions often fail because of a misconception about the nature of discussion.* Discussion is not a simple, undirected, purposeless conversation. It is not another name for a "bull session." Nor is it a tightly structured, formalized meeting in which everyone raises his hand to recite or tries to make motions. No one calls for a hasty vote in a determination to "win."

On the contrary, informal discussion is (a) directed by a leader, (b) with serious intent, (c) to achieve purposeful ends, (d) through cooperative speech.

2. *Informal discussions often fail because of apathy.* If the participants are apathetic — have little interest in the topic or have no equity or concern in the outcome — they will not strive to make the discussion successful. Coercion may lead to apathy: if, within our classrooms, our businesses, or our industries, the teacher-boss-director says, "Everyone *will* discuss this next Friday," we are not likely to discuss it with enthusiasm. Apathy may arise from hopelessness: if a decision made by the group cannot or will not be implemented, if we discuss after a decision has already been made by another person or group, we are likely to say, "What's the use?" The best discussions

grow quite naturally out of the needs of the participants. We talk best about our own beliefs, poorest about someone else's. We reason best when there is a chance our decisions will be put into effect and when we are held responsible for them.

3. *Informal discussions often fail because of personality factors.* One participant may be "slow of speech" because he is afraid he will hurt someone's feelings or will appear childish or foolish. Another may be aggressive, positive, dedicated to forging ahead in order to "get things done." He seems to have everything worked out. Neither timid nor unreasonably aggressive, the ideal participant assumes his fair share of the discussion and helps others assume theirs.

4. *Informal discussions often fail because of poor leadership.* Leaders come in assorted sizes and dispositions — ranging from extreme, undirected permissiveness to extreme, tightly-controlled authoritarianism. Neither of these is a really capable leader; yet there are also many in between who do not know how to help people cooperatively. There are few "natural" leaders who know how to guide a discussion, and the qualities that make up a good leader are indefinable. This much can be said: a good leader calls forth the best in each participant. He plans a discussion carefully, sees that all points are presented, and keeps the group's attention on the discussion. Through his direction the group arrives at the solution or understanding of problems.

5. *Informal discussions often fail because of lack of purpose.* Because group deliberation is considered an essential need of a free society, discussions often become ends in themselves. We frequently discuss merely to discuss — without knowing what we want˜or the direction in which we should progress, without information, or without a determination to stick to the point. Discussions then become a kind of convenient entertainment so that busy men and women can pride themselves on being "democratic."

Joint purposelessness — whether in education, business, industry, or politics — should never pass as democratic behavior. If discussion is democratic, it seeks understanding of people and issues. It seeks meaningful answers to questions important to the people who are doing the talking.

☐   **SELECTING AND PHRASING**
                                               THE DISCUSSION QUESTION

The first requisite for any effective discussion is selecting and phrasing a subject which members of a group may pursue with interest and profit. To accomplish this, several points must be kept in mind.

1. *Select a subject growing out of experienced difficulties.* Consider the family, for example. Things go along normally for a time, but one evening at dinner Father says, "This family hardly seems a family any more. Mother is busy with the Auxiliary. Jill has her Cheering Block, her dance club, her art work for the yearbook. With Mike, day and night it's basketball. And for me, there seems to be nothing but trips out of town. Let's try to get back to being a family again. What do you say? How can we do it?" Here the father voices a problem he believes to be of mutual concern, and he invites the others to join in solving it.

The story repeats itself many times daily in our communities. The public school administrators experience similar difficulties in working with civic officials, teachers, and pupils. Civic officials experience difficulties in working to improve traffic conditions, check juvenile delinquency, or plan community expansion. The chairman of the board, the owner of the small business, the president of the lodge — all experience difficulties and seek satisfactory answers. When we can sense our difficulties or phrase our needs, we are in a position to select a subject for profitable discussion.

2. *Phrase the subject in the form of a question.* The father asks, "What can we do to become a family again?" The high school principal asks, "Should we continue our present support of high school basketball?" The Chairman of the City Council asks, "What can we do to improve our city streets?" A question seeks answers of many kinds without suggesting that *one* answer should be presented and subsequently discussed. The question avoids the suggestion that there are only two answers — "for" and "against" — and admits the possibility and the desire that an answer may arise from the group deliberation which never once occurred to the participants individually.

3. *Phrase the question unemotionally.* In our everyday lives we

often emotionalize our difficulties. We say, for instance, "Who was the wise guy who said Anthropology C120 was a snap?" "What are we going to do with those left-wing kooks?" As we noted earlier, few of us want to be without emotional language — it is colorful, interesting, thought-provoking, and often delightfully humorous. And occasionally it is the very kind of language that goads us into progressive action. Yet for serious discussion, a topic should be phrased in words that are free of bias, words that speak clearly without flying the "red flag" of supercharged emotion.

4. *Phrase the question in terms that are easily understood.* When we engage in purposeful discussion, we are interested in arriving at understandings and solving problems. We hope for results. Consequently, if we get lost in a maze of vague and ambiguous words, we have to spend an inordinate amount of time on definitions. This means correspondingly less time on precise answers to the question. For example, consider the following questions:

"Has the sun really set on the British Empire?" This is an interesting question, one that might be pleasant to discuss at an idle moment in the coffee shop. But because of the metaphor, it belongs more to the poet than to the reflective thinker. Does the question ask if England has lost some colonies, or does it say that England is no longer a powerful nation?

"Should a college seeking to give meaningful experiences to its students adopt a policy of selective admission or a policy of selective retention"? This question obviously is longer than necessary. The whole phrase "seeking . . . students" is unnecessary, and the words "meaningful experience" are vague and virtually useless. Furthermore, the question limits the discussion to the two possible policies, neither of which makes sense apart from specific proposals for action.

"Does progressive education better prepare the student to live productively in contemporary society?" In such a question, "progressive education" is a nebulous term. "Better," of course, is useless until we know what "good's" are being compared. "Productively" seems to have an agreed-upon meaning, but once discussion begins we soon learn that the term is slippery and has many subjective meanings.

In summary, and recalling in reverse order, *a good subject for discussion should be a clear and unemotional question arising from the experienced difficulties of the discussants.*

In examining the discussion question, the student will find two procedures quite useful: analyzing the question in terms of *immediate goals,* then approaching the goals *logically* and *systematically.*

Once a question has been phrased, we want first to know: "Where are we headed? In which direction must we travel? What is our objective?" Admittedly, as we suggested earlier, there are times when the goal is merely to listen to the boss, to provide a "space filler" for a conference or convention, or to break the ice and become acquainted with others. If this *is* the goal, our task is simple. We need only to learn to say, "Yes, sir, B. J.," or draw on our supply of verbal social courtesies. When we are truly approaching serious group discussion, we may define our goals as finding satisfactory answers to questions of (1) fact, (2) value, or (3) policy.

1. *The question of fact is concerned with a search for the probable truth in a particular situation.* In the 1960 Presidential Campaign, for example, the two candidates were in effect asking the question, "What is the present status of United States prestige in foreign countries?" or "Has United States prestige declined in the past eight years?" Approaching the second of these as a discussion question, we cannot remain satisfied with a simple "yes" or "no." We discuss it at greater length — objectively, fairly — adding factually descriptive materials to help us complete an analysis. It should be appaient that some questions of fact are not discussable. "What is Mickey Mantle's lifetime batting average?" "Does Emily Post say it is permissible to eat fried chicken with the fingers?" "Who won the 1960 Summer Olympics?" These "facts" are matters of record, fixed and unchanging, and it is pointless to subject them to extended analytical discussion.

2. *The question of value seeks to discover or appraise merits.* College students are constantly asking, "What *value* is there in an economics course?" or "Is it worth it to enter graduate school right after graduation?" Weekly and monthly magazines print articles with such titles as "How shall we evaluate the last Congress?" "How shall we appraise the platforms of the opposing parties?" or "How may we

best measure the nature and effectiveness of the Johnson administration?" Such questions do not seek to describe or discern fact; rather, they seek to estimate the value of the thing or event in question. When the question is answered in a discussion, we conceivably have an enumerated list of values as well as an estimate of the weight of each — as arrived at by the deliberative efforts of the group.

3. *The question of policy seeks to discover or propose a course of action.* It often implies that the status quo is not good enough — that the future could be better if we followed a different course of action. The key words are "Should we . . . ." "Should we provide medical care for the aged?" "Should we extend Federal aid to education?" Note that for these two questions we limit our discussion to particular recommendations, while for the following two there may be any number of possible policies: "What should be our policy toward Cuba?" "What should be our attitude toward the Communist bloc?"

In our brief analysis of the three goals of conventional discussion questions, we have referred to questions faced by presidential candidates. It should be pointed out with emphasis that the goal-seeking procedures of the candidates are not the same as those of discussion participants. Candidates debate; discussants discuss. Candidates seek to win through persuasion; discussants seek to understand through reflective deliberation. Candidates are committed to a single course of action; discussants are committed to openness of consideration. By no means should this be construed as unfavorable to the candidate. On the contrary, his decisions and the bases of his argument may have been reached through the methods of group discussion. Often debate, argumentation, and persuasion are the end results of reflective deliberation.

Having investigated the three immediate goals of questions for discussion, we must ask: What is the most satisfactory method of arriving at those goals?

☐   **THE LOGICAL DEVELOPMENT OF DISCUSSION**

We attempt to solve our difficulties in many ways:

The *defeatist* accepts problems as his lot: "Yes, the situation is bad, but what can I do about it? Once I get adjusted it will no longer hurt."

The *optimist* dreams them away: "Never fret. Things always get better, and they'll get better again."

The *misanthrope* retreats from them: "The world has gone to the dogs. I'm leaving for a hermit's cave."

The *mystic* rises above them: "Troubles, yes, but the spirit will come through."

The *pseudo-democrat* transfers them: "I'm sending a letter to my Congressman about that."

It takes no more than a hasty glance to realize that such actions do not solve problems; they are refusals to face them, think about them, and do something with them.

The classic "pattern" or procedure to use in problem solving was formulated by John Dewey at the turn of the century. Dewey indicated that there were five necessary steps in an act of "reflective thinking":

1. Becoming aware of a difficulty or problem
2. Describing and defining the problem
3. Considering possible solutions
4. Selecting the best solution
5. Testing the solution by action

Virtually all thinking progresses through these five steps. First, a stimulus interrupts our normally smooth progression of life. We sense something. We ask, "What is happening? What can I do? I'll try one idea and if that doesn't work, I'll try something else." Consequently, out of the initial shock, stimulus, or *sensation* comes an *awareness* followed by *clarification, adjustment,* and *verification* through observation.

Because the Dewey system is natural and life-like in its approach to problem solving, it lends itself exceptionally well to informal group discussion. There are, of course, times when certain of the steps may be omitted. The library staff, for example, *knows* that its budget is just too small to continue all its services, so the librarians may wisely choose to devote their energies to solutions rather than to the problem. The Juvenile Aid Division *knows* the kind and extent of juvenile crime; so the Division personnel may think chiefly in terms of solutions. The Sigma Sorority knows that *freshman* girls do not want to pledge Sigma; so the officers may choose to discuss only the solutions. But to discuss solutions without accurately describing the symptoms and causes of the problem is to follow a simple hit-or-miss pattern. A group should carefully consider each step if possible, omitting one only with reluctance. Problem solving by the five-step pattern of reflective thinking is a synthesis, a composite of all five aspects.

Now, let us construct a question outline based on the five steps. Such an outline will prove useful for a participant's analysis of the question before the discussion begins, or for the leader responsible for orderly progress during the discussion period itself.

PRELIMINARY OUTLINE

Question: Should Tadoma Tech subsidize varsity athletes?

Step 1. Awareness   **I.** Chairman's introduction
       A. What is the history of the question in brief?
       B. What recent event increases its importance?
       C. Why is this particular group concerned with the problem?

Step 2. Description of problem   **II.** How shall we define the key terms?
       A. What is meant by "subsidize"?
       B. Who is included in "varsity"?
       C. Who is included in "athletes"?

      III. Does a problem exist in our present policy of non-subsidization?
       A. What is the purpose of this institution?
       B. What is the purpose of its athletic program?
         1. Training professional athletes?
         2. Building strong bodies?
         3. Instilling school pride?
         4. Improving public relations?
         5. Demonstrating athletic superiority?
       C. How successful have we been in attaining these goals?
         1. Do our graduates succeed as professional athletes?

2. Do we build strong bodies?
3. Do we instill school pride?
4. Do we improve public relations?
5. Do we demonstrate athletic superiority?

D. Does our policy of non-subsidization affect our academic program?
E. Does our policy of non-subsidization limit alumni support?
F. What aspects of problem analysis have we ignored?

Step 3. Consideration of solution

IV. What two significant choices are implicit in the discussion question?
A. Shall we continue with the present policy?
B. Shall we consider a policy of subsidization?
   1. Plan A. May we subsidize by scholarships only?
   2. Plan B. May we subsidize by room, board, and tuition?
   3. Plan C. May we subsidize to the full extent allowable by our conference regulations?

Step 4. Selection of the best solution

V. Which policy appears most desirable?
A. What are the criteria for our best policy?
B. Which policy seems best to meet those criteria?
C. What are the anticipated outcomes?
   1. Will the solution create other problems?
   2. Will the solution remove or adjust to present difficulties?
D. Do we have the funds to put the plan into effect?

Step 5. Verification Ideally, the decisions of the group (at this point) should be put into action, observed, and modified as the need arises.

A preliminary outline will do much to help the participant. In the first place, when forced to put his thoughts on paper, he may easily realize how little he knows about the problem. Second, the outline, even though sketchy, helps to organize his thoughts. Third, it may spur the participant to gather more factual materials before meeting with others in the discussion situation. And fourth, such planning, subsequently reinforced with factual materials, stimulates a more active and interesting interplay of ideas during the discussion. In short, it does matter a great deal what a participant says and in what order he says it.

☐   **THE DISCUSSION LEADER**

Leadership is a marvelous thing, and most of us would like to possess it in abundance. It gives us the opportunity to be creative, to make the nothing that we have the something that we want. It produces new energies, new concepts, and new actions out of old and somnolent facts. Leadership in discussion requires energy, experience, and knowledge of human nature. A good discussion leader has at least three definite responsibilities: (1) planning adequately, (2) encouraging full, free discussion, and (3) persisting toward a group-determined goal. Examine each of these separately.

PLANNING ADEQUATELY

There are, of course, the obvious tasks which must be taken care of before the meeting: phrasing the question, choosing the room, the time, and place (the comfort of the room, the convenience of the hour, the "energy potential" of the participants at that hour), giving advance notice, and formulating statements of the group's concern and the general goal of the first discussion. Not quite so obvious, judging from current practice, are other equally important responsibilities.

1. *Arranging the chairs in a face-to-face pattern.* Such an arrangement suggests that the leader is simply one of a group made up of

equally important people. Thus, discussion should pass freely within the circle without having each comment directed to the leader. Such a seating arrangement leads to ease of communication of ideas and information.

2. *Arranging to talk with participants prior to the discussion.* This kind of preliminary conversation should enlarge the leader's perspective. Through these preliminaries, he may measure the degree of concern, become acquainted with the several individual personalities, and estimate the amount of cooperation or conflict which may appear at the time of the meeting.

3. *Studying the question.* If there are minutes of the previous meeting, read them. If a street paving is under consideration, know the cost, possible contractors, and laws about paving streets. In other words, research the topic. The leader might further enrich the discussion by distributing copies of pertinent factual material or by providing visual aids. Both of these help to keep the discussion progressing toward satisfying conclusions.

4. *Preparing an outline.* An outline helps to keep the discussion on the main track, and moving steadily ahead. Some discussion leaders duplicate an outline of ideas or problems to be met and place it before the group for their consideration. The chairman, however, must always safeguard the right of members to raise additional questions and present other ideas. He must not consider his own outline sacred or absolute.

ENCOURAGING FULL AND FREE DISCUSSION

The leader is the one who sees to it that the issues — the ideas, assertions, feelings — are presented. He must further see to it that they are presented *reasonably* — that is, fairly and fully.

1. *By respecting the opinion of others.* Though it is perfectly natural for the leader to want to enhance his own self image, he must frequently rein himself in in order to encourage others to participate in discussion. The other participants have an equity in the decision, and that equity should assure them the right to express their ideas fully. Indeed, they have not only the right but also the responsibility to bring their opinions freely into the open. Sometimes, however, the

leader must draw participants into the discussion by asking direct questions such as "What information do you have, Henry, about insurance rates?" or "Do you feel, Mr. Irving, that this solution would be acceptable to the group you represent?"

2. *By requesting deeper investigation of issues.* It is not enough merely to talk, especially when participants have to be encouraged to talk; the discussion must penetrate more deeply into important matters. The leader may say, "Very good, but is there some factual basis for that statement?" or "This seems to conflict with much that we have already said. Can you reconcile the conflict?" or "We have looked at this problem only from our point of view. Suppose we try to see it from the other fellow's." The leader is calling for supporting materials, for consistency of treatment, as well as for objectivity. At this point, he meets his greatest responsibility — that of checking shallow, hasty decisions and assuring full, objective consideration of the issue before the group.

PERSISTING TOWARD GROUP-DETERMINED GOALS

People sometimes grow weary of a discussion topic. When no immediate progress is apparent, they become eager to drop the discussion and turn to activities which seem more fruitful or, at least, more pleasant. A leader who is sensitive to the signs of weariness or impatience will help the discussion participants if he insists on a clear statement of objectives and persists toward them in the following ways.

1. *He defines the goals early.* Any group of persons talking together likes to know how much it must accomplish in one hour — or one meeting. The chairman should help the group by defining this goal clearly early in the meeting. He then must continue to remind the group members of ends to be met before adjournment. A definite task mutually agreed on will often overcome fatigue and assure progress.

2. *He summarizes and synthesizes often.* As a rule, the leader summarizes at the conclusion of each of the five steps of problem solving. As discussion continues, he brings together the ideas of

agreement or shows how they clash. He calls for continued deliberation until each of the several goals has been determined.

3. *He stimulates discussion.* Often it is not enough merely to "call" for further discussion; the leader must stimulate it. He may challenge a statement, insert a point of view contrary to popular belief, or cite a particularly dramatic example. He may quote an unusual opinion or set up a straw man which must be torn down by further discussion.

4. *He refuses to accept evasion.* Many times we do not speak to the point. We try to insist that our problems are "nothing more than human nature" or that they are not half as bad as the problems of others. Such answers provide little comfort. The leader should note evasiveness and firmly insist on meeting the issue squarely.

5. *He follows through.* If the discussants are also charged with the responsibility to act after the decision has been reached, the leader should remain in touch with his group, confer with them often regarding the progress being made, and see the recommended action through to completion.

SUMMARY

Informal discussion is the talk of the dinner table, the classroom, the conference, and the committee. Most of our issues are met and our problems solved within the framework of this speech form. It is one of the bases of democratic action and therefore worthy of serious study if our society is to become more orderly and efficient in the decision-making process. Both the leader and discussants have a stake in the outcome of the discussion and should take their respective obligations seriously. Effective discussion is possible only if there is harmonious interplay between the leader and the discussants themselves. The skills to be learned and practiced in discussion are:

1. Selecting and phrasing the question for discussion
2. Defining and understanding the immediate goals of the meeting
3. Mastering the problem-solving technique
4. Becoming a skilled and respected discussion leader

The principles of good informal discussion are also applicable to the more formal speech forms that follow.

■   **THE PANEL**

In informal discussion we find a small circle of people talking
together in the hope of solving a problem. If we break open the circle,
change all the discussants into "experts," and add an audience, we
have a form of discussion known as *the panel*. Just as in a committee, there may be any number of persons on the panel. By tradition, however, there are usually only four or five members. They
sit facing an audience rather than in a circle. A chairman, previously
selected, introduces the participants to the audience and briefly describes the issues or problems to be discussed. The panel members
then address their discussion to one another, being careful to speak
loudly enough so that the audience can "listen in." The chairman
keeps the discussion moving toward definite goals. At the end of the
time limit, the end of the program, or when the arguments have
been covered, the chairman usually presents a summary, thanks the
participants, and sometimes urges questions or further discussion by
members of the audience.

In some instances the objectives of the informal discussion and
the panel may be identical. Both forms are often committed to
following the steps of reflective thinking. Both may work for greater
understanding or to solve a problem. Both depend on the rapid give-
and-take of ideas instead of the prepared speech.

The two, however, have some significant differences. The informal
discussants are often "laymen" — from the custodian up through the
president — while the panelists are normally "experts." The discussion is often solely for the benefit of the people doing the talking;
the panel speaks to inform an audience. The discussion usually seeks
agreement; the panel often seeks only a presentation of conflicting
points of view. Viewed in this light, the panels on television or radio
are more similar to debate than to informal discussion.

Panel members must possess the skills of public speaking. Since
they are speaking to an audience, they must adapt to that audience.
And since the "experts" are often professionally committed to a
particular program or point of view, they feel duty-bound to persuade
their listeners. In fact, panelists often turn from their fellow members
and speak directly to the audience in order to inform, convince, or
entertain.

■   **THE SYMPOSIUM**

Originally the symposium was a drinking party in ancient Greece at which the host served his finest wines and encouraged equally fine conversation. The symposium has a different meaning today. Three or four authorities are seated on a stage, or at least in front of an audience. Each is expected to discuss one aspect of a general topic. The chairman, not himself a participant, addresses the audience first to explain the subject to be discussed. He normally provides a brief background statement, attempts to show the relevance or timeliness of the topic at hand, and then introduces the first of the "experts." The length of their speeches depends, of course, on the scheduled time and on whether or not the audience is permitted to ask questions. The purpose is generally informative rather than persuasive.

A symposium may become a debate, but at its best it remains an attempt to present and describe aspects of a particular event or condition rather than argue them. For example, if the question of a symposium were "Is television meeting its potential for public instruction?" three speakers might present the separate viewpoints of a TV network, a sociologist, and a city school superintendent. If the opinions of the television expert are likely to clash with the others' opinions, he might present the problem while the others present solutions to avoid the win/lose atmosphere of debate and keep within the descriptive objectives of the symposium.

■   **THE DEBATE**

A debate is a meeting of opposing forces, two sides agreeing to disagree. In debate, the individual speaker is determined to convince his audience that his point of view is "right," that his analysis of the problem is the "correct" one, or that his solution to that problem is the one most likely to remove existing difficulties.

The subject for debate is best stated as a resolution rather than a question. For example:

> *Resolved:* That this school should abolish campus fraternities and sororities.

Resolved: That late hours for women students should be extended.

Resolved: That the United States should adopt a program providing increased medical care for the aged.

The resolution thus channels the speaking along particular lines. Instead of encouraging investigation of every conceivable solution, the resolution forces each side to come to grips with a particular or specific solution.

As with the other forms of group speaking, the chairman helps to get the debate under way by introducing the subject and the speakers. In intercollegiate debate there are usually four speakers. The first normally upholds the affirmative, that is, he *affirms* that conditions should be changed and that we should adopt the proposal as stated in the resolution. The second speaker takes the negative, that is, he *negates* the existence of a problem or denies that the proposed solution is the one most desired. The third and fourth speakers have the same respective roles.

The most frequent order of speaking in intercollegiate debating is as follows:

CONSTRUCTIVE SPEECHES. The four speakers "construct" a case for their side. They build argument and support it with information. The first affirmative speech is entirely prepared ahead of time; subsequent speeches, although supported with prepared material, depend for their arrangement and emphasis on the previous speeches in the debate. They argue, refute, and further support what has gone before. The usual sequence of speakers and the time allotted to each for constructive speeches in "team debate" are as follows:

1. First Affirmative   (10 minutes)
2. First Negative   (10 minutes)
3. Second Affirmative (10 minutes)
4. Second Negative   (10 minutes)

REFUTATION. To refute an argument is to show how or why it will not stand up under careful examination. The refutation may be an objection (pointing out errors or weaknesses in the opponent's reasoning) or a counter-proposal (offering a solution which is more practicable or solves the problem more fully). Speeches of refutation are sometimes called rebuttals because the speakers attempt to rebut or destroy the opposing arguments. It is important to remember that the affirmative or the negative may — in fact, *must* — engage in rebuttal or refutation to strengthen its own position. Effective refutation demands analytical skills of a high order and a thoroughgoing knowledge of both sides of the question. Obviously, it also demands unusual ability as an extemporaneous speaker.

The usual sequence of speakers and the time allotted to each for refutation in "team debate" are as follows:

1. First Negative   (5 minutes)
2. First Affirmative   (5 minutes)
3. Second Negative   (5 minutes)
4. Second Affirmative (5 minutes)

In the political area, however, no such order appears to have been accepted. The Lincoln-Douglas debates and the Kennedy-Nixon debates both established special "ground rules."

By devoting so much space to cooperative speaking, we may have created the impression that "non-cooperative" speaking or "direct-clash" debate is non-democratic. Nothing could be farther from the truth. Debate, persuasion, advertising — all are as democratic as buttermilk and chawbacon. If the listener is to operate freely, he must be convinced through argument or persuasion, not force. If he is to remain free, he must be free to listen or not to listen, to agree or not to agree. And the speaker, aware of his listener's freedom, must acknowledge the challenge and meet the listener on his own terms. Our choice, as Professor Brigance enjoyed putting it, is to "talk it out or shoot it out." Fortunately, modern Americans seem to prefer the former.

■   THE FORUM

The forum is an enlargement of the communication circle to include the audience. Here the members of the audience become participants by commenting on issues or asking questions. The forum may be used in conjunction with each of the group speaking procedures. Thus we may have a panel-forum, a symposium-forum, or a debate-forum. In addition, we may also have a lecture-forum or a film-forum. Whenever the audience members become the speakers and by their questions and comments share in the process of public decision making, we have a forum.

It is not easy to turn an audience into a group of speakers. After all, the audience is composed largely of "laymen" who find that disagreeing with the expert requires at least a modest amount of courage. The layman's lesser knowledge of the subject, his place in the group as contrasted to the expert's place on an elevated stage, the impromptu and unrehearsed nature of his remarks, and the restriction of time necessarily placed upon him all frequently check his desire to speak. Yet throughout our country, audiences are frequently given the opportunity to speak out. City councils are faced with "citizen groups" who object to bond issues or speak up for new storm sewers in the south end of town. School boards expect to hear from "interested parties," such as tax study groups, the PTA, and the teachers' federation. In many of these instances, the members of the audience expect to speak up. They often have certain persons to speak for their group. They are not intimidated when their favorite topic is raised for discussion.

The moderator and the experts, however, often must provoke audience participation. The moderator must at the very outset indicate his desire to hear audience questions and remarks. He must provide what might be called "psychic comfort" — an atmosphere which clearly expresses concern for what the audience hears as well as what it chooses to say in reply. The experts must, of course, proceed in similar vein by speaking in a manner which welcomes discussion and suggests a willingness to test idea with idea.

SUMMARY

1. Group speaking is deliberative and cooperative.
2. Informal discussion sometimes fails because of:
   a. Misconceptions abouts its nature
   b. Apathy
   c. Differing personalities
   d. Poor leadership
   e. Purposelessness

3. Informal discussion is more likely to succeed if the discussants:
   a. Carefully select and phrase the question
   b. Understand the discussion goals
   c. Follow the problem-solving pattern
4. An effective leader will:
   a. Plan adequately
   b. Encourage full and free discussion
   c. Persist energetically toward the group-determined goal
5. Some ways to face issues and involve the audience in the discussion are the panel, the symposium, the debate, and the forum.

EXERCISES

1. Divide the class into several groups, each containing four or five members, and prepare for informal group discussions in the following manner:

   a. Call a meeting before the date assigned for the discussion. During this meeting, select a chairman and phrase a question for group discussion.
   b. Each member should prepare a discussion outline which reveals his best thinking on the selected topic. A copy of the outline should be given to the instructor prior to the discussion. This will serve as minimum evidence that the participant has given the subject adequate consideration.
   c. The members of the class not involved in the discussion should eavesdrop inconspicuously and evaluate the discussion toward the end of the hour. This evaluation should consider (1) the discussion organization, (2) the contribution of each participant, and (3) the effectiveness of the group leader.

2. Write a two-page critical analysis of the action recently taken by a group (committee, family, class) of which you were a member. Be sure to answer these questions:

   a. Did the group have trouble getting started?
   b. Did each member assume his full share of the group responsibility?

    c. Did the group's discussion progress effectively?
    d. Did the chairman demonstrate good leadership?
    e. Did the group arrive at satisfactory conclusions?

If you have not recently been in a discussion situation, write a similar analysis of a radio or television discussion.

3. Do we make as much sense as we think we do? Frequently, in our discussions, we feel that we utter only truly significant thoughts. To test this assumption, record or tape a group discussion; then select a person to transcribe the tape. A little study of the written words should prove helpful — as well as embarrassing. It is surprising how we sometimes say the opposite of what we intend.

4. Select a discussion question which pertains to your campus and about which there are reasonably strong feelings. Then prepare a symposium-forum. The appointed chairman and speakers should discuss the basic issues for twenty to twenty-five minutes before receiving comments from the audience.

5. Phrase a debate resolution which pertains to campus problems and about which there are clear differences of opinion. Restricting the opening speeches to four minutes and the rebuttals to two, conduct a short debate. Following the presentation, turn the occasion into a forum by calling for comments and questions from the audience.

CHAPTER 15

INTRODUCTION TO
PARLIAMENTARY PROCEDURE

Many now reading this book and pursuing a college education will, in a few years, be chosen to lead the organizations within their communities. Some will preside at the mayor's Committee for City Planning or the Board of Public Works. Some will preside at a meeting of the School Board or the City Council. Some will be elected president of Rotary, Kiwanis, Altrusa, the Lion's Club, the Exchange Club, or the Country Club. Others will serve as vice-presidents, secretaries, and treasurers of the CIO, the AAUP, the PTA, the AAUW, and the IOOF. A few will gain special recognition by being elected to a state or national legislature. In all these organizations, parliamentary procedure of some kind will be used to assure orderly and efficient action.

There is, of course, no need to wait; the reader, even at the present, has abundant opportunity on campus to use the rules of parliamentary procedure. How many honoraries are there? How many departmental clubs? How many Greek letter fraternities and sororities;

"dorm floor councils"; coalition political parties; and how many organizations to welcome the hikers, the bikers, the skiers and fliers, the players of bridge and checkers and chess? Many! And in each of these a form of parliamentary procedure is the rule rather than the exception. Quite naturally, then, the question arises: Why is parliamentary procedure so much with us?

■   THE PURPOSES OF PARLIAMENTARY PROCEDURE

Parliamentary procedure, whether practiced by rules of the British Parliament, the United States Senate, or a well-organized campus fraternity, has four purposes. Three of them serve to protect rights; the fourth serves to assure deliberative action.

1. *Parliamentary procedure helps to determine the will of the majority.* In our conversational speech or in our small-group discussions, we have relatively little difficulty in expressing our points of view. Seated around a table, or in a classroom, we experience the quick, easy informality of the occasion; and out of the give-and-take of ideas, we can easily note the consensus of the group. When, however, the group increases to twenty-five or thirty, it is much more difficult to determine what the group action will be and who constitutes the democratic majority. Parliamentary rules help us solve such a difficulty by establishing an intelligent discussion and voting procedure.

2. *Parliamentary procedure helps to protect the rights of the minority.* Believing as we do in the exercise of debate, we could not endorse any system of rules which would force the minority into silence or deprive its members of the right of free expression. Certain rules, such as the two-thirds rule to close debate, are designed to protect the minority. The minority must remain *in attendance* and *free* — free to discuss, to join the majority, to change the majority, to compromise with the majority, or to overthrow it by peaceful means and become the majority through good reasoning and sound evidence.

3. *Parliamentary procedure helps to protect the rights of individuals.* Parliamentary procedure exists not only to protect groups;

it extends an equal protection to the individual. It assures him his *personal* right to freedom from abuse. It gives him the opportunity to speak without interruption, to ask questions of procedure, or to object to a consideration of any proposed action which constitutes a restriction of his personal rights as a member of a deliberative group. It even gives an individual the right to nominate a "Joe Smith" as the Republican candidate for President.

4. *Parliamentary procedure helps to expedite business in an orderly manner.* All of us have had opportunity to doubt the truth of this statement. At fraternity or sorority meetings or possibly at a meeting of a departmental club, we have seen a "parliamentary" group come to a complete halt because of confusion or indecision. The presiding officer, a stumbling leader, offered little help to the members wrestling with the numerous motions that had been entertained simultaneously. The windbag of the group seemed to be constantly on his feet misdirecting the legislative traffic. And noise rather than discussion became the order of the day. This was not the result of parliamentary procedure, however; it was the *result of its absence.* When the members of a group, or even the chairman of the group, understand and use a few major rules of parliamentary procedure, there will be an orderly progression of business.

■ GETTING A GROUP ORGANIZED

To illustrate the major rules of procedure, let us imagine that a community or school club is about to be organized. We must make certain assumptions about our organization. We must assume that a small group of interested people has announced that there will be a meeting of all who share their interests. At the announced time and place, a member is asked to assume the role of temporary chairman. He calls the group to order, states the reason for the meeting, and presides as the group elects temporary officers. Usually the temporary chairman remains the leader of the organization until the Constitution Committee has completed its work of drawing up a constitution acceptable to a majority of the membership. Among other things, the constitution will specify the permanent officers to be elected.

☐   **THE ELECTION OF PERMANENT OFFICERS**

Making nominations. Since the temporary chairman is still presiding, he will be the one to say:

"The floor is now open for nominations for the office of President."

A member choosing to nominate someone for the office usually stands, addresses the chairman by saying, "Mr. Chairman," and announces:

"I nominate Hillary Dale."

Since it is not necessary to second a nomination, the chairman immediately says:

"Mr. Hillary Dale has been nominated. Are there other nominations?"

This procedure continues until everyone has had an opportunity to nominate his candidate.

Closing nominations. When the chairman is confident that everyone has had his opportunity to speak, he may declare the nominations closed:

"If there are no objections, the nominations are closed."

A member, however, may, after recognition by the chair, introduce a motion to close the nominations:

"I move that nominations be closed."

This motion must receive a second, and, in order to pass, a majority of two-thirds.

Voting. Unless specified in the constitution or by-laws, officers are usually elected by a *plurality* rather than a *majority* vote. A plurality is simply the greatest number of votes cast, while a majority refers to "over half." For example, if there are thirty voting members, sixteen of them need to vote for a candidate in order to elect him under the majority rule. As few as seven votes could elect an officer in a similar meeting of thirty persons if at least five candidates have been nominated. The following example contrasts the election of an officer under the two rules:

Plurality Rule Votes			*Majority Rule Votes*	
Robbins	4		Robbins	16 —Elected
Hoops	3		Hoops	(eliminated)
Bloom	5		Bloom	(eliminated)
Gallagher	6		Gallagher	7
Thiry	7	—Elected	Thiry	7
Farling	5		Farling	(eliminated)

As the examples above suggest, the group must establish the rule to be followed before proceeding with the election.

Four methods of voting are in common use: (1) *voice vote,* by saying "yes" or "no," "aye" (pronounced "eye") or "nay"; (2) *physical expression,* by raising the hand or standing; (3) *ballot,* a form of written voting which allows for secrecy; (4) *consent,* a particularly useful method when the presiding officer senses that no one in the group is likely to challenge his ruling. For example, if there were only one nomination, the chair might feel perfectly free to say:

> *"If there are no objections, the chair rules that nominations are closed and that Mr. Mimsley has been elected by a unanimous vote."*

If the chair hears an objection at this point, he is obliged to choose one of the other three courses of action.

Once the permanent presiding officer has been elected, nominations and elections continue for each of the additional officers.

☐   **AN ALTERNATE METHOD**

Many organizations provide for a nominating committee, which is responsible for preparing a slate of nominees for the offices to be filled. Even though a slate is presented, the chair must provide opportunity for members to make additional nominations from the floor. When other nominations are made, the method described above is followed; when none are made, it is appropriate for the chair to rule the nominees elected or to entertain such a motion as:

"Mr. Chairman, I move that the slate be accepted and that the nominees be declared elected."

This motion requires a second and a simple majority to pass.

■   **CONDUCTING A REGULAR MEETING**

Once a group has been organized, has a constitution and duly elected officers, it is ready to hold a "regular" meeting. How does the group proceed? What comes first and what comes last?

☐   **THE ORDER OF BUSINESS**

Though any organization is free to establish the order best suited to its purpose, the one most commonly used is as follows:

1. *Call to order* by the president

    Chair: *"The meeting will come to order. Will the secretary please call the roll?"*

2. *Roll call* — often to determine whether enough members are present to conduct business. Such a number is called a quorum. A group may establish the number for a quorum in its constitution. If it does not, the usual number established by rules of order is a majority of the qualified members.

3. *The reading of the minutes*

    Chair: *"May we hear the minutes of the last meeting?"*

    The minutes comprise a record of all motions, committee reports, and general agreements arrived at by the organization.

    Chair: *"Are there any corrections? If not, the minutes are approved as read."*

    But if there are corrections to be made, members or officers may suggest changes or additions. Any correction is made with consent or with a vote of approval of the members. The chairman then says: *"The minutes stand as corrected."*

4. *Reports from officers, boards, and standing committees* — followed by group approval or rejection

5. *Reports from special committees*

6. *Unfinished business*
7. *New business*
8. *Announcements*
9. *Setting the time for the next meeting* (unless there is a regular meeting time)
10. *Adjournment*

☐   **THE PRESIDING OFFICER**

From our italics above, the presiding officer may appear to be a mechanic — that is, by saying the right thing at the right time, he keeps the gears in operation so that business may proceed with a minimum of disorder and delay. But his chief responsibility is considerably less mechanical and far more creative. He is responsible for conducting the meeting in such a manner that the will of the group may be discovered and that no individual be denied his right to participate in the process of decision making. Normally, especially in more formal groups, the presiding officer neither enters the debate nor declares himself for or against a particular motion. He presides impartially and impersonally — so impersonally that he refers to himself as "the chair."

The major responsibilities and duties of the chair are these:

1. To open and adjourn meetings.
2. To keep order, with the help of a sergeant-at-arms if necessary.
3. To follow parliamentary procedure with the help of a parliamentarian.
4. To help the group understand the business at hand.
5. To conduct an orderly discussion, permitting and encouraging a variety of points of view.
6. To help the group arrive at an orderly decision and see that it is implemented.
7. To follow the criteria of good chairmanship as outlined in the previous chapter.

☐   **PRESENTING A MAIN MOTION**

The individual member is the central figure of parliamentary practice. It is he — not the chairman or president — who intro-

duces motions, speaks for their passage or defeat, and votes on
their final disposition. How should he proceed?

He stands and says, *"Mr. Chairman."*
The chair replies, *"Mr. Kitt."*
He states his motion: *"I move that we sponsor a chess tournament
for all male upperclassmen during the month of May."*
The chair says, *"You have heard the motion. Is there a second to
this motion?"*
Another member stands and says, *"Mr. Chairman, I second the
motion."*
The chair summarizes: *"It has been moved and seconded that this
organization sponsor a chess tournament for all male upperclassmen during the month of May. Is there any discussion?"*

Presenting a main motion, then, is very simple. An individual (1)
stands and addresses the chair, (2) the chair acknowledges him, (3)
he states his motion, (4) another member seconds it, and (5) the
chair repeats the motion and calls for discussion. If any one of
these items of procedure comes out of sequence, the group is in
error.

Let us take another look at the main motion which Mr. Kitt introduced. Is the motion acceptable, properly phrased to facilitate meaningful discussion?

1. *A motion should be stated in correct parliamentary form.* It
should begin with the words *"I move that —"* or *"I move to —"*
rather than *"I make a motion —"* or *"I make a move —."*

2. *A motion should be stated impersonally.* In more formal groups,
the personal pronouns *I, we,* and *you* should be used sparingly. Mr.
Kitt's motion would have been less personal had he said, "I move
that *this club* sponsor a chess tournament . . ." rather than "I move
that *we* sponsor . . . ."

3. *A motion should be definite.* Mr. Kitt's motion is definite
enough to merit discussion. He suggests a specific kind of tournament for a definite group during a particular month. True, he has
not included the precise time and place, nor has he mentioned the
rules by which the tournament may be conducted. These things are

better handled by a committee. He has, however, given the group
enough of the essentials to reach a decision.

4. *A motion should contain a single item of business.* For illustration, let us assume that Mr. Kitt had stated:

In error: *"I move that we sponsor a chess tournament for all male*
            upperclassmen during the month of May and that we
            sponsor a Summer Festival of Progressive Jazz."

Obviously, such a motion would not meet the criterion of "a single
item." Discussion of this motion would be confusing, to say the
least, inasmuch as some members could speak to support one of
the ideas and defeat the other. In this instance, the organization
would have been wiser to entertain two motions, each handled separately.

5. *A motion should contain no argument.* On this count, too, Mr.
Kitt's original motion passes the test. Realizing that it is foolish to
ask the group to vote on the suitability of his reasoning, he wisely
reserves his arguments for the moment of discussion. He presents
his motion without impassioned appeals, calmly and objectively,
clearly and briefly.

6. *A motion, if passed, should be stated so that it involves group*
action. Again, Mr. Kitt's motion passes the test. He clearly wants
his group *to do something* — not to endorse some principle, commend someone, or support a candidate. While it is possible to do
these things, they should be presented in the form of *resolutions* rather
than as main motions.

■   **AMENDING MOTIONS**

After the motion has been made, seconded, and repeated by the
chair, the discussion period follows. During this time members may
rise to a *request for information* in order to be sure about the precise
nature of the motion. They may rise to speak in support of the
motion, to speak against it, or to express a desire to change some
particular provision of the motion. This latter expression is called an
amendment.

Often an individual who is displeased with a main motion may know how he would like to change it but not know how to request the change. As a result he might state his amendment —

In error: *"I move to amend the motion so that it will not necessarily be limited to male upperclassmen and so we can play canasta if the social committee says it is all right."*

Obviously, such an amendment would lead to confusion. It is wordy. It lacks precision. It introduces the added consideration of the social committee. In short, it is a poorly stated amendment.

Then how shall we go about it? There are several forms in which amendments are correctly stated.

1. By *inserting* — that is, by inserting a word or words within the motion. For example:

"Mr. Chairman, I move to amend the motion by inserting the word 'early' before the word 'May.'"

2. By *striking out* — that is, by removing a word or words from the motion.

"Mr. Chairman, I move to amend the motion by striking out the word 'male.'"

3. By *striking out and inserting* — that is, by substituting new words for those which should be removed.

"Mr. Chairman, I move to amend the motion by striking out the word 'chess' and inserting the word 'canasta.'"

4. By *adding* — that is, by adding words *to the end of the motion.*

"Mr. Chairman, I move to amend the motion by adding the words 'of next year.'"

5. By *dividing* — that is, by separating ideas within a motion so that separate votes might be taken on each idea.

"Mr. Chairman, I move that this motion be divided so that we might consider the tournament first and the matter of the time second."

In addition to these accepted forms for amendments, there are other rules which must be observed: (1) A motion to amend requires a second. (2) It may be debated. (3) It requires a simple majority to pass and thus change the main motion. (4) There may be only one *primary* amendment — such as the examples above — on the floor at any one time. (5) There may be only one *secondary* amendment (*i.e.,* an amendment to an amendment) at any one time. (6) Amendments are voted on before main motions.

Once the chair senses that the motion has been sufficiently discussed or amended to shape it to the preferences of the group, he may initiate the voting procedure:

Chair: *"Are you ready for the question?"*
Group: *"Question."*
Chair: *"The question as amended is: That this organization sponsor a chess tournament for all upperclassmen during the month of May. All those in favor say 'aye.'* (He pauses to listen.) *All those opposed say 'no.'* (And he pauses again.) *The 'aye's' have it. The motion passes."*

This, then, is one simple method of introducing, debating, amending, and voting upon an item of business. This procedure becomes slightly more involved, however, when we introduce other motions to hasten or delay action.

■ DELAYING ACTION

Several safeguards against hasty, impetuous action are built into the structure of parliamentary procedure. Four of them are considered here.

□ REFERRING A MOTION TO COMMITTEE

When referring a motion or an idea to a committee, care must be taken to include four necessary elements: (1) the matter which the committee is to consider, (2) how many members are to serve, (3) how they are to be selected, and (4) when the committee is to report back to the group. For example:

"I move that this motion be referred to a committee of three appointed by the chair to report no later than Thursday of next week."

If there is a standing or permanent committee, such as the Social Committee, the motion could specify this and avoid the appointing of another. This motion requires a second; it may be debated and amended; and it requires a simple majority to pass.

☐   **LAYING A MOTION ON THE TABLE**

The purpose of laying a motion on the table (figuratively, not literally) is to postpone, to delay immediate consideration. In some instances laying a motion on the table is the equivalent of preventing action altogether. The motion may be stated like this:

> *"Mr. Chairman, I move to table the present motion regarding the chess tournament."*

or

> *"Mr. Chairman, I move that the motion regarding the chess tournament be laid on the table."*

The "chess tournament motion" may be taken from the table by a motion to that effect later in the same meeting or during the meeting which follows. A motion to table requires a second, is neither debatable nor amendable, and requires a simple majority to pass.

☐   **POSTPONING TO A STATED TIME
                                  AND POSTPONING INDEFINITELY**

The difference between the intent of the two postponement motions is obvious. The individual making the motion to postpone to a definite time suggests that he is interested in the main motion but that it would be better discussed at another time. The individual making the motion to postpone indefinitely may have no interest in it and be thinking not only of delaying action but of preventing it altogether. The motions are simply stated:

> *"Mr. Chairman, I move that consideration of this motion be postponed until the March meeting."*

and

"Mr. Chairman, I move that consideration of this motion be post-poned indefinitely."

Both motions require seconds. Only the first is amendable. Both are debatable and require a simple majority to pass.

☐   **MAKING SPECIAL ORDER OF BUSINESS**

When a member senses that a motion has been introduced which might be more suitably handled at a later date, he may make a motion creating a special order by saying —

> *"Mr. Chairman, I move that this matter be made a special order for the March meeting at the time immediately following the Social Committee report."*

The motion may be amended as well as debated. To pass, it must have a majority of two-thirds. If the motion should pass, the chair or a member may call for the "order of the day" at the time specified during the March meeting. The "call" is a convention which reminds everyone that a special matter is to be considered at that particular time.

☐   **OBJECTING TO CONSIDERATION**
                        WITHDRAWING A MOTION

We consider here two other procedures which are useful in delaying action on a main motion. Like the motion to postpone indefinitely, these two procedures have the effect not of delaying but of permanently suppressing. Both of them seek to remove a motion before it reaches the point of discussion. Neither requires a second and neither is amendable nor debatable, and a ruling by the chair may make voting unnecessary. The objection is different, however, from the withdrawal in that it requires a two-thirds majority to pass, and it may interrupt a speaker. To object, one must propose that a motion is (1) immoral, (2) irrelevant, or (3) unconstitutional. To object, a member arises before debate has started and says:

> *"Mr. Chairman, I object to a consideration of this motion on the grounds that a chess tournament is frivolous and removed from the purposes of this organization."*

To withdraw, the originator may say before discussion has started:

> *"Mr. Chairman, I ask permission to withdraw my motion."*

If the chair has not repeated the main motion, the originator needs no permission to withdraw or change it. If the main motion has been stated for the sake of discussion, the chair may grant permission to withdraw or may put the request to a majority vote of the group.

■   **HASTENING ACTION**

Many of us tend to talk too long once we are challenged by an idea. If our enthusiasm is unchecked, the business of the group is long delayed. In order to avoid prolonged consideration or unnecessary delay, parliamentary law provides us with motions which help to speed up the action. Four such motions are discussed here:

☐   **MOVING THE PREVIOUS QUESTION**

This motion intends to bring discussion to a close by calling for an immediate vote on "the previous question" — *i.e.,* the question or motion being debated. It is simply stated:

> *"Mr. Chairman, I move the previous question."*

or

> *"Mr. Chairman, I move that we vote immediately on the motion."*

Such a motion must be seconded. It is neither debatable nor amendable and requires, like most motions which terminate discussion, a two-thirds majority to pass. If the motion passes, debate stops immediately and a vote is taken on the motion previously discussed.

☐   **LIMITING DEBATE**

To hasten action during a meeting with a crowded agenda, members may limit the time allotted for debate. For example:

"Mr. Chairman, I move that debate on this motion be limited to fifteen minutes."

or

"Mr. Chairman, I move that debate cease at 10:15 p.m."

The motion may be amended but not debated. Like the motion calling for the previous question, it requires a majority of two-thirds for adoption.

☐   **SUSPENDING THE RULES**

When haste is desired and a matter of particular importance should be brought to the immediate attention of the group, a member may rely on the motion to "suspend the rules." Thus:

"Mr. Chairman, I move that we dispense with the reading of the minutes and the reports from officers and committees in order to discuss the motion calling for a chess tournament."

This motion is neither debatable nor amendable and requires, like the two previous motions, a majority of two-thirds for adoption. If the motion passes, normal rules of procedure immediately yield to a consideration of the pressing matter of importance. Once the item of special importance is settled, the presiding officer asks the group to return to its regular rules of procedure.

☐   **TAKING A MOTION FROM THE TABLE**

In effect, this motion is like introducing a main motion since it recalls a main motion previously tabled. It is phrased:

"Mr. Chairman, I move to take from the table the motion concerning the chess tournament."

It is neither amendable nor debatable, and it requires a simple majority for adoption. If it passes, the motion to which it refers is handled as though it were a main motion.

■ MAINTAINING RIGHTS AND PRIVILEGES

During any regular meeting of an organization, occasions may arise when there is need to object to action taking place, or to request information about pending action. The five such motions, procedures, or requests now discussed are alike in that none of them may be amended or debated and all of them may interrupt a speaker. Of the five, only one — appealing from the decision of the chair — needs to be seconded or even voted upon. All others are ruled on by the chair with the approval by the group.

☐ RISING TO A POINT OF ORDER

Whenever a member believes that an error in procedure has been committed, it is his responsibility to correct it.

Member: *"Mr. Chairman, I rise to a point of order."*
Chair: *"Please state your point."*
Member: *"This main motion is out of order inasmuch as we already have a main motion on the floor."*
Chair: *"Your point is well taken."*

At this point the chair withdraws the second main motion and directs discussion to the first motion.

☐ RISING FOR PARLIAMENTARY INQUIRY

A situation may arise in which a member, unacquainted with the rules of a particular organization or of parliamentary law, wishes to question a matter of procedure.

Member: *"Mr. Chairman, I rise to a parliamentary inquiry."*
Chair: *"Please state your inquiry."*

Member: *"I wish to know if Mr. Clearborn's motion is debatable."*

The chair then answers the question, or if he is unable to do so, he may rely upon the group parliamentarian. If there is no procedural rule to cover the situation, the chair could ask the group to vote an answer to the member's inquiry.

☐   **RISING TO REQUEST INFORMATION**

This motion, though quite similar to the one preceding, is different in that it usually seeks information beyond that of parliamentary procedure.

Member: *"Mr. Chairman, I rise to a request for information."*
Chair: *"Please state your request."*
Member: *"Does Mr. Tomlinson expect to offer a prize to the winner of the chess tournament?"*
Chair: *"Will Mr. Tomlinson answer Mr. Gwyn's question?"*

If the chair knows the answer to the question, he may state it. A wise chairman, however, turns to his group when the members possess information equal — or nearly so — to his own.

☐   **APPEALING FROM THE DECISION OF THE CHAIR**

Any chairman will be called upon from time to time to pass judgment or to make rulings. When the chair makes a ruling to which a member objects, that member may test the judgment by appealing the decision.

Chair: *"Your discussion is out of order, Mr. McCabe; this motion is no longer debatable."*
Member: *"Mr. Chairman, I appeal from the decision of the chair."*
Another: *"Mr. Chairman, I second the appeal."*
Chair: *"Please state the grounds for your appeal."*
Member: *"The motion calling for the previous question was defeated; therefore debate on the main motion is in order."*
Chair: *"The chair stands corrected. Thank you."*

If the chair, in this or any similar instance, believes that he — and
not the member — is correct, or if he is uncertain about the decision,
he may ask for a vote of the group to sustain his decision. Such a
vote must be definite — by ballot, standing, or a show of hands —
not merely by "aye's" or "nay's." It should be counted and announced. A majority vote sustains a decision of the chair.

It is not unusual for a member to appeal from the decision of the
chair when there is a close voice or show-of-hands vote. A wise
chairman will "double check" a doubtful vote if for no other reason
than to assure the group of honest decision making. If a member
doubts the announced result of a voice or hand vote, he may request
a recount or a vote by ballot or standing. The chair usually grants
these requests. The member may also appeal from the decision by
saying:

Member: *"Mr. Chairman, I appeal from the decision of the chair."*
Another: *"Mr. Chairman, I second the appeal."*
Chair: *"The chair announced that the 'ayes' had it and that the
motion has been passed. All those who sustain the decision of the chair please stand."* Following the tally of
the vote, *"All of those who do not sustain the decision
of the chair please stand."*

The chairman usually asks another officer or member to count the
votes. If the decision is sustained, the chair announces, *"The decision
of the chair has been sustained. The motion is passed."* If the members do not sustain the decision, a new and definite vote must be
taken on the original motion. This motion requires a second and a
simple majority for adoption.

☐   **RISING TO A QUESTION OF PRIVILEGE**

This motion is designed to secure action pertaining to the comfort
or personal welfare of a member or of the entire group.

Member: *"Mr. Chairman, I rise to a question of privilege."*
Chair: *"Please state your question."*
Member: *"I request that the members seated in the front of the*

> *room speak louder or turn slightly so that we may hear in the back of the room."*

Chair: *"The request is reasonable. If possible, will the members down front try to abide by Mr. Behr's request.*

Such a motion could as easily pertain to the lighting, heating, ventilation, or anything which affects the comfort and well-being of the members.

■ REVIEWING A PREVIOUS MOTION

Few organizations remain completely fixed and unyielding to change; consequently, they must have the privilege of reversing a decision previously made. Two motions are useful at this point.

□ RECONSIDERING A MOTION

The motion to reconsider permits a group to ignore a vote previously taken on another motion. For example:

"Mr. Chairman, I move to reconsider the motion to sponsor a chess tournament."

This motion must be seconded. It cannot be amended but may be debated. It can be made the same day or at the meeting following the original vote on the motion. If the motion is adopted by the simple majority required, the voting to which it refers is ignored as though no vote had ever been taken. As a result, the "chess tournament motion" is again up for discussion and subsequent vote during that or the following meeting.

□ RESCINDING A MOTION

To rescind is to make void; therefore, this motion, unlike the previous one, intends not so much to reconsider as to nullify. Since, however, the motion to rescind may be debated, it does have the effect of reconsidering. It is stated:

"Mr. Chairman, I move to rescind the motion passed during the February meeting providing for a chess tournament."

It must be seconded, may be debated, may not be amended, and requires a simple majority for adoption. Unlike the motion to reconsider, the motion to rescind cannot be made at the same meeting as the original motion it is designed to repeal. The motion to rescind, if adopted, immediately repeals any motion previously passed.

■   **CLOSING A MEETING**

Two motions deserve consideration at this point.

□   **TO RECESS**

The purpose of this motion is to provide for a "break" in the business of the meeting, not to terminate it.

"Mr. Chairman, I move that we recess until 10:20 a.m."

or

"Mr. Chairman, I move that we recess for twenty minutes."

The motion requires a second. It may be amended with respect to the time or length of the recess. It may not be debated.

□   **TO ADJOURN**

The purpose of the motion to adjourn is to bring the meeting to a close.

"Mr. Chairman, I move that we adjourn."

or

"Mr. Chairman, I move that this meeting be adjourned at 11:00 a.m."

Many groups meet at regularly scheduled times. Some do not, however, and in order to avoid the necessity of another motion — to fix the time for the next meeting — the motion to adjourn may be stated:

"Mr. Chairman, I move that we adjourn until March 14 at 9:00 a.m."

The motion to adjourn requires a second. It may not be debated or amended, except in relation to time, and requires a simple majority for adoption.

■   **PRECEDENCE OF MOTIONS**

From the previous discussion it becomes apparent that there are times when several motions are permitted on the floor at the same time. As we have observed, only one *main* motion may be "on the floor" but there may be several subsidiary or privileged motions in some way associated with the main item of business. For example, let us say that we have the following motions presented in the order indicated below:

1. A main motion
2. An amendment
3. An amendment to the amendment
4. A motion to refer to committee
5. A motion to take a recess
6. An amendment to the motion to take a recess

In this instance there are six motions on the floor. All of them are in order and must be voted on in orderly fashion.

To dispose of motions in an orderly way, we rely on an established *order of precedence,* which specifies which motions may be in order and which motions must be voted on first. To illustrate, in the above example we would begin with the amendment to the recess and work in reverse fashion until we arrived at the main motion. The chair calls for a vote to amend the length of the recess; it fails. He then directs the vote to the recess; it fails. He calls for a vote on referring the secondary amendment to a committee, and so on through the vote on the main motion. He finally announces:

"The 'noes' have it. The motion to sponsor a chess tournament is defeated."

The established precedence of the motions discussed in this chapter is as follows:

    A. PRIVILEGED MOTIONS
        1. Adjourn
        2. Recess
        3. Question of privilege
    B. INCIDENTAL MOTIONS — Order, Appeal, Object, etc. (These have no order among themselves.)
    C. SUBSIDIARY MOTIONS
        4. Lay on the table
        5. Previous question
        6. Limit debate
        7. Postpone to definite time
        8. Refer to committee
        9. Amend
       10. Postpone indefinitely
    D. MAIN MOTIONS

A motion toward the bottom of the list has the lesser precedence and must therefore yield to the motions above it. A detailed chart about precedence and other items is provided at the end of this chapter.

■   **A CONCLUDING STATEMENT**

The material presented in this chapter is by no means exhaustive in its treatment; it is, as the title suggests, an introduction to the basic rules most frequently used by those small organizations which conduct their business by parliamentary procedure. Even the motions included here have not been completely discussed, and other motions have been omitted altogether. This is but a beginning. The student is encouraged to study *Parliamentary Procedure* by Alice F. Sturgis, or the "bible" of parliamentary procedure, *Robert's Rules of Order*.

EXERCISES

1. Examine and report on either of the books listed below:

   Alice F. Sturgis, *Sturgis Standard Code of Parliamentary Procedure* (New York: McGraw-Hill Book Company, Inc., 1950).

   or

   General Henry M. Robert, *Robert's Rules of Order,* Revised 75th Anniversary Edition (Chicago: Scott, Foresman and Company, 1951).

2. Set aside *six class meetings* for an introductory study of parliamentary procedure. Assume at the outset that the group has already been organized, that a constitution has been prepared, and that the standard committees and officers have been specified.

   First Day: Conduct an election of the usual officers of a group, such as a president, vice-president, and secretary-treasurer. Make appropriate nominating speeches. Understand and use the motion to close nominations. Everyone should stand to speak at least once during all class meetings dealing with parliamentary procedure.

   Second Day: The chair should follow the order of business indicated in this chapter. Each member should be prepared to stand and make a main motion which is in acceptable form. Likewise each member should be prepared, purely as a mechanical exercise, to stand and present an amendment to his neighbor's motion.

   Third Day: Following the order of business, each member should prepare to introduce a main motion, to speak briefly for the passage or defeat of a motion, to amend a motion, and to refer a motion to a committee.

   Fourth day: One half of the class should present main motions and then use all motions which suppress debate and hasten action. The other half should work to delay action in order to assure more thorough consideration of business.

Fifth and Sixth Days: During the business of each of these two days, make sure to engage in good, energetic parliamentary debate. Make certain — just for the experience — that every motion in the following table of motions is used meaningfully.

TABLE OF MOTIONS AND REQUESTS DISCUSSED IN THIS CHAPTER LISTED ACCORDING TO PURPOSE

	Is it a Motion or a Request?*	*May it interrupt a speaker?*	*Does it need a second?*	*Is it amend-able?*	*Is it debat-able?*	*What vo is required*
DELAYING ACTION						
1. Refer to committees	Motion	No	Yes	Yes	Yes	½
2. Lay on the table	Motion	No	Yes	No	No	½
3. Postpone to stated time	Motion	No	Yes	Yes	Yes	½
4. Postpone indefinitely	Motion	No	Yes	No	Yes	½
5. Special order of business	Motion	No	Yes	Yes	Yes	⅔
6. Object to consideration	Request	Yes	No	No	No	⅔
7. Withdraw a motion	Request	No	No	No	No	Chair
HASTENING ACTION						
8. Previous question	Motion	No	Yes	No	No	⅔
9. Limit debate	Motion	No	Yes	No	No	⅔
10. Suspend rules	Motion	No	Yes	No	No	⅔
11. Take from table	Motion	No	Yes	No	No	½
MAINTAINING RIGHTS AND PRIVILEGES						
12. Point of order	Request	Yes	No	No	No	Chai
13. Parliamentary inquiry	Request	Yes	No	No	No	Chai
14. Request for information	Request	Yes	No	No	No	Chai
15. Appeal from the decision	Request	Yes	Yes	No	Yes	Chai
16. Question of privilege	Request	Yes	No	No	No	Chai
REVIEWING A PREVIOUS MOTION						
17. Reconsider	Motion	Yes	Yes	No	Yes	½
18. Rescind	Motion	No	Yes	No	Yes	½
CLOSING A MEETING						
19. Recess	Motion	No	Yes	Yes	No	½
20. Adjourn	Motion	No	Yes	No	No	½

* We define a "motion" as a procedure starting with the words, "I move. . . ." Note with one exception, the "requests" need no seconds and are not amendable or deba and that, with two exceptions, the chair *may* decide the outcome without a vote.

AN INTRODUCTION TO PHONETICS

When a child is born, he immediately inherits the culture of his family and his society. Part of that culture is a language which, except in the most primitive of societies, has an orderly written form as well as a system of spoken sounds. The child learns to speak before he knows anything about writing, spelling, and reading. In fact, about 95 per cent of all children develop a complete sound system before beginning to read.

When a child goes to school, he is taught to assign to sounds the written symbols we know as the letters of the alphabet. He learns to recognize the combinations of letters that produce syllables so that he can both read and write words correctly. This is called the phonics method of teaching reading, because the child learns to "sound out" the letters and syllables in a word. As any English-speaking person knows, however, it is nearly impossible to learn to read and write English using only phonics as a guide, for the language has very few hard and fast phonetic rules. Words which sound the same are spelled differently; different combinations of letters often have the same sound. The following example illustrates the problem: "As she stands among the boughs, she bows to a beau named Bowie who shoots arrows at the bows on her dress." German, Spanish, Portuguese, and Italian are all simpler languages phonetically, and it is thus somewhat easier to pronounce their written words on sight.

Phonetics, the study and systematic classification of spoken sound, uses a set of symbols which represent the sounds of our language much more accurately than the twenty-six letters of the English alphabet. Each symbol represents one sound and one sound only. This sound is called a *phoneme* and includes all members of the same sound family. Thus, the phoneme whose phonetic symbol is [k] represents any sound in the *k* sound family. To illustrate, there are two *k* sounds in the word "creek," but the phonetic symbol [k] is used for both the *c* and the *k*.

Though the phonetic alphabet is not meant to replace our standard alphabet, it is used more and more frequently in the study of language.

373

English grammarians now use it in teaching the principles of structural linguistics. Dictionary makers have begun to use a combination of phonetic symbols and the less accurate diacritical markings to show acceptable pronunciations. And many elementary schools have made basic phonetics an integral part of their reading programs, with excellent results. In short, an acquaintance with phonetics is coming to be, and indeed should be, part of everyone's educational background.

This introduction to phonetics is necessarily brief. For more detailed information, the student should consult the reference books listed at the end of this appendix.

THE PHONETIC ALPHABET

A simplified phonetic alphabet and examples for each symbol are given below. The list is divided into three parts, *consonants* and *vowels* — the two basic kinds of sounds — and *diphthongs*, two vowels combined. The consonants are subdivided according to the way they are articulated: *plosives*, produced by momentarily blocking the breath stream with the lips or tongue and then releasing the trapped breath with a slight puff or explosion; *fricatives*, produced by partially blocking the breath stream, with the result that the breath escapes with the sound of friction, or sometimes of hissing; *nasals*, produced by emitting the sounds through the nose instead of the mouth. The consonants listed under *miscellaneous* are often referred to as *glides* ([r] and [j]), *laterals* ([l]), and *affricates* ([tʃ] and [dʒ]).

The phonetic vowel is the key to spoken language. It is the voice element that determines the syllable, which, in turn, carries the meaning of audible thought. We clothe the vowel with consonants which change — sometimes ever so slightly — the message of the vowel. To illustrate, look at the vowel [i]. Even if we give it a static beginning consonant, [s], the final consonant can change its meaning: [sim], [sik], and [sit].

The name of most of the phonetic symbols is the same as the printed, or orthographic, name; the name of vowels and diphthongs, however, is usually the name of the sound they represent. The names of unfamiliar symbols are shown in parentheses at the right.

CONSONANTS

	Symbol		As in . . .	Transcribed as . . .
Plosives:				
	1. [p]		put	[p ʊ t]
	2. [b]		bone	[b o n]
	3. [t]		tell	[t ɛ l]
	4. [d]		done	[d ʌ n]
	5. [k]		crude	[k r u d]
	6. [g]		give	[g ɪ v]
Fricatives:				
	1. [f]		fine	[f a ɪ n]
	2. [v]		vine	[v a ɪ n]
	3. [s]		sign	[s a ɪ n]
	4. [z]		zoo	[z u]
	5. [θ]	(theta)	both	[b o θ]
	6. [ð]	(thorn)	that	[ð æ t]
	7. [ʃ]	(esch)	shove	[ʃ ʌ v]
	8. [ʒ]	(zsa)	Hoosier	[h u ʒ ɚ] *
	9. [h]		high	[h a ɪ]
	10. [ʍ]	(wha)	when	[ʍ ɛ n]
	11. [w]		weep	[w i p]
Nasals:				
	1. [m]		man	[m æ n]
	2. [n]		name	[n e m]
	3. [ŋ]	(bong)	sing	[s ɪ ŋ]
Miscellaneous:				
	1. [r]		red	[r ɛ d]
	2. [l]		leap	[l i p]
	3. [j]	(yot)	you	[j u]
	4. [tʃ]	(chay)	cheap	[tʃ i p]
	5. [dʒ]	(jay)	jam	[dʒ æ m]

* As said by the majority of Americans

VOWELS

1. [i]		eat	[i t]
2. [ɪ]		hit	[h ɪ t]
3. [e] [1]		hate	[h e t]
4. [ɛ]		bed	[b ɛ d]
5. [æ]		ask	[æ s k]
6. [a] [2]		ask	[a s k]
7. [ɑ]		trot	[t r ɑ t]
8. [ɒ] [3]		trot	[t r ɒ t]
9. [ɔ]		hawk	[h ɔ k]
10. [o] [1]		showed	[ʃ o d]
11. [ʊ]		book	[b ʊ k]
12. [u]		cool	[k u l]
13. [ʌ]	(accented)	cup	[k ʌ p]
14. [ə]	(unaccented)	along	[ə l ɔ ŋ]
15. [ɝ] [5]	(accented)	bird	[b ɝ d]
16. [ɜ] [4]	(accented)	bird	[b ɜ d]
17. [ɚ] [5]	(unaccented)	mother	[m ʌ ð ɚ]

DIPHTHONGS

1. [ɔɪ]		boy	[b ɔ ɪ]
2. [aʊ]		mouse	[m a ʊ s]
3. [aɪ]		typed	[t a ɪ p t]
4. [ɪu] [2]		new	[n ɪ u]

There are three things to remember about writing the phonetic alphabet:

1. Phonetic symbols are *printed* as they are presented here (unless the instructor specifies differently).

2. There are *no capital letters* in the phonetic alphabet.

[1] Also a diphthong.
[2] A sound ordinarily used in the Eastern United States.
[3] A sound ordinarily used along the Atlantic Coastal areas.
[4] A sound ordinarily used by Eastern and Southern speakers.
[5] A sound ordinarily used by Northern and Western speakers.

3. Most consonant symbols, and all vowels, just as in orthographics, are printed *on top of a line*. There are a few exceptions, such as [g], [p], [ŋ], [ʃ], [ʒ], and [j].

If he follows these simple rules, the student should have little difficulty in forming the phonetic symbols correctly. A word of warning is in order. In practicing the exercises that follow, the student may run into two problems. First, he may find it difficult to write accurate phonetic equivalents without *hearing* a person's speech. He can only guess what the speaker *might* say. Second, he may have trouble recognizing and transcribing speech from a dialect area other than his own. (See pages 268–269 for a discussion of dialects and dialect areas.) If he does, he must rely on his instructor for help in transcribing the two unfamiliar dialects.

EXERCISES

The following English words are to be transcribed into phonetic symbols. Exercises for learning vowels are followed by exercises for diphthongs and, finally, for unfamiliar-looking consonants. The student should transcribe these words again and again until he can hear the different sounds clearly and use the phonetic alphabet with ease and confidence.

Vowel #1 [i] as in "eat" [it]

peep, peek, keep, geese, mean,
feast, Pete, sneeze, heap,
leaned, fiend, meat, trees,
lease, keen

Vowel #2 [ɪ] as in "hit" [hɪt]

sick, kicked, wicks, rid,
leaked,[6] click, mixed, gift,
knicked, fizz, team, slick,
clipped, TV, picks

---

[6] A few "test" words are included in the practice lists to keep the student from responding automatically without thinking of the sounds involved. For example, *leaked* does not contain the [ɪ] sound in "hit" but the [i] sound in "eat."

Vowel #3 [e] as in "hate" [het]

saved, paste, fate, hay, bale, tape, April, May Day, gaze, namesake, lately, details, scrape

Vowel #4 [ε] as in "bed" [bεd]

Ted, care, red-tailed bear, spear, stared, fair trade, wear, hairy, head, creeds, nest, still

Vowel #5 [æ] as in "ask" [æsk]

    #6 [a] as in "ask" [ask]

cast, aunt, pass, capped, packed, snappy, can't, knee, trapped, halves, red caps, tap dance, wrapped, bath

Vowel #7 [ɑ] as in "trot" [trɑt]

    #8 [ɒ] as in "trot" [trɒt]

cop, topped, fox, knotty, strapped, Prague, olive, mobbed, Bombay, red top, back stop, Bonnie

Vowel #9 [ɔ] as in "hawk" [hɔk]

caught, law man, gnawed, wall, crawled, sawed off, dawn in East, ball bat, bought bread, raw meat

Vowel #10 [o] as in "cold" [kold]

post, roll in dough, loafed, rope, stay at home, Zorro,

Southern, Northern, Western

Eastern under certain circumstances, such as when the sound ordinarily would be an [æ] but is followed by an [f], a [v], an [s], [θ], or an [n] plus another consonant.

Some Eastern Coastal speakers as far south as Charleston, South Carolina. Is halfway between [ɑ] as in "top" and [ɔ] as in "Paul." Is sometimes referred to as the "short o."

ham bone, zero, caught cold,
red coat

Vowel #11 [ʊ] as in "book [bʊk]

cooked meat, wade in brooks,
poor man, made cookies,
good eats, calf, look at Harry,
played rook, sipped

Vowel #12 [u] as in "cool" [kul]

too many cooks, bought tools,
moved to Westville, hoot,
noon, east bedroom, many
moons, sit loose

Vowel #13 [ʌ] as in "cup" [kʌp]

run, stunned, hot cross buns,
meat is done, struck, nipped,
some fun, gum tree, strum
guitar

There are two "uh" sounds.
This one is used to show when
"uh" is accented. The unaccented "uh" is vowel #14.

Vowel #14 [ə] as in "away" [əwe]

above, sofa, a button, a reason, balloon, pulled a rope,
aloof, a can of coffee, prepare,
select

This is the symbol that represents the unaccented "uh"
sound. It is called *schwa*.

Vowel #15 [ɝ] as in "bird" [bɝd]

#16 [ɜ] as in "bird" [bɜd]

curves, he turned away from
her, astern, he ate a portion
of roast beef, a man and
woman drew two circles

There are three "er" sounds.
The two symbols listed here
represent the "er" sound when
it is accented. The #15 sound
is more common and is used
in the North and West in General American Speech. The
#16 sound is used by standard
Eastern and Southern speakers. The unaccented "er"
sound is vowel #17.

Vowel #17 [ɝ] as in "runner" [rʌnɝ]

eastern, western, prefer a custard, He spent a hundred dollars, His sister had very pleasant manners

This sound is more often used in General American Speech. The Southern and Eastern speaker often uses the schwa [ə] in its place.

Diphthong #1 [ɔɪ] as in "boy" [bɔɪ]

toys, enjoyed, coiled a rope, Lloyd, It was boiled in hot water, fish and poi, He avoids big cities

Diphthong #2 [aʊ] as in "mouse" [maʊs]

drown, around a town, clowned, He vowed never to go away from home, A black cloud went over town at noon

Diphthong #3 [aɪ] as in "typed" [taɪpt]

dine and dance, a sign of prosperity, He climbed a telephone pole twenty times, Mighty Mouse moved Times Square ninety miles from London

Diphthong #4 [ɪu] as in "new" [nɪu]

Tuesday, newspaper, duty, student, dew, Sue, snoop, true, doom, due, tooted, movie, high noon, zoomed

In parts of the country, mainly the East, whenever a phonetic [u] sound is preceded by a phonetic [t], [d], or [n], an [ɪ] is used before the [u].

Plosive #1 [p] as in "put" [pʊt]

Pat, typed, trip, Pete, sapped,
pepper, plowed, exploit, soup,
hoop, pleased, Paul, hopped,
poles, placed

Plosive #2 [b] as in "bone" [bon]

Bob, beaver, braves, boasted,
rob, bicker, rebels, cabaret,
corn cobs, robes, about,
bruise, clubbed, boil

Plosive #3 [t] as in "tell" [tɛl]

Tom, steamed, toiled, stick,
bet, about, stacked, timed,
caught, top, lettuce, turnip,
Pete, tombs, stoves

Plosive #4 [d] as in "done" [dʌn]

Don, drew, deeper, deserved,
doom, drip, spread, ragged,
cracked, taped, ribbed, allowed, David, divide, drove

Plosive #5 [k] as in "crude" [krud]

kicked, cows, deck, spike,
spoken, cakes, calves, corn,
cavalry, brook, cooled, coils,
caves, cot, caught

Plosive #6 [g] as in "give" [gɪv]

get, gone, leg, guide, given,
bags, glows, growl, geese, golf,
gave, ground, goose, good, got

Fricative #1 [f] as in "fine" [faɪn]

feet, foot, fight, fought, cough, freight, fool, muffin, turf, elf, finder, flounder, fall, firmer, leafy

Fricative #2 [v] as in "vine" [vaɪn]

vesper, vim, vigor, vitality, ever, leave, vase, investment, void, voter, vows, advice, devoted, veer, vodka

Fricative #3 [s] as in "sign" [saɪn]

seal, sound, sighs, kisses, stews, Mississippi, steamboats, soiled, certain, sea, passes, said, sad, say

Fricative #4 [z] as in "zoo" [zu]

zoom, advise, zero, news, buzzer, xylophone, nerves, resolve, Missouri, ease, despise, carouse, lovers, papers

Fricative #5 [θ] as in "both" [boθ]   The name of the symbol is
                                            theta.
thin, Athens, three, ether, bath, thread, earth, booth, thrive, Beth, thrown, throne, thug, thermometer, death

Fricative #6 [ð] as in "that" [ðæt]   The name of the symbol is
                                            thorn.
there, that, bathe, then, these, father, mother, brother, rhythm, this, either, rather, those, lathe, thou

Fricative #7 [ʃ] as in "shove" [ʃʌv]   The name of the symbol is
shoot, shout, efficient, fish, *esch.*
flesh, shine, Chicago, Sho-
shone, sheet, shoes, shaved,
clashes, flush, shindig, shops

Fricative #8 [ʒ] as in "Hoosier" [huʒə]

Asia, Zsa-Zsa, pleasure, mea-   The name of the symbol is
sure, usual, vision, hosiery, *zsa.*
leisure, rouge, beige, garage,
conclusion, persuasion

Fricative #9 [h] as in "high" [haɪ]

hot, heap, howdy, headstart,
hid, hoses, horses, heels,
hated, hood, hoodlum, raw-
hide, heard, height, haughty

Fricative #10 [ʍ] as in "when" [ʍɛn]

which, where, somewhat, who,   The name of the symbol is
wheat, whine, whisper, whale, *wha.*
white, shredded wheat

Fricative #11 [w] as in "weep" [wip]

water, wisp, wish, weather,
woo, wine, swoon, sweater,
wore, wasp, waiter, swish,
wither, swat, wise

Nasal #1 [m] as in "man" [mæn]

meat, motion, made, maid,
mixed, mustard, matter,
model, moose, smeared,
mirth, mouse, mice, matrix

Nasal #2 [n] as in "name" [nem]

neat, notion, name, noun,
number, Nash, Neal, Neely,
Nelson, Nixon, Newman,
Nichols, Niles, Norton

Nasal #3 [ŋ] as in "sing" [sɪŋ]

The name of the symbol is *bong.*

sting, tongue, running, eating,
ink, rang, anchor, calling,
shouting, strong, longer, sang,
wrong, bank, strength

Miscellaneous #1 [r] as in "red" [rɛd]

rude, tread, tearing, various,
wrong, Racine, Detroit, Rich-
mond, Grand Rapids, Baton
Rouge, raid, riding, railroad

Miscellaneous #2 [l] as in "leap" [lip]

living, line, alone, boiled,
lapsed, slaves, loaves, leak,
left, shells, Lily, Alice, Louis,
Lloyd, Sally

Miscellaneous #3 [j] as in "you" [ju]

youth, young, music, union,
few, yellow, yesterday, yeast,
yawning, Jugoslavia, yes,
onion, imbue, beauty, yo-yo

The name of the symbol is *yot.*

Miscellaneous #4 [tʃ] as in "cheap" [tʃip]

cheese, chance, church, chalk,
cherry, coach, chapel, birch,
couch, choose, Charles, Ra-
chel, Chip, Richard, Butch

The name of the symbol is *chay.*

Miscellaneous #5 [dʒ] as in "jam" [dʒæm]

joy, fudge, ledge, giraffe, July, George, June, Joe, Joan, Jesus, jest, bridge, jeep, soldier, jerking

The name of the symbol is *jay.*

Transcribe the following paragraph into phonetic symbols. Assume that the speaker is talking rapidly between the // signs, which show pauses.

Paul and Eugene were singing under the window of the sorority house when Beth learned about Agnes. // She jumped out of bed //, clutched her beige robe with her fists //, got a three-gallon bucket of water //, and poured it all on her boy friend //. She stopped their fine music with the water // and ran them off by saying //, "I never wish to see you again // if you date Agnes //, or Lucille //, or Wendy // or Jeannie //, or . . . ."

REFERENCES

Carrell, James, and William Tiffany. *Phonetics.* New York: McGraw-Hill, 1960.

Huckleberry, Alan. *Beginning Phonetics.* Dubuque, Iowa: Wm. C. Brown, 1961.

Kenyon, J. S., and T. A. Knott. *A Pronouncing Dictionary.* Springfield, Mass.: G. & C. Merriam, 1953.

Wise, C. M. *Applied Phonetics.* Englewood Cliffs, N.J.: Prentice-Hall, 1957.